LEST WE FORGET

A History of The Last Post Fund 1909–1999

Serge M. Durflinger

The Last Post Fund
Montreal
2000

Canadian Cataloguing in Publication Data
Durflinger, Serge Marc, 1961-
        Lest We Forget: a History of the Last Post Fund 1909-1999
Published also in French under the title: Je me souviens
Includes bibliographical references.
ISBN 2-9806532-0-9 (English edition)
        1. Last Post Fund-History. 2. Veterans-Canada.
        I. Last Post Fund. II. Title
UB395.C2D87 2000   353.538   C00-900224-3

ISBN 2-9806532-1-7 (Édition française)
        1. Fonds du Souvenir-Histoire. 2. Anciens combattants -Canada.
        I. Fonds du Souvenir II. Titre.
UB395.C2D8714 2000   353.538   C00-900329-0

Legal deposit second quarter 2000
        National Library of Canada
        Bibliothèque nationale du Québec
Publisher: Last Post Fund
with financial support from Veterans Affairs Canada.

Printed in Canada on acid-free paper
Typeset in Bembo 11 points over 13 pts leading
by Anlo inc.

Front cover: "Grieving Soldier" stained glass window, Gate of Remembrance, Field of
Honour, Pointe-Claire, Québec. Created by Montreal artist Nicole Gascon, presented to the
Last Post Fund in 1998 by the Royal Canadian Legion Dominion Command. Copy
presented to Veterans Affairs Canada in Charlottetown to commemorate 90 years of service
by the Fund to Canada's war veterans and their families.

The crest shown overleaf was officially unveiled in 1921 and is used in the corporate seal of the Last Post Fund.

Designed in collaboration with the College of Arms, it represents Canada's three armed services, the army, the navy and the air force.

In 1909, the fund adopted the motto, "Lest We Forget," from Rudyard Kipling's poem, "The Recessional."

Pro Patria et Defensoribus is translated as "For the Nation and its Defenders."

Lest We Forget:

A History of The Last Post Fund 1909–1999

TABLE OF CONTENTS

FOREWORD

As Patron of the Last Post Fund, I am pleased to be associated with the publication of a book devoted to the organization's history. This work traces the remarkable and often moving history of an important Canadian agency that continues to have its *raison d'être* after 90 years of work.

Since its creation in 1909, the Last Post Fund and its members have believed that veterans must receive recognition for their military service, and they have dedicated their efforts to ensure this happens. Their mission is to provide veterans in need with a dignified burial, preferably beside their comrades in arms.

As its founder, Arthur Hair, said, the Last Post Fund is a genuine "war memorial". It owns and manages the Field of Honour in Pointe-Claire, Québec, the only cemetery in Canada reserved exclusively for veterans. It is a true memorial garden and a place of rest for those who have made immense sacrifices in the service of Canada and democracy.

The history of the Last Post Fund is typically Canadian. It is the story of people motivated by patriotism and compassion working together to take care of those who have shared the same values: morality, dignity, and the profound desire to serve our country.

I congratulate Dr. Durflinger on his work. I encourage veterans, the general public, and everyone interested in Canada's history to read it. In this book they will find further proof that our country is worth protecting and that we must honour those who have defended it.

October 1999

Roméo LeBlanc

PREFACE

In many ways the founding of the "Last Post" Imperial Naval and Military Contingency Fund by Arthur Hair in Montreal in 1909 reflected the times in which he lived. The social ideals then prevalent helped advance the organization's early goals and sustain its principles. Patriotism, fealty to the monarch, and service to the empire were accepted and encouraged in Canada, especially among those of British origin. The military establishment was held in high esteem.

That penniless former soldiers and sailors of the empire might not find a proper resting place seemed ungracious and shameful. Yet few Canadians were even aware that this deplorable situation existed, and fewer still were prepared to prevent it. In fact, the most common public attitude was that unfortunate victims of poverty, veterans or not, should be cared for by philanthropic organizations and buried by the municipality in which they died.

Without Arthur Hair's determination and overwhelming sense of duty, the Last Post Fund (LPF) would neither have been created nor survived. Hair, a British immigrant, veteran of the South African War, and patriot, devoted his life to the Fund and its objectives. Acting as secretary-treasurer, he steered the LPF through its difficult early years and attracted many distinguished associates to serve with him in carrying out its mission.

For the first 13 years of its existence, the LPF depended on the generosity of benefactors; it never publicly appealed for funds. Despite the patronage of the governor general of Canada, Hair's organization found substantial financial assistance difficult to obtain. However, members remained determined that no friendless veteran would be consigned to oblivion and abandonment in a pauper's field. Throughout the trying years of the First World War, the proudly patriotic Hair and the LPF's executives and trustees engaged the Fund in charitable work in aid of the war effort.

By 1922 there were hundreds of thousands of demobilized veterans in Canada, and a growing number were passing away in indigent circumstances. As a consequence, the federal government recognized the importance of the Fund's work. In exchange for the organization's expansion from its base in Québec to a national level, Ottawa began granting annual subsidies to cover the costs of burials. The LPF had come of age as a national institution. Hair's persistence had ensured its continuation.

The lean years of the Great Depression increased the value and need of an organization to bury needy veterans, and the LPF filled this role admirably. This difficult period was immediately followed by the Second World War. Again, under the inspired leadership of Norman Holland and Arthur Hair, the LPF earned a name for itself as a patriotic organization and became increasingly devoted to maintaining older military burial plots.

Its work continued to grow in the postwar period with the reintegration into civil life of nearly one million Canadian veterans. There was a continuing need for the Fund in the 1950s and 1960s as many of the old soldiers who had served in South Africa or manned the trenches of the Western Front began to pass away in larger numbers. In the 1980s and 1990s a similar trend has occurred with Canada's veterans of the Second World War and the Korean War.

On the threshold of the 21st century, the LPF will maintain its social relevance by continuing to see to the funeral and burial needs of poor or abandoned veterans. In addition, a new challenge awaits the LPF as it assumes greater administrative responsibilities for all veteran burial benefits supported by the federal government. It is also expected that the LPF's involvement in the maintenance of all military burial sites across Canada will become even more prominent.

After 90 years of operation, the Last Post Fund remains a dynamic and evolving institution whose main assets are its devoted employees and dedicated volunteers. In 1999, the LPF created the Award of Merit to recognize outstanding achievement and meritorious service. The Award consists of an engraved Plexiglas image of the illustration appearing on the front cover of this book. It was my great pleasure to present the inaugural awards to the following worthy recipients: Lieutenant-General Gilles Turcot, Canon Arthur Wilcox, Lieutenant-Commander (N) James Lattimer, Captain (N) Peter

Langlais, Lieutenant-Colonel Harvey Bishop, and Mr. David Nicholson. All these men have contributed immensely to the success of the LPF in the last few decades. They are symbolic of the spirit of the Last Post Fund and fully representative of those many men and women whose stories of hard work and dedication fill the pages of this book.

The Last Post Fund has always remembered those who have served, and it always will.

Lest We Forget.

Jacques Morneault
Brigadier General (retired)
National President
Last Post Fund

December 1999

AUTHOR'S PREFACE

This book is a history of the Last Post Fund (LPF), a fascinating and important institution. The Last Post Fund is not well known by the Canadian public or even by the academic community. This is unfortunate. The LPF has carried out its good works across the country for decades, and many well-known figures in Canadian history considered themselves privileged to have been associated with it. The Fund's story is one of adversity, achievement, and, ultimately, triumph. Yet until this publication the story has gone untold.

Since 1909, the Last Post Fund has existed principally for one purpose: to provide dignified funerals and burials to Canada's veterans whose estates were insufficient to cover the costs of proper interment. The LPF is an organization motivated by patriotism and driven by its respect and gratitude for those who served Canada. The Fund is not a charity or a veterans' group. From a private body conducting a handful of burials each year, the LPF has evolved into a fully-funded agent of the Department of Veterans Affairs. In 1998, the Fund began carrying out veterans' burials that traditionally had been Ottawa's responsibility. This is an impressive record of growth and institutional maturity.

The following narrative examines a number of issues and topics, including the Last Post Fund's founding and goals, its administration and financing, its services and benefits, its organizational growth, its co-operation with government and other organizations, the role of personalities in the evolution of the Fund, and the inauguration and maintenance of the Field of Honour, Canada's only dedicated military cemetery. Along the way this book describes the challenges that have confronted the organization in peace and war. I have organized the text into chronological chapters. Nevertheless, the historian's traditional conundrum of when to subjugate the flow of chronology to topical coherence, or vice-versa, occasionally manifests itself. Because the Last Post Fund is still very much in existence and continues to evolve, it is perhaps understandable that the history of its earlier decades can be more fully assessed than that of recent years.

In some ways, this is an 'official history'. The Last Post Fund commissioned this work and hired me to research and write it. The manuscript has been read and commented on by an Editorial Committee struck by the Fund. Nevertheless, at the very outset of this project I insisted on retaining complete control over the organization, content, and tone of the book. I also asked for unfettered access to archives and documents. As a professional historian, I could hardly be expected to write the book otherwise. The LPF immediately granted all my requests and the working relationship has been fruitful. The Editorial Committee has been the source of helpful advice and minor suggestions for revision, nearly all of which I gratefully accepted and implemented.

This history of the Last Post Fund is meant for a general reading audience. Its style and presentation are not academic in nature, as the absence of citations indicates. It was my intention from the start that the book evoke individuals and events, not analyze bureaucratic decisions and administrative minutiae in a blow-by-blow account of committees tinkering with corporate by-laws. The latter sort of information, of necessity, occasionally slips into the narrative, but not, I trust, in lethal doses.

To a large extent, my approach has meant subordinating analysis to information, and simply recounting the story. Wherever possible I have attempted to place various aspects of the Fund's history into a broader perspective. While my mandate was to write the history of the Last Post Fund as an institution, I quickly became aware that the organization's past was intimately linked to the unfolding of Canada's general history this century. Accordingly, I refer to, but do not elaborate on, such themes as death and burial practices, social class, immigration, patriotism, Canada's linguistic duality, the role of the state in regulating the lives of Canadians, the status of women, and the effects of war on Canadian society. I hope that *Lest We Forget* will make some scholarly contribution to Canadian institutional, veterans', and socio-military history. I have provided a note on sources and a select bibliography at the end of the book for the use of readers interested in further exploring these subjects.

A number of people have assisted me in preparing this history. The executive and staff of the Last Post Fund's national office and of its Québec branch have been extremely co-operative and generous of their time. I would especially like to mention Colonel Pierre Richard, past-president of the Québec branch and co-ordinator of this publication; Colonel René Pothier, the manager of the Québec branch of the Last Post Fund; and Colonel Alex Bialosh, the executive director of the Last Post Fund. Arthur "Chip" Hair, grandson and namesake of the Fund's founder, provided useful material covering his grandfather's early years. Dr. Janine Stingel helped me with research in Ottawa. John Parry perceptively copy-edited the manuscript and vastly improved its presentation. I am grateful to them all, although I alone bear responsibility for the narrative and any of its shortcomings.

Serge Durflinger
Gatineau, Québec
November 11, 1999

ABBREVIATIONS

CASF	Canadian Active Service Force
CB	Companion of the Order of the Bath
CBE	Commander of the Order of the British Empire
CCA	Canadian Corps Association
CEF	Canadian Expeditionary Force
CMG	Companion of the Order of St. Michael and St. George
CPF	Canadian Patriotic Fund
CWGC	Commonwealth War Graves Commission
DCM	Distinguished Conduct Medal
DFC	Distinguished Flying Cross
DFM	Distinguished Flying Medal
DND	Department of National Defence
DPNH	Department of Pensions and National Health
DSCR	Department of Soldiers' Civil Re-establishment
DSO	Distinguished Service Order
DVA	Department of Veterans Affairs
GOC	General Officer Commanding
GWVA	Great War Veterans' Association
HQ	Headquarters
IODE	Imperial Order Daughters of the Empire
IWGC	Imperial War Graves Commission
LPF	Last Post Fund
MBE	Member of the Order of the British Empire
MC	Military Cross
MD	Military District
MLA	Member of the Legislative Assembly
MM	Military Medal
MOU	Memorandum of Understanding
MP	Member of Parliament
NATO	North Atlantic Treaty Organization
NRMA	National Resources Mobilization Act
OBE	Officer of the Order of the British Empire
RCAF	Royal Canadian Air Force
RCEME	Royal Canadian Electrical and Mechanical Engineers
RCMP	Royal Canadian Mounted Police
RCN	Royal Canadian Navy
RCNVR	Royal Canadian Naval Volunteer Reserve
RCOC	Royal Canadian Ordnance Corps
RNR	Royal Naval Reserve
SAVA	South African Veterans Association
UN	United Nations
VAC	Veterans Affairs Canada
VBR	Veterans Burial Regulations
VC	Victoria Cross

Arthur Harold Douglas Hair,
founder of the Last Post Fund, c. 1915

1

BEGINNINGS, 1908–1914

The Last Post Fund is not a charity, it is a duty.

ARTHUR HAIR

The modern political era for Canada began in 1867, when several colonies in British North America agreed to merge into a new Confederation. The resulting 'Dominion of Canada' grew to vast geographic proportions in the following years, incorporating other colonies and attracting large numbers of immigrants, mainly from the British Isles, to settle its sparsely-populated territory. Within a generation, the country's Atlantic and Pacific coasts were linked by a transcontinental railway. By 1900, most of Canada's 5.3 million inhabitants still lived in rural areas, although increasing industrialization led to greater urbanization and a denser concentration of road and rail networks. Montreal was Canada's largest city, with a population of 267,000 in 1901, rising to 406,000 in 1911; Toronto was a distant second. Canada was a confident, growing, and comparatively affluent young country. In 1904, Prime Minister Sir Wilfrid Laurier uttered his oft-repeated boast that "the Twentieth Century shall be the century of Canada." Most of his compatriots agreed with him.

Yet, even though nearly 30 per cent of Canadians were of French ancestry, Canada was also very much a 'British' country. Confederation had in no way altered the fact that Canada was a member of the British Empire and that the British monarch was also Canada's sovereign. The official flag remained the Union Jack, and Canadian citizenship was unknown, all Canadians being British subjects. The governor general was always a British nobleman selected by London.

Since the 1870s, the British Empire had grown to form an immense world-wide territorial and economic unit. Britain was the world's most powerful naval and commercial nation. Given Canada's overtly British character, English-speaking Canadians generally took pride in the fact that their country belonged to the empire. Despite occasional violent opposition to British rule in some colonies, most Canadians of British ancestry considered the empire a progressive, civilizing, and stabilizing force in the world. Stirring popular accounts of imperial adventures and conquests filled books, journals, and newspaper articles. The stories and verses of well-known British writer and poet Rudyard Kipling and pieces by many other writers, journalists, and essayists promoted the idea that Britain's armed forces were heroic and worthy of the empire's undying gratitude. Patriotism was a strong social principle. Imperial fervour in Canada reached its zenith at the time of the South African War (1899–1902), in which Canada participated. Duty to the empire and to the sovereign was sacrosanct for many English Canadians and for most of the many British immigrants residing in Canada. The Canadian military maintained and usually cherished the pomp and pageantry of British military traditions.

As a result of this ingrained sense of patriotic duty, all those serving or having served in the military stood high in public esteem throughout the empire. Being a 'Soldier of the Queen' was a noble pursuit and, given the often sacrificial nature of war service, received social acclaim not normally accorded to civilian vocations. However, it was also true that once military service had been completed, society just as quickly forgot its ageing veterans. It is within this context of late Victorian and Edwardian imperial and patriotic zeal, very strongly felt in much of Canada, that the Last Post Fund (LPF) came into being.

The Spark Ignited

At the turn of the twentieth century, it long had been the practice in Canada, as in many other countries, for municipalities to inter society's thousands of indigent dead in unmarked civic plots. These cemetery plots were often referred to as 'pauper' graves or a 'potter's' field. Civic authorities also commonly consigned the bodies of these poor and often friendless persons to hospitals, universities, or the coroner's office for anatomical study. In short, according to the customs of the time, only the ability of an individual's estate or survivors to pay for a proper burial prevented a pauper burial.

Despite public recognition for the military's role in building and sustaining the empire, society made no distinction between deceased persons who had been civilians all their lives and those who had served in the army or navy on active service. Discharged British or Canadian veterans dying in Canada, if penniless, received a pauper burial as a matter of course. Moreover, the British military paid little attention to the selection of final resting places for soldiers and sailors serving with the colours at the time of their deaths; burials were haphazardly organized and often not even recorded. Although dignified battlefield burials normally followed military operations, there was no contingency planning for the future upkeep of the burial sites. Few marked graves existed from the Napoleonic Wars or the Crimean War, for example. British and Canadian military establishments had no organization in place to register and maintain permanently the gravesites of their fallen. While a start had been made during the South African War, such a system would have to await the First World War and the organization in May 1917 of the Imperial War Graves Commission (IWGC). In the meantime, most battlefield burial sites remained abandoned and neglected.

These, then, were the conditions governing military and indigent burials in Canada when, at Christmastime in 1908, two policemen found an elderly and obviously destitute man huddled on the ground in a doorway on St. Alexandre Street in downtown Montreal. The man was unconscious. The policemen took him to the nearby Montreal General Hospital, then located on Dorchester Street (now René Lévesque Boulevard), where, with the single curt remark: "Drunk!", they hastily left the unfortunate derelict in the care of hospital staff. A doctor quickly agreed with their diagnosis and detailed some orderlies to cart the man to a room where unconscious drunks were allowed to 'sleep it off'.

While the so-called drunk was being wheeled away, the head orderly, a British immigrant named Arthur Hair, noticed a blue envelope protruding from the man's coat pocket. Since Hair was a pensioned veteran of the South African War, he recognized it as the kind issued by Britain's War Office to soldiers on their discharge from military service. Opening it, he found the honourable discharge and good conduct certificate of one Trooper James Daly, 2nd Dragoon Guards (the Queen's Bays). Daly had served 21 years in the British army and seen active service throughout the empire, including during the Crimean War, in which Britain had participated from 1854 to 1856. The old veteran clearly cherished this document, for it was his *only* possession, save for several crusts of stale bread wrapped in an old red handkerchief stuffed into one of his pockets. Besides his obvious poverty, no hints about his life could be deduced.

While standing beside the former trooper and reading his discharge papers, Hair detected no smell of liquor about him and could not help but notice his sadly emaciated condition. Another doctor was called. Hair's suspicion was confirmed: Daly was not drunk at all, but suffering from exposure and starvation. He never regained consciousness and died two days later. As hospital staff could obtain no information on the whereabouts of any of his family or friends, Daly's body went unclaimed. Accordingly, hospital officials arranged for his remains to be removed to the city morgue for disposal.

On Daly's death, Hair, who had taken a personal interest in this sad case, contacted the Montreal branch of a veterans' association of which he had been a member to inquire whether it would take charge of the old veteran's burial. (The organization in question has not been clearly recorded, though it might have been the Army and Navy Veterans Association or the South African Veterans Association (SAVA).) The veterans' group declined to assist in the matter, citing as its principal reason the fact that Daly had not been a contributing member. Though sympathetic, one member explained to Hair that the association had no funds or even an institutional mandate to handle such a case as that of the unfortunate Daly, who, like others before him, simply 'fell through the cracks'.

Hair considered this a "miserable excuse", and he was outraged by the callous disregard for the deceased man's past military service displayed by other veterans, especially since it was well known that Québec's Anatomy Act dictated that the remains of the indigent dead be turned over to the authorities for anatomical study. Hair likely would have conceded there was nothing philosophically objectionable with the Anatomy Act. After all, the medical benefits of examining cadavers were obvious and the province's thousands of indigent dead annually provided a ready laboratory for study. Moreover, according to widely accepted middle-class values and social standards, poverty was normally the outgrowth of irresponsibility, mismanagement, and social failure. Destitution was strongly associated in the public eye with alcoholism or some other form of social 'evil' and was therefore considered a character flaw. People had to make their own ways in life, and death, presumably. But Hair made a clear distinction between the veteran and non-veteran indigent dead. As far as he was concerned, military service ennobled the one character in a manner from which the other could not benefit. The military dead, no matter what their lot had been in life, were worthy of more reverential treatment than civilian dead. In this patriotic, imperially-minded era, Hair set out to convince others that he was right.

Although rarely publicized, cases such as Daly's were common in Canada. Military pensions for British soldiers were notoriously low and never sufficient to support a man, as thousands of discharged veterans learned. Historian Desmond Morton has pointed out that "the British...seemed to pauperize veterans, as any visitor to London discovered when beset by the bemedalled and disabled veterans of the Empire's wars, selling pencils or begging." In Canada, too, many veterans were reduced to charity cases. The United States, by contrast, had been arguably overly-generous with its Civil War veterans and paid out enormous sums for pensions which many budget-conscious legislators came to regret.

Hair himself understood the problem: following his active service in South Africa, the British government granted him the minuscule pension of one shilling, six pence per day – the equivalent in Canadian funds of about 35 cents, a ludicrously low amount even by the standards of the time. Compounding the difficulties, there were few veterans' organizations and none was able to bury indigent ex-servicemen on a regular basis. With his strong sense of patriotism aroused, Hair threw himself into the task of ensuring a proper burial for a man he had never known but with whom he shared that bond of military service that only veterans can fully comprehend. Hair soon raised enough money from among fellow hospital workers and friends to remove Daly's body from the morgue, just before it was to be turned over for anatomical study, and arrange for its proper burial.

Hair would later claim that the scene unfolding before his eyes that December day reminded him of the old English nursery rhyme:

> Rattle his bones
> Over the stones
> He's only a pauper
> Whom nobody owns.

For Hair, the very empire that he himself had undertaken to safeguard at the time of the South African War seemed terribly ungrateful to this needy veteran, and all others like him, at the hour of their deaths. Surely provision could be made to ensure the proper burial of those risking their lives in the service of their country? In a letter to the editor of *The Gazette* (Montreal) he recounted the entire sorry episode. He expressed his feelings of revulsion that no one seemed much to care about the final days of Canada's and the empire's destitute soldiery. Hair gave vent to his sense of outrage and, in so doing, publicized perhaps for the first time the plight of impoverished veterans and the lack of gratitude shown them by society in general. The letter, published on December 28, 1908, constitutes a founding document for the Last Post Fund.

A BRITISH SOLDIER'S DEATH

Sir, Will you permit me to narrate the following incident, the facts of which I personally vouch for, in the hope that it may prevent the recurrence in any city that has a strong representation of British ex-army men.

A few days ago a British Pensioner without friends or relatives within location, sank in a doorway ill and comatose. The Police removed him to an Hospital where he died shortly afterwards without regaining consciousness.

Another soldier approached a "British" soldier's organization who expound the theory of good comradeship, with a view to respectable interment at a minimum cost, and was told by one of the Executive that there were "no funds" for such a contingency, and that not being a member, or having contributed to the organization's funds, they could do nothing in the matter. Consequently the body was handed over to the Inspector of Anatomy for disposal.

The Executive member's retort was presumably prompted by this particular man being a non-member, but as an ex-member of that particular organ-

ization, I have heard the sentiment expressed, that they should never allow a British soldier or sailor fall ill and die without decent burial, if brought to their notice.

I would strongly advocate a "Voluntary Burial Fund" being organised for this purpose, which from my personal experience of British soldiers and sailors, I feel confident would be kept in such a condition as to meet such local contingencies and provide a resting place for the Empire's fighting "derelicts."

Arthur H.D. Hair

Hair later remarked that he was motivated to raise funds for Daly's burial mainly out of a sense of "sympathetic camaraderie of one soldier for another".

Twenty years later, one newspaper account stated that "the pathos of the incident impressed [Hair] so strongly that it … changed the whole plan and course of his life." He thereupon launched a personal crusade to ensure that, in Montreal at least, no veteran would go to a pauper's field. All veterans deserved a respectful burial service and a marked grave. Hair was a man of modest means and to put his idea into practice, he needed the patronage of the city's wealthier patriotic families. Between December 1908 and April 1909 he devoted a great deal of time to canvassing the opinions and seeking the public support and financial assistance of prominent citizens, philanthropists, and social workers. Sir Hugh Graham, Sir Montague Allan, Henry Birks, and other well-known Montrealers pledged their support and provided small amounts to help get the project started. Allan gave $50 for example. What Hair hoped to build was a truly "Practical War Memorial", one of "gratitude" for military services rendered. His guiding inspiration, and that of his associates, was that "to honour and protect in death, seems but a small return to him who has protected the nation's honour in life." Since no precedent existed to guide him, Hair embarked on a venture whose challenges and implications he could only imagine. His brief and chance encounter with Daly had proved the catalyst for the creation of the Last Post Fund and, Daly might be considered, unofficially, the first of over 100,000 Canadian, Imperial, Commonwealth, and Allied veterans whom the LPF would bury in its first 90 years of operation. But who was Arthur Hair?

The Driving Force

Arthur Harold Douglas Hair was born June 14, 1873, in London, England. His Scottish father, James, was a civil engineer employed by the East India Company. His mother, the former Katherine Tooze, was the daughter of an Anglican minister from Devonshire. While Arthur was still a boy, his parents divorced and he and his four siblings, two of whom died in youth, were separated. Hair attended an Anglican school at Llanthony Abbey, Wales, for two years but was otherwise taught informally by his mother, who was educated.

At the tender age of 13, Hair left England for reasons that remain unclear, although it can be surmised that his disintegrating family situation made it perhaps preferable that he seek a better life abroad – and what better place than in bountiful Canada, the senior British Dominion? Hair was perhaps one of over 80,000 British children, most under the age of 14, who were dispatched to Canada by various groups in Britain to work as agricultural labourers or domestic servants. As historian Joy Parr has noted, these "British boys and girls were taken away from their native country before the age of knowledgeable consent." Whatever the case, Hair arrived alone in this country in 1886, lodged with a Huguenot farming family north of Montreal, and for a while attended a country school in Lachute, Québec. It was a rude awakening. Hair worked long hours as a labourer and household servant for the farmer who kept him. He earned the pittance of $2 a month. Late in his life, he recalled that during this time he had been "bewildered and lonesome"; in fact, he was wretched. The hardship and harsh treatment proved too much for him, and he ran away, preferring to take his chances on his own in this strange land. He eventually made his way to the Québec City area, where he lived in the bush for a time with a Native community.

Arthur Hair's military career began in 1889, when, at the age of 16, he enlisted as a trumpeter in the Regiment of Canadian Artillery in Québec City. In 1891, he transferred to the Permanent Force as a gunner in "B" Battery, Regiment of Canadian Artillery, which was reorganized as the Royal Canadian Field Artillery in 1893. "B" Battery was also located in Québec City. In 1898, Hair took his discharge and, failing to pass the physical examination for service in the North-West Mounted Police, returned to Britain, possibly seeking the adventure that Canadian military service could not provide. Landing at Glasgow, he immediately enlisted in the Royal Horse Artillery. He trained at Woolwich and St. John's Wood, London, after which he was drafted to "A" Battery, Royal Horse Artillery, for imperial garrison duty at Meerut, in northwest India (where his parents had been married).

In early 1900, with war raging in South Africa, Gunner Hair's unit was despatched to Colenso, Natal, where it joined General Sir Redvers Bullers's field force. Subsequently, Hair's battery saw service in Durban with Lord Dundonald's 1st Cavalry Brigade. Hair fought throughout the length and breadth of South Africa, but the strain of continuous duty took its toll. In February 1902, three months before the end of the war, Hair collapsed while on a reconnaissance patrol and was invalided to Herbert Military Hospital in England, suffering from "nervous disability". He was released following several months of rest and convalescence, and the army discharged him on medical grounds. For his services in the field, Hair received the Queen's South Africa Medal with seven battle clasps – an unusually high number, testament to his battery's strenuous campaigning.

Hair, who was tall and lank, almost frail, and of a reserved disposition, had met his future wife, Janet McIntyre, in England following his return from Canada in 1898. He maintained an active correspondence with her while in South Africa. Following his discharge in 1902, they agreed that Hair should seek permanent work in Canada since Britain was experiencing high unemployment. Janet would join him later.

The 30-year old Hair disembarked at Québec City in January 1903. However, his fragile health forced him to seek complete rest in a rural setting, some 40 kilometres north of Québec City. Later that year he tried his luck in Montreal. He found employment at the Montreal General Hospital, where he rose to be head of the hospital orderlies. He received room and board but little in the way of salary. Despite this shaky start, Janet joined him and they married before the end of 1903. They would raise a family and be together for over 40 years, until Hair's death in 1947.

The largely self-taught Hair was energetic and resourceful. In addition to his job at the hospital, he maintained a link to military life by joining No. 5 Field Ambulance, Canadian Army Medical Corps,

Non-Permanent Active Militia where he served from 1906 to 1909, eventually reaching the rank of sergeant-major. When the growing demands of his job obliged him to give up his military duties, his discharge certificate noted that he had "performed his duties efficiently, and his conduct was exemplary". Hair was a charter member of the Canadian branch of the South African Veterans Association, and he helped veterans of that conflict resettle into civilian life. He was a religious man and an active member of the congregation of Trinity (Anglican) Church in Montreal. He read extensively and indulged a wide variety of interests, including church history and criminology. This, then, was the man behind the Last Post Fund.

The Founding of the Last Post Fund

One immediate and immensely valuable supporter of Hair's proposal to create a veterans' burial organization was the Reverend John MacPherson Almond, rector of Trinity Church since 1904. He too was a veteran of South Africa, where he had served in 1899 and 1900 as Anglican chaplain to Canada's first contingent, the 2nd Battalion (Special Service), Royal Canadian Regiment of Infantry. He understood military matters, sympathized with veterans' difficulties readapting to civil life, and had a long-standing interest in social issues. Almond was instantly seized by Hair's proposal; he had in fact observed similar situations himself as a military clergyman. He used his numerous clerical and military contacts to garner even more local support for Hair's ambitious plan. Almond would later recall the "great indignation" with which Hair approached him over the callousness of allowing veterans' bodies to go unclaimed. The two men would be close partners in the affairs of the Fund for the next 30 years, until Almond's death in 1939, at which time he had risen to the status of Honourary Colonel, the Venerable Archdeacon John MacPherson Almond, C.M.G., C.B., V.D., M.A., D.C.L. Almond saw to it that Hair's ideas came to fruition.

On April 19, 1909, six men and two women met in the vestry of Trinity Church, at the northwest corner of St. Denis and Viger. The church was an impressive landmark, built in 1865, with a 168-foot steeple (a gift from the Molson family) and seating for 1,250 people. Among those present that evening were Arthur Hair, John Almond,

Arthur Hair and his wife Janet, née McIntyre, 1908. Hair is wearing the uniform of a wardmaster (sergeant-major), Canadian Army Medical Corps. Courtesy Arthur Hair, Ottawa.

Venerable Archdeacon John M. Almond,
president of the Last Post Fund,
1909-15; 1932-39.

and Brigadier-General Lawrence Buchan, C.V.O., C.M.G., A.D.C., the General Officer Commanding (GOC) the Québec military district and a veteran of the South African War. Others present to pledge their organizations' fund-raising support were Lucien C. Vallée, of the South African Veterans Association; Alex Mackay, of the Imperial South African Veterans Association; W.W. Marsh, of the Army and Navy Veterans Association; and Mrs. R. Hemsley and Miss Borthwick, representing the Imperial Order Daughters of the Empire (IODE). Hair later recalled it as "a little gathering with patriotic ideas and fervour, and no money."

Nevertheless, this meeting founded the "Last Post" Imperial Naval and Military Contingency Fund. The three original trustees, responsible for the Fund's direction and finances, were Almond, Buchan (who died later that year) and Commander J.T. Walsh, Royal Naval Reserve (RNR), who subsequently accepted his nomination as a naval representative. Walsh, marine superintendent of the Canadian

Pacific Railway's steamship service, was also a Catholic – an important consideration in his selection. Buchan became involved with the Fund by the expressed wish of Governor General Earl Grey, who had generously agreed to act as patron-in-chief of the new organization, a considerable *coup* for Hair and Almond.

Those present at the inaugural meeting also chose the original executive committee of the Fund: Almond was named president; Hair, representing the militia, served as secretary; Lucien C. Vallée, formerly of the *65e Carabiniers Mont-Royal*, became treasurer. Vallée also represented the Army and Navy Veterans Association. Five other members, not all of whom were present, were appointed to the governing body, including Mrs. R. Hemsley, head of the Montreal IODE; a Mrs. F.W. Slater, and Sergeant-Major T. Leblond, Royal Canadian Dragoons, representing the Permanent Force (the regular army). Officers of the Fund received no salaries or honoraria and only a few allowable expenses. For the next 13 years Hair worked out of his home, receiving no remuneration for his tireless efforts until 1922.

Minutes of the inaugural meeting indicate that Buchan, who made one of the earliest cash donations to the Fund for preliminary expenses, selected the unwieldy name, the "Last Post" Imperial Naval and Military Contingency Fund. No one expressed dissatisfaction. From the beginning, many called the new organization simply the Last Post Fund, a practice followed here. Hair fittingly described the "Last Post" as the "last summons of the day in barracks, in camp or on the quarterdeck", as well as the ceremonial farewell sounded on the burial of a former soldier or during commemorative services.

In partnership with Arthur Hair, John Almond exerted a great deal of influence over the direction of the LPF in its early years. By 1909, he had built up a rock-solid reputation in Montreal. He was an excellent administrator and natural leader who worked untiringly on behalf of the Fund (and many other patriotic and philanthropic associations) for most of the next three decades. The organization's growth owed as much to his labours as to those of any other person. Almond was born in 1872 in Skigawake, Bonaventure County, in the Gaspé region of Québec. He was a graduate of Bishop's College, Lennoxville, and was ordained in 1897. For a time, he served as priest-in-charge in Labrador, responsible for a vast territory, including a rugged 700-kilometre coastline. In 1899, church authorities assigned him to the Anglican cathedral in Québec City, where he arrived just in time to be appointed Anglican chaplain to the Canadian contingent embarking for South Africa in October. Almond found campaigning in South Africa arduous, often monotonous, and generally difficult as he had had virtually no time to prepare for the assignment. Nevertheless, he persevered and took an interest in the welfare of the men, ministering to them following a number of major engagements. The fighting men remembered him most for the sporting and recreational activities that he organized behind the lines. Following his service in South Africa, he returned to Québec City at the end of 1900, and moved then to the small pulp and paper town of Grand Mère. In 1904, he became rector of Trinity Church.

As with Hair, the LPF became Almond's passion. Near the end of his life he claimed that "there is nothing with which I have been connected of which I am so proud as the inauguration and development of the Last Post Fund. I would rather be connected with that than with anything else ... in my career." During those same years, members of the LPF would have occasion to express the same sentiment about him.

The Last Post Fund adopted as its original logo a wreath of olive leaves enclosing the word "Pax", Latin for "peace". Over the wreath was the Latin inscription "Pro Patria et Defensoribus", (For the Nation and Its Defenders). On the left a bugler in full dress uniform of the Fusilier Regiment, partly turned towards the wreath, is sounding his bugle. Below him were the words "Last Post" and the motto "Lest We Forget", drawn from Rudyard Kipling's poem "The Recessional", first published in 1897, of which the first two stanzas are:

> God our fathers, known of old,
> Lord of our far-flung battle-line,
> Beneath whose awful Hand we hold
> Dominion over palm and pine –
> Lord God of Hosts, be with us yet,
> Lest we forget – lest we forget!
>
> The tumult and the shouting dies;
> The captains and the kings depart:

Still stands Thine ancient sacrifice,
An humble and a contrite heart.
Lord God of Hosts, be with us yet,
Lest we forget – lest we forget!

The "Last Post" Imperial Naval and Military Contingency Fund obtained its letters of incorporation in the Province of Québec on June 11, 1909. According to its 1909 constitution: "the primary object of this Fund is to provide Christian burial for ex-Army or Navy men who die in a hospital or public institution, or in any way become a public charge after death, and to provide it in such a way as to show the citizens of the British Empire that respectful provision in the last extremity is made for those who loyally have served the Flag." Thus was honourable sepulchre provided to any ex-soldier or sailor who had been on active service and who might at death be in destitute circumstances, friendless, or indigent. His remains would be shown dignity, and his military service gratitude. While Canadian in origin, the benefits offered were not confined to Canadians alone: any member of the imperial army or navy, nursing service, or British colonial forces was eligible provided that it could be established to the satisfaction of the directors that an individual had been a *bona fide* serving member of the military, had been honourably discharged, and had become a public charge after death. The LPF would also bury, at that person's expense, any non-indigent veteran desiring a military funeral and grave marker.

Early Operations

To be credible, the fledgling organization had to put its plans into action. After all, the inaugural meeting had been widely reported in Montreal's English-language press. The first formal burial sponsored by the Last Post Fund took place in Mount Royal Cemetery in April 1909, when it laid to rest a 40-year old indigent British veteran of the South African War, ex-trooper A. Walter Walters, an apparent suicide, in the cemetery vault. The respectful ceremony was attended by several of the Fund's leaders and supporters. The LPF buried Walters in this temporary location pending acquisition of its own plot. Its first burial in the Catholic Côte-des-Neiges Cemetery, again in the cemetery vault, occurred on October 20, 1909, for former Private Patrick

Brosnan, late of the British Army's 2nd West Yorkshire Regiment. From this modest beginning, numbers increased steadily until the outbreak of the First World War. In several instances, the LPF actually removed the unclaimed bodies of veterans from university and hospital dissecting facilities for honourable burial. It took time for the public, mortuary officials, and veterans' organization to learn of the Fund's existence, its burial facilities, and its services. Most of all, perhaps, it took money to inter dispossessed veterans.

In January 1910, once money was available, Hair wrote to the Mount Royal Cemetery to inquire about purchasing some plots at a special rate set aside for philanthropic and patriotic societies. He confidently noted in his letter that "we aspire to making the Last Post Plot a National landmark and something for the citizens of Montreal to point with pride to as having originated in their midst". In April the cemetery offered the LPF its "lowest possible price" of $20 per gravesite, which the Fund accepted. That month, and with the financial assistance of the IODE, the LPF purchased two burial plots – one Protestant and one Catholic – on the slopes of Mount Royal. The Protestant plot was part of Mount Royal Cemetery, while the Catholic was in Côte-des-Neiges Cemetery, which matched the Mount Royal Cemetery's price. Each small plot contained 10 gravesites, and the two were conveniently adjoining, separated only by a wrought-iron fence. The LPF made subsequent additions by purchasing individual or groups of gravesites, with each grave costing $20.

Regardless of their race, colour, creed, or gender, impoverished veterans could henceforward obtain an honourable funeral and burial alongside their comrades. Each simple grave would be similarly marked. In 1919, Hair was moved to write that: "our plots are...a tribute to the untiring devotion of [our] association...The plots are in the most beautiful location of both Cemeteries...are well kept and each grave is marked by a dignified granite Memorial Tablet flush with the ground on which is inscribed the Rank, Name, Age, and Regiment of those interred therein." Notwithstanding the rank of the deceased, individual graves could not be decorated by surviving family members beyond an occasional arrangement of cut flowers. In death, all former comrades would lie in peace together on equal terms, an interesting 'levelling' which was not reflected in the social prominence normally afforded military officers. That Hair was himself not an officer veteran might have had something to do with the adoption of this policy, though no objections seem to have been raised by the higher-ranking members constituting the Fund's leadership. There was no need, or money, for lavish burials, although all funeral ceremonies would be conducted in a dignified manner.

On Saturday afternoon, May 7, 1910, a large crowd gathered at the LPF's new burial plots on Mount Royal. A strong military contingent and dozens of veterans representing conflicts from the Crimean War to the South African War were present to witness the LPF's first formal interments. The Fund buried five ex-soldiers in Mount Royal Cemetery, followed by two others in Côte-des-Neiges. John Almond officiated at the first service and the chaplain of the *65e Carabiniers Mont-Royal* at the second. The British Army and Navy Veterans Association fired three volleys over the gravesites. The colourful military ceremony, which the press considered grand and quite unusual, was heavily reported on in Montreal's newspapers and illustrated weeklies. If positive publicity was any indication, the LPF was well on its way to respectability.

Hair was anxious to add a martial appearance to the Fund's new plots and so, in 1910, wrote to local military quartermaster authori-

Inaugural burial ceremony at the LPF's plot in Mount Royal Cemetery, May 1910, Reverend John Almond officiating. Arthur Hair is lower far right.

ties and even to Colonel Sam Hughes, the minister of militia and defence, to seek some obsolete smooth bore muzzle-loading 9-pounder guns and shot to adorn the sites. While the cannons would prove difficult to obtain, Hughes explained that the obsolete shot was available from large stocks in Kingston. The minister authorized the transfer of some to the LPF. In 1911, three small pyramids of 9-pounder shot were set up in each of the Protestant and Catholic cemetery plots.

Although the Mount Royal Cemetery was worried that the cannons "might be tampered with by youth", Hair, the former gunner, insisted on obtaining some for the site. But even Colonel R.W. Rutherford, master general of the ordnance, could not come up with any cannons for the persistent founder of the LPF. Most of the old muzzle-loading 9-pounders were being retained for use as saluting batteries and were not available for decorative purposes. Finally, in July 1912, the Department of Militia and Defence authorized the transfer to the Fund of four 9-pounder field pieces and their carriages from St. Helen's Island, in the St. Lawrence River opposite Montreal. The transfer was approved by the minister himself, and the military delivered the cannons, two to Mount Royal Cemetery and two to Côte-des-Neiges. The project had taken over two years, but these vintage guns, which had been cast in Britain in 1875, would guard the Fund's mountain-side plots.

In 1909, the LPF began a tradition that it still maintains, though in a modified form. In its early years, every May 24, (Victoria Day, or Empire Day), the LPF organized a joint commemorative ceremony at its Mount Royal burial plots. (In 1909, lacking plots, it held its ceremony at the old Papineau Avenue Military Cemetery.) The event became known as 'Decoration Day'. Each year, local military, civic, and ecclesiastical authorities gathered to honour those veterans buried there – and indeed all the empire's military dead. Military bands played, the lament was piped, and a bugler sounded the Last Post. Beforehand, LPF volunteers cleaned the gravesites and decorated them with small Union Jacks. Following the outbreak of the First World War these moving events became larger and better attended, and they seemed to take on a significance in the community far out of proportion to the number of impoverished veterans interred there. The LPF began earning a social niche for itself as a patriotic body. The

Montreal press always fully reported the Decoration Day ceremonies; the Fund's activities were not going unnoticed.

Despite the reference to "Christian burial" in the Fund's original constitution, and its Protestant and Catholic burial plots, the LPF was ready to attend to non-Christians as well. But religion was often a divisive subject in those pious times, even among Christians of different denominations. 'Mixed marriages' normally referred not to race, ethnicity, or language but to religion, and Catholics were forbidden from entering non-Catholic places of worship. Perhaps recognizing the potential for inter-denominational tensions, the executive deemed it advisable to introduce the following clause in the revised 1912 constitution: "Denominational discussion is strictly forbidden during meetings or any function and the spirit of forbearance in all matters pertaining to the ritual of all and any denomination is to prevail at all times, patriotism and comradeship predominating to the exclusion of denominationalism." So serious did the directors consider this matter that any transgression against this rule could lead to the ouster from office of any member whose behaviour, through imprudent expression, was found to be "objectionable to the interests of the cause".

The original rules governing the Fund's meetings appear stiff, even draconian, in other respects as well. For example, a member desiring to speak had to rise and "respectfully address" the president, who thereupon formally announced the member by name. A member could speak no more than twice on any subject and for no more than five minutes at a time. If a non-member was present at a meeting, no member could discuss the affairs or transactions of the Fund, under penalty of expulsion from the Fund. All members were obliged to wear their Fund insignia and any military service medals and decorations to which they were entitled. These regulations were compatible with the social standards of the time and also bespoke the seriousness with which the Fund approached its business. They also bore the unmistakable imprint of the overly formal Arthur Hair, whose dealings with others were usually unnecessarily complicated.

Like James Daly and Walter Walters, most indigent veterans residing in Canada before the outbreak of the First World War were former British soldiers who had subsequently immigrated to this country. This is clearly reflected in the backgrounds of those men initially buried by the Fund. The actual number of Canadians who had seen active service in the Canadian militia was relatively small at this time. While over 30,000 militiamen had been temporarily mobilized for border defence at the time of the Fenian Raids (which occurred spasmodically between 1866 and 1871), few had seen any action. Some 400 Canadians took part in the Red River Expedition of 1870, in a mainly British effort to contain Métis leader Louis Riel's first acts of resistance against Ottawa's authority. During the Northwest Campaign of 1885, mounted to suppress Riel's second rebellion, Ottawa mobilized 8,000 troops for active service, and from 1899 to 1902 over 7,300 Canadians served in South Africa. These numbers are minuscule compared to the hundreds of thousands of British troops who served throughout the empire in hundreds of campaigns and engagements during the same period. For example, half a million men served during the South African War. Hundreds of thousands of Britons immigrated to Canada between 1902 and 1914, with 150,000 arriving in 1913 alone. Many had difficulty finding adequate employment or lacked family support in Canada. A considerable number among them were former service-men. It is not surprising, then, that the LPF's early burials would mainly be of immigrants.

Given the imperial impulses of its creators, and because most early burials were of former British troops, in early 1910 the LPF sought support for its ideals in Britain. Hair dispatched an informa-tion leaflet to prominent British military leaders, many of whom offered unstinting praise for the goals of the Fund. The founder of the Boy Scout movement, Lord Baden-Powell, opined that the Fund strengthened the bonds of empire. Hair's own sense of patriotism went beyond Canada's boundaries, looking as he often did to Britain for his inspiration. Few English Canadians would have objected.

While chiefly providing a service to the dead rather than concen-trating on the needs of the living, the LPF also sometimes acted as "friend and advisor" to the survivors of a deceased veteran. In doing so, the Fund was crossing the line between a patriotic society and a social welfare organization, a role outside its mandate which it assumed occasionally, on a case-by-case basis, throughout the first half-century of its existence. For example, Hair frequently wrote to the Department of Militia and Defence on behalf of impoverished veterans' families regarding pension questions or claims. He also routinely assisted desti-tute survivors in obtaining the aid of one or more of Montreal's many charitable agencies to enable them to survive. He directed South African War veterans' families to patriotic and benevolent organizations such as the Canadian Patriotic Fund and the Soldiers' Wives' League. In one early case, the LPF took on the responsibility, with the Canadian Patriotic Fund, of financially assisting a disabled veteran of the South African War who finally passed away in 1912.

In accordance with Québec's Anatomy Act, in June 1910 the province granted the LPF "special privilege and power to act as 'next of kin' where it can be established that a man, who has become a public charge after death, was previously at any time a member of His Majesty's Army, Auxiliary or Colonial Forces." The Fund also became custodian of the deceased's personal effects, if any, if no next-of-kin could be located before interment. Normally, it sold these items to recover burial costs. In 1911, for example, the LPF publicly raffled a deceased veteran's watch and ring, a measure that yielded an impressive $92 for the Fund. This was a necessary expedient: money was in short supply. It almost always would be.

The activities and responsibilities of the fledgling organization grew rapidly. Within a few years the LPF had also interested itself in the restitution, marking, and care of neglected and forgotten graves of deceased naval and military veterans. The inaugural constitution also mentioned that an "effort will be made to gradually extend the Fund to all cities throughout the Dominion". It was expected that any new branches outside Québec would maintain their own burial plots. Hair, extremely proud of the LPF, even dared hope that similar groups would be organized throughout the empire. In October 1909, Hair tabled his first semi-annual report to the executive members of the Fund. He was optimistic and concluded: "I think you will agree with me we have matter for congratulation and the prospect of a successful future". This assessment was prophetic, to say the least. But for the time being, the Fund would have to show that it could fulfill the growing number of objectives that it had set for itself.

Financing

Arthur Hair and John Almond had forged a credible organization. In early 1909 Hair wrote to Earl Grey, the governor general, to request the favour of his official patronage for the Fund. It was a bold but shrewd move. Grey's patronage would provide the LPF with instant respectability. Hair's letter to Grey was endorsed by a number of well-to-do Montrealers, including Sir Hugh Graham, powerful proprietor of *The Montreal Daily Star,* whom Hair had visited in connection with the founding of the Fund, and who provided free advertising space in his newspaper for this novel venture. Perhaps because of Hair's evident sincerity and the obviously patriotic nature of the proposed endeavour, Grey granted his patronage. Thus was born the Fund's enduring tradition of having as its honorary patron the governor general of Canada. With this official sanction from Rideau Hall, the LPF was well on its way to success. The lieutenant-governor of Québec, Sir Alphonse Pelletier, also consented to associate his name with the Fund, as have all of Québec's and subsequently all other provinces' lieutenant-governors. Soon the mayor of Montreal, J.J. Guérin, and the lord bishop of Montreal, the Rt. Reverend J.C. Farthing, added their official support, as did Graham and Sir Montagu Allan, the Montreal shipping magnate. During the First World War the Catholic archbishop of Montreal, Mgr. Paul Bruchési, and Sir Sam Hughes added their names as well. In 1912, the respected Anglican clergyman, Reverend Canon F.G. Scott became honourary president of the LPF. Scott would later gain fame, along with Almond, for his extraordinary services as a military chaplain during the First World War.

But Lord Grey imposed an important condition in exchange for the considerable weight of his patronage. He insisted that the LPF remain a purely naval and military patriotic fund and not become a public charity. In other words, if the LPF hoped to maintain vice-regal support, it would have to limit its fund-raising to contacting active and retired military personnel and, as Hair phrased it, "patriotically disposed citizens" in Québec. A widespread public appeal or highly visible solicitation would have implied a popularizing of the noble sentiments to which the organization was pledged. This inability to canvass publicly would cause the LPF some financial distress in its early years. But no one in the organization wanted to lose the governor general's patronage, and so they carried on as best they could.

The Fund had, in fact, some considerable initial and ongoing expenses for funerals (strictly limited and controlled though they were), printing and stationery, postage, and incorporation fees. Hair originally raised money by sending a circular letter to the commanding officer of every military unit in Québec asking each to assist the LPF financially and to encourage his men to become members, paying minimal annual dues. But Hair also understood that government parsimony and reduced funding for militia training would lessen the ability of units and their members to contribute to the Fund. Lucien Vallée, the original LPF treasurer and later its recording secretary, noted in his first financial report, for the year ending March 31, 1910, that most contributions came from individuals "through the influence of [an LPF] member". The bank balance stood at a mere $150.02. In 1911, Vallée moved to the Québec City area, and for several years he was no longer very active in the Fund's affairs. He recommended merging the positions of secretary and treasurer and Hair became secretary-treasurer – a position that he held for 36 years, except for a brief hiatus in 1920-21.

In the five years leading up to the First World War, the LPF survived in large part as a result of the generosity of the cash-starved Montreal militia units, whose members might one day benefit from the LPF's services. The busy and devoted secretary-treasurer arranged numerous speaking engagements for himself at militia messes. Sometimes the officers permitted him to leave behind a collection box on behalf of the Fund. These boxes were distributed in naval and military canteens, armouries, military clubs and institutes, and barracks. Hair himself at first went around and gathered the proceeds. Although money was scarce, some units held special fund-raising events, usually light entertainments, and turned the proceeds over to the LPF. For example, in March 1912 the Sergeants' Mess of the Montreal Heavy Brigade, Canadian Garrison Artillery, held a "Euchre and Dance" and later sent the LPF a cheque for $60. The LPF developed particularly close relations with certain local units, such as the Victoria Rifles of Canada. Many sympathetic associations, drawn from both major language groups, did what they could. For example, *L'Association des vétérans canadiens* occasionally helped with small donations. With time, the LPF's contacts widened and its friends and supporters grew in number. In 1914, local expressions of generosity allowed the Fund to post a surplus of $488. In this manner did Hair's brainchild survive its infancy.

Public opinion, however, even when roused, produced little tangible financial effect. Another letter-writing campaign publicized the good works of the Fund and, as usual, also solicited financial assistance. In 1911 and 1912, Hair wrote to, among dozens of other prominent men, Sir Wilfrid Laurier, Sam Hughes, Sir Herbert Ames, Sir Hugh Graham, and Lord Strathcona, Canada's wealthy high commissioner in London, with whom Hair met in 1911. All received a copy of a small booklet describing the Fund's *raison d'être* prepared by Hair, who wrote most of the LPF's promotional literature produced during his lifetime. In November 1912, Sam Hughes replied to one of the Fund's trustees, Commander J.T. Walsh, stating that he was "fully in sympathy with the objects of your Association and consider that you are doing a very valuable service to the Imperial idea in Canada." Hair and other members of the LPF executive met with Hughes in December to discuss his department's financial assistance to the Fund, but little seems to have resulted. Officially, the cash-strapped Department of Militia and Defence provided cannons and shot, but no funding.

In September 1911, Hair penned a laboured letter to none other than Rudyard Kipling, a Nobel laureate (Literature), staunch defender of British imperialism and perhaps the most popular writer in Britain:

Rudyard Kipling Esq.,
Batemans, Burwash, Sussex, England
September 11, 1911

Respected Sir,

Appreciating your lifelong experience of "the Service man" and particularly Tommy Atkins in every phase of his existence – I feel sure that there is nobody who would lend a more attentive ear to "Tommy's" needs, than the one who has evidenced the ability to analyse his character and peculiarities with such vivid truism as we know you have. To be brief as possible and to avoid tiring you with appeals I presume you are the constant recipient of, I would respectfully submit that the object of my communication is to ask your kind perusal of the accompanying pamphlets explanatory of the work of this Organization which has only been in existence for a little over two years, is unique in its character and laudable of its purpose, but working against odds in a part of the Empire which (unfortunately for the general welfare of the same) is anti-Military in spirit. In short we are in need of money to erect appropriate and identical monuments on the two Plots (Protestant and Catholic) we now own on Mount Royal, and in accordance with the wishes of our Patron in Chief – His Excellency Earl Grey, Governor General, when giving us his patronage we were to abstain from making it a Public Charity as much as possible, and maintain it a distinctly "Service Fund" appealing to the Militia of the country for support – In this we have been successful to a certain extent, and as result have been able to purchase two very nice plots in the Protestant and Catholic Cemeteries in which we have given "six feet of ground" to no less than thirteen of the Empire's Defenders who saw active service in the Empire's Wars covering the period of the Crimea to the present date, and who, but for the existence of this Fund would have been relegated to a Pauper's grave or the Inspector of Anatomy, an ignominious end for any man who has offered his life's blood as a sacrifice (if need be) for his country.

Incidentally, I may also say, many are the letters of gratitude and even re-imbursement from Mothers, Sisters, Brothers, and loved ones we have received even from distant lands, Australia amongst other places.

Now, Sir, it seems to me that there is nobody can grasp the noble ideal of this work in the dual effort to save our Empire's Defenders from the ignominy of a Pauper's Grave or Dissecting Room, and encourage the spirit of true "Camaraderie" as well as yourself, and being imbued with this feeling, I am taking the liberty to ask your kind consideration of composing an Ode or Ballad to the denomination of this Fund viz. – "The Last Post" allowing us the Copyright for sale, as a donation to the Memorial Fund.

Appreciating that little is obtained without the asking, while also appreciating the many calls you have on your generosity, and apologising for the intrusion,

> *I have the honour to be, Sir,*
> *Very Respectfully Yours,*
> *Arthur Hair*
> *(Late of the Gunners' R.H.A.)*
> *Secy. Treas.*

Kipling's reply was not long in coming.

September 19, 1911

Dear Sir,
Very many thanks for your letter of September 11th, and much as I am
interested in any scheme of the nature which your Imperial Naval and
Military Contingency Fund sets out to accomplish, I am afraid it is
impossible for me, with my present engagements, to write you an Ode or
Ballad of the kind which you ask, and which I am sure your work so well
deserves.

Yours truly,
Rudyard Kipling

Such early financial strains were one reason Hair implored the federal
government to assume what he believed to be its legal and moral
responsibilities in the matter of indigent veterans' burials.
Notwithstanding the Fund's initially private nature, Hair intended all
along to pressure the government to recognize the need for the services that the LPF was providing. He believed that the enterprise could
survive only with regular injections of government grants and an official commitment to furthering the goals of the organization. When no
such support was forthcoming, Hair grew increasingly bitter and came
to consider all levels of government hypocritical; governments paid
lip-service to the valuable contributions of veterans, he thought, but
suffered from a convenient lapse of memory at the veterans' hour of
need. There was some truth to this, but, in this case, the government's
attitude reflected that of much of society. It had never been the role of
government to finance the burials of its impoverished citizens – veterans or not. Turn-of-the-century industrial society had created large
numbers of urban labourers, for example, who, because of the vicissi-
tudes of life and for want of pensions or appropriate government welfare legislation, died in abject poverty. Since municipalities, churches,
and various benevolent organizations had traditionally dealt with their
interment, Ottawa saw little reason to establish by its intervention in
the case of veterans what might evolve into a precedent with wider
application. Hair faced an uphill battle.

Making a Difference

Not long after the founding of the LPF, Hair left his position at the Montreal General Hospital. He worked for several years as an office manager with the Montreal firm of Gault and Ewing, real estate and insurance brokers, and later in the front offices of a coal company. During this period Hair was able to develop and nurture the organization that he had instigated. His employers understood the demands that it made of his time, and, as Hair later indicated, he was fully aware of the debt that he owed them. The work of the Last Post Fund, in fact, began to consume most of his time and energy.

The LPF received much correspondence in the first few years of its existence. Many letters sought information regarding its services, while others passed on details of veterans' deaths, especially as appreciation for the LPF's role grew in the veterans' communities, among those engaged in the mortuary business, and by individuals and organizations concerned with the care of the poor and aged. For example, Father Ray Pennafort, a Catholic priest in Montreal wrote: "I the undersigned priest certify that Michael Mangan, pensioner of the British Army, having served 21 years and 75 days in the Seaforth Highlanders, died this morning June 15, 1912 at the Home of the Little Sisters of the Poor... Said pensioner has no one to defray the expenses for his funeral and should be given the burial of a veteran." Father Pennafort wondered if the LPF could help. It could; the LPF buried Mangan in its military plot in Côte-des-Neiges Cemetery. The Last Post Fund was making a difference.

Other correspondents, often from the underclasses of society, expressed gratitude for the work that the Fund was accomplishing. Many of their often-poignant letters provide the true measure of the importance of the LPF for the impoverished families left behind by deceased veterans. In April 1912, the Manchester widow of ex-trooper James Robert Pilling, formerly of the British army's 15th Hussars, wrote to the LPF: "I beg to tender you my sincerest thanks for your kind letter received last Wednesday informing me of the death of my husband. The news has come as a terrible shock to me. I also wish to thank the Executive of the Fund for undertaking the burial of my husband and especially for the military honours paid him. He was always proud of his connection with the Army... Words fail to express my deep feelings of gratitude for all you have done. I am so thankful that my husband's remains fell into such kindly hands." The LPF, as was its legal right, sold off Pilling's meagre belongings, although it returned his medals and watch to his widow. There is an interesting footnote to the story. The LPF requested a copy of Mrs. Pilling's declaration of next-of-kin and her marriage certificate. On receipt of these items it would dispatch a death certificate enabling her to apply for her deceased husband's meagre pension. She duly sent the documents but, nothing being received by the Fund, she inquired about the status of her letter at the Post Office. There she was informed that her envelope "very likely went by the [Royal Mail Steamer] *Titanic*. If that is so it will be lost." She obtained replacement copies and eventually received her husband's death certificate from the LPF.

In September 1911, Patrick Kelleher, of Cork, Ireland, wrote a note of appreciation to the Fund for having buried his uncle. "What a grand thing it is to have such a[n] Association as yours to look after the interests of strangers", he wrote. Similarly, Mrs. Grace Wills of Edinburgh wrote in 1912 that the news conveyed to her by the LPF of the death of her son, ex-trooper Robert Wills, formerly of the 2nd Dragoon Guards, "came as a painful surprise to us all and we were grateful indeed to know...that your Society had carried out the last sad rites and that he was followed to the grave by comrades in the absence of his own Kith and Kin." She enclosed a small sum as a token of her appreciation. This was also an era in which almost all veterans deaths and LPF funeral cortèges and burials were described in the press. Few interested readers could escape growing knowledge of the Fund.

By the summer of 1914, the "Last Post" Imperial Naval and Military Contingency Fund had been in existence over five years. It had defined a place for itself as a small but growing benevolent organization devoted to recognizing the patriotic sacrifices of the empire's defenders. The LPF had obtained the public support of some of the most powerful men in Québec and indeed in Canada. It had buried several dozen ex-servicemen, and Arthur Hair realized that, in his LPF work, he had found his true vocation.

But for Arthur Hair, Canada's military community, the Last Post Fund, and the entire country, the greatest challenge loomed just around the corner. War would shake Canada to its very foundations and, in a few short years, legitimize the Last Post Fund as Canada's leading authority on veterans' burial planning.

2

THE FIRST WORLD WAR AND ITS AFTERMATH, 1914–1919

Nor was their agony brief, or once only imposed upon them.
The wounded, the war-spent, the sick received no exemption.
Being cured they returned and endured and achieved our
redemption.

RUDYARD KIPLING,
INSCRIPTION IN MEMORIAL CHAMBER,
PEACE TOWER, OTTAWA

In the summer of 1914, the First World War broke out following years of mounting political and military tension in Europe. On June 28, the heir to the Austro-Hungarian throne, Archduke Franz Ferdinand, was assassinated in Sarajevo by a Serbian terrorist. One month later, on July 28, Austria–Hungary declared war on Serbia. Germany moved in support of Austria–Hungary, while Russia mobilized in defence of Serbia. Within days, all these nations were embroiled in war. France, allied with Russia, also mobilized, prompting a German declaration of war. For a few days Britain remained neutral. But on August 4, once German forces invaded Belgium, whose security Britain had pledged to uphold, Britain declared war on Germany. All Europe was aflame.

Canada could not remain immune from the conflict. While Confederation in 1867 had given Canada the right of self-government, and nearly complete domestic independence, the country's international status had remained the same: constitutionally, and in the eyes of the world, it remained a British colony. When Britain was at war, Canada was too.

Canada's military response was nothing short of outstanding. At the outbreak of hostilities, it had a standing army of only 3,100 men. However, through a herculean effort, and not without political controversy, the nation mobilized for war. Canadian military historian C.P. Stacey has claimed that Canada's immense contribution to the Allied cause in terms of men deployed and victories scored during the First World War may have been the country's greatest single achievement. Strange-sounding places such as Ypres, the Somme, Vimy, Passchendaele, Amiens, Arras, and Mons would assume enormous importance in the annals of the nation's military history and become etched in the collective memory of Canadians for generations.

From a 1914 population of approximately 7.8 million, over 620,000 men and a few thousand nursing sisters were on active service during the war. Some 425,000 of these served overseas with the Canadian Expeditionary Force (CEF). Another 25,000 fought in the British air services, while 5,000 joined the Royal Canadian Navy. The cost to Canada in human lives was appalling: before the guns ceased firing, more than 60,000 of its soldiers had been killed and another 170,000 wounded.

Going to War

Immediately on the outbreak of war, the leading members of the "Last Post" Imperial Naval and Military Contingency Fund met in emergency session to discuss the war situation and decide on how the LPF could help with "war relief". The Fund's executive unanimously decided that the organization could play a constructive and patriotic role by assisting servicemen's families left in straitened circumstances. Given the patriotic impulse that had stimulated the Fund's creation, this new mission was entirely in character with its founding principles.

Arthur Hair, along with W.H. Atherton, Ph.D., Montreal historian and social reformer, and the other members of the executive present at the meeting (Almond was absent), hoped that all military units and patriotic associations active in the Montreal area would co-operate to assist those on active service as well as their families. The goal was to avoid needless duplication of effort and expense. Accordingly, on August 12 the Last Post Fund hosted a meeting of local patriotic groups and organizations and those attending decided to establish a Montreal branch of the Canadian Patriotic Fund (CPF) led by representatives from large financial institutions.

Public-spirited citizens and groups had set up the CPF in 1900 to assist the needy families of Canadian soldiers who had volunteered to serve in the South African War. At the national level, the CPF was re-formed in 1914 at the suggestion of the governor general, His Royal Highness the Duke of Connaught. In the absence of their principal breadwinner on active service, the CPF would assure families of servicemen a basic minimum standard of living. From 1914 to 1919, nation-wide fund-raising by the CPF yielded an astonishing $50 million.

The Last Post Fund appointed Arthur Hair and W.H. Atherton, who was born in England and immigrated to Canada in 1907, to sit on the general committee of the CPF's Montreal branch (eventually the largest in Canada), and the LPF proved to be an early fund-raiser on behalf of this organization. Many local charitable or philanthropic groups contributed to the Canadian Patriotic Fund, canvassed for it, or held special events in its name to raise money. In September 1914, the City of Montreal gave the enormous sum of $150,000. The same month, the LPF did what it could by organizing an exhibit of military artifacts in a vacant downtown storefront. The show, made up of loans from private collections, was designed to attract attention to the Fund and raise money for the CPF. With visitors paying an entry fee of 10 cents, it raised the handsome sum of $626, which included the proceeds of a raffle for a piano donated by William H. Leach, an executive of the LPF, in whose piano store some of the Fund's early meetings were held.

The close co-operation between the CPF and the LPF did not last through the war. In 1915, Hair complained that the Montreal CPF had invited Atherton and him to only two of its meetings. Despite the LPF's auspicious start in assisting soldiers' families, the CPF very rapidly eclipsed it in this role. For the remainder of the war, the two groups co-operated indirectly and the LPF did not try again to organize a special event on the CPF's behalf. The Fund had itself to think about as well.

The LPF was fully committed to assisting the war effort in any manner not inconsistent with its charter purposes. In fact, despite its tiny budget, the LPF often ventured well beyond its original mandate. For example, in August 1914 it distributed hundreds of cards to all Montreal-area armouries, garrisons, and recruiting centres inviting men enlisting for overseas service to use the LPF as their forwarding address in the absence of any family or friends to assume this role. In keeping with its concern for soldiers' welfare, in September 1914 the Fund also went on record as decrying the "inadequacy" of Ottawa's meagre pension plans for discharged men. This would not be the last time the LPF criticized Ottawa's veteran policies. At the same time the LPF petitioned the government to establish "Soldiers' Homes" for those troops, undoubtedly numerous, who would return from the front maimed and in need of special care. These Soldiers' Homes would serve to house impoverished veterans as well.

Perhaps in an attempt to make the LPF more relevant and immediate to the sentiments of philanthropic and sympathetic Montrealers, Hair reminded readers of the LPF's promotional literature that the organization was interested in the welfare of the living as well as the dead. A contingency clause in its constitution empowered the LPF to assist ex-servicemen or their families in instances of serious financial distress. When the Fund's leaders deemed such aid to fall more appropriately within the purview of other bodies (such as the Canadian Patriotic Fund and the Soldiers' Wives' League), they directed the unfortunate families to these organizations. But, because of the LPF's growing renown, veterans and their families approached it for various forms of assistance and services, and money was often in short supply. During the war the LPF occasionally 'loaned' $5 or $6 to a veteran's family to help it through a particularly stressful period. At the end of each fiscal year, the Fund invariably wrote off the money as an expense.

In the autumn of 1915 the LPF assisted the Citizens' Recruiting Association in its general publicity campaign held at the Montreal Arena. The Fund contributed a display consisting of a group of military wax figures collectively entitled "A Silent Appeal", which attracted many viewers and resulted in the dissemination of a large amount of recruiting literature. Always a patriotic organization, the LPF took on the added and urgent goal of promoting the prosecution of the war to its fullest possible extent, including supporting the controversial and culturally divisive policy of conscription of manpower for overseas service.

One member of the Last Post Fund in particular made an enormous personal contribution to the war effort. Enlisting in August 1914, the president of the LPF, the Reverend Canon John Almond, was appointed chaplain of the divisional artillery in the 33,000-strong First Canadian Contingent, which sailed from Gaspé on October 3, 1914. Despite his mixed fortunes in South Africa, Almond, who had since become enormously respected in Montreal religious and military circles, was offered a prominent place in the First Contingent. So, too, was the better-known Reverend Canon F.G. Scott, who was the honorary president and chaplain-major of the Last Post Fund. Since Almond had helped to found the LPF, his overseas posting with the Canadian Expeditionary Force merely cemented his long-standing interest in veterans' and military affairs. Commander J.T. Walsh assumed the presidency of the Fund during Almond's wartime absence.

In August 1915, the energetic and capable Almond was promoted major and appointed assistant director of Chaplain Services at the Headquarters (HQ) of the Canadian Corps overseas. By the end of 1916, Almond, by this time a lieutenant colonel, was directly supervising the four divisional chaplains (including Canon Scott with the First Division), who in turn oversaw the work of dozens of other chaplains. Almond's efficiency and abilities caught the eye of the commanding officer of the First Division, Major-General Arthur Currie, who would become commander of the famed Canadian Corps in June 1917 and, after the war, president of the LPF. Currie's personal regard for Almond and his eventual involvement with the Fund were no mere coincidence. The war provided a stimulus for men of like mind to work closely together and also to become united in common causes afterwards. The LPF was one such cause, and Currie and Almond developed a friendship based on mutual respect that lasted until Currie's death in 1933. In early 1917, the erratic and ineffectual director of Chaplain Service, Richard Steacy, was dismissed by Corps HQ (at Currie's near-insistence), and Almond, promoted to colonel and strongly supported by Currie, replaced him. Almond's first task was to reorganize and reinvigorate the Chaplain Service in order to raise the chaplains' morale and also their profile in the Canadian Corps. In this goal he was entirely successful.

In 1917 Almond found himself in charge of 276 military chaplains overseas. He proved a determined administrator, who also could be hard-nosed when occasion demanded. Historian Duff Crerar has written of him: "During his first year in office [as director] Almond forged a highly visible, versatile and disciplined religious agency that earned the confidence and respect of most senior officers." Crerar has also described Almond as "congenial and sensible". General Currie was so appreciative of Almond's efforts that he vowed to help the chaplaincy in any way he could in the postwar period. With his subsequent, very active commitment to the Last Post Fund, Currie kept his word. In 1918, Almond was created a Companion of the Order of St. Michael and Saint George (CMG). Prior to the armistice he was also made a Commander of the Order of the British Empire (CBE).

Almond's military service overseas also enabled him to lay the groundwork to assist Canadian soldiers after the war. He felt that only chaplains who had worked overseas and seen the horrors of trench warfare could truly understand veterans' needs. In fact, the war helped shape Almond's own views towards both society and Christianity. He became a vocal advocate of the "social gospel" movement, which sought to involve the church directly in alleviating all types of social problems. Almond's postwar work with and on behalf of veterans and their families became inseparable from his notion of employing "social Christianity" for the spiritual and material betterment of the less fortunate. His involvement with the Last Post Fund is an excellent example of this very precept. In September 1915, Almond returned to Montreal on a short leave and attended a meeting of the LPF's executive committee. There he stated that he frequently discussed the Fund overseas with the troops as well as with fellow chaplains. He firmly believed that a great deal of interest in the LPF would be forthcoming following the cessation of hostilities and that the need for its services would grow enormously.

Arthur Hair, by this time in his early 40s, also became active in the war effort. He organized a cadet corps out of Trinity Church and, using his expertise acquired in the Canadian Army Medical Corps, served as a first aid instructor with the Montreal Harbour Police. He also acted as an artillery recruiting sergeant, providing preliminary drill to the raw recruits and shepherding them to Valcartier for further training. As if this was not enough, Hair also took on the duties of quartermaster sergeant with the McGill University Canadian Officers' Training Corps. In attempting to attract notice to the work of their organization, the patriotically driven members of the LPF's board led by example.

Curiously, however, very early in the war, in September 1914, Hair notified the executive of the LPF in a letter that he was, as the minutes of a committee meeting record, "reluctantly tendering his resignation" as secretary-treasurer, owing to "unavoidable circumstances." Perhaps belying some form of internal conflict within the organization, Walsh requested Hair to take no action for the time being and allow the executive an opportunity to "consider" the matter. No meetings took place for two months, until November, at which time the matter of Hair's resignation was conspicuously *not* discussed, Hair being duly present as secretary-treasurer. It would not be the last time that Hair threatened to resign, and, as discussed below, he actually did resign on one occasion.

On May 8, 1916, the Last Post Fund inaugurated, under the patronage of the governor general, a Supplementary Memorial Fund to raise money to erect memorials, in Canada, Europe, or elsewhere "to perpetuate forever the memory of our fallen heroes". LPF promotional literature insisted that "moneys received for this particular Fund [will] NOT [be] applied to the general work of the 'Last Post Fund'". The idea for such a wartime collection was a measure of the growing pride felt throughout Canada at the battlefield achievements of the Canadian Expeditionary Force. It was also meant to be a testimonial to the enormous casualties that Canadians were suffering on the Western Front.

In order to raise funds for its new project, and also to help pay for postwar veterans' convalescent homes, the LPF arranged for the sale to the general public of a special seal meant to be affixed to the back of postal envelopes to signify the user's support for the new Memorial Fund. Postal authorities approved the scheme. For the remainder of the war, these special seals, comprising the LPF logo superimposed on the Union Jack, were sold at LPF special events and through a variety of other outlets, including the headquarters of local military units. Money was raised in modest amounts, but the seals publicized the LPF – a secondary though clear objective of the campaign.

In the summer of 1916, the Montreal Soldiers' Wives' League invited the LPF to participate in a major fund-raiser that it was planning to hold that autumn. The League hoped to collect money to assist the struggling local families of men away on active service. Following some considerable debate, in September the LPF

Illustration in the LPF publication, The Mail Bag, *October 1916.*

announced that it would publish a bulletin for public sale at the function and would turn over two-thirds of the proceeds to the League. As a *quid pro quo,* the LPF was allowed to sell its envelope seals at the exhibit and retain full proceeds. *The Naval and Military Mail Bag/Souvenir de la Kermesse militaire*, the LPF's illustrated 46-page "Military Benefit Souvenir" booklet containing articles in English and French, served as the official organ of the elaborate event held from October 17 to 21 at the Montreal Arena, a common venue for patriotic and war-related events.

The publication of *The Naval and Military Mail Bag* in October 1916 was one of the LPF's major wartime endeavours. The handsome booklet helped publicize the organization as one of Montreal's foremost wartime patriotic societies – and this after only seven years of under-funded existence. In order to produce *The Mail Bag*, the LPF organized an editorial committee under Hair's tutorship and successfully solicited the assistance of Montreal-area stationers, publishers, and advertisers, who patriotically contributed their services and materials free of charge. The authors of articles were also willing to 'do their bit' on a voluntary basis during this time of "universal sacrifice". *The Naval and Military Mail Bag* contained original contributions from historians W.H. Atherton, Benjamin Sulte, and L.-O. David, as well as by Arthur Hair, Canon F.G. Scott, Lucien Vallée, and Charles Marcil, Member of Parliament and former Speaker of the House of Commons, and other well-known public figures.

The Last Post Fund used this publication also as a promotional tool. Hair admitted in a brief introduction that the LPF was not well understood. "There are naturally many who do not even know of the objects of this association", he wrote, "or what it has done to organize its existence." He then went on to outline the LPF's *raison d'être*, which exercise he felt would be "interesting and instructive". "Our *primary* object is obitual", Hair wrote. "We urge the establishment of National Military Cemeteries where any man who has served the Empire honourably may find respectful sepulchre…wherein his weary bones may rest at the sounding of the 'Last Post'." "In the past", Hair continued, "the Nation's gratitude to its Defenders when they die friendless has been reflected in the Civic Morgue, the Potters Field and the College Dissecting Room – truly an ungrateful reward." Hair was far-sighted enough to realize that if an organization

MILITARY   BENEFIT   SOUVENIR

The Naval and Military
MAIL BAG

SOUVENIR DE LA KERMESSE MILITAIRE

A collection of original articles written for this publication on the occasion of the military benefit of the

Série d'articles inédits, écrits pour cette revue à l'occasion de la kermesse militaire tenue au bénéfice de la

SOLDIERS WIVES' LEAGUE

Arena, 17th to 21st October 1916

· LEST ·
WE
FORGET

"JE ME SOUVIENS"

PAX
LAST POST

"Last Post" Imperial Naval and Military Contingency Fund

P. O. BOX 1382   MONTREAL

Cover of The Mail Bag, *1916.*

like the Last Post Fund had proven necessary before the First World War, its utility would be much magnified in the years ahead.

An LPF "Ladies Committee" had been set up in September 1914 to assist in raising funds. Its members assumed leadership roles in the LPF in this regard for the period of the war. With respect to the Soldiers' Wives' League fund-raiser in October 1916, Mrs. Leila Morrison, later convener of the LPF's Ladies' Auxiliary, acted as liaison with the League and almost single-handedly negotiated the LPF's successful participation in the event. Dozens of organizations, societies, and military units set up booths and stalls there. Some displayed items for sale or auction, sometimes including valuable artwork and antiques. Other groups provided entertainment or refreshments. All the work and proceeds were on behalf of impoverished military families. While the LPF had its own prominent booth, its principal involvement was to sell *The Mail Bag*. The LPF raised a total of $677, including receipts from the sale of seals. This enabled the Fund to purchase a $400 Victory Bond the following year – the LPF's first long-term investment.

Attempts at Inclusiveness

The LPF noted in *The Mail Bag* that as the publication was "issued in the Province of Quebec, these offerings will be found to be in every way an admirable bilingual tribute…and one proffered by representatives of the two great races to whose hands the destinies of Canada are entrusted." In fact, the booklet was the LPF's first significant public appeal to a French-Canadian audience. The motto, "Lest We Forget", was cleverly translated as Québec's provincial motto, "*Je me souviens*".

But while the Fund sought inroads into the French-Canadian community, it would take more than a few bilingual articles in a patriotic publication for it to succeed. Political and cultural differences were heightened in Québec during the war, and any organization, such as the LPF, that promoted conscription for overseas service, and which had no high-profile French-Canadian members, could hardly have expected widespread support from that community. The Last Post Fund was in appearance and fact very largely an English-language institution, catering to the needs of a veteran community overwhelmingly of British origin. Several among its executive were British born, including Arthur Hair himself. Under these circumstances it was difficult for the Fund to appear relevant to Québec's French-speaking majority, few of whom had recently seen active service. French-Canadian militiamen had been mobilized at the time of the Fenian Raids (1866–1871) and during the Northwest Rebellion in 1885. Several hundred French Canadians had enlisted for service in the South African War, and a few others had campaigned with British forces in the service of the empire. Perhaps 20,000 served during the course of the First World War. Overall, the pool of French-Canadian veterans in Québec (the only province in which the LPF operated at that time) was not nearly as large as that composed of English-Canadian and British immigrant veterans. To October 1916, only one of the LPF's 54 burials had been of a French Canadian: J.B. Ouellette, a veteran of the South African War. It is likely, however, that other benevolent groups, Catholic or fraternal, interred at least some indigent French-Canadian veterans. The trend did slowly change. By the end of 1919, about 17 per cent of LPF burials had been of French Canadians, most of whom died in that year's massive influenza epidemic.

Canada's cultural differences were magnified during the war over the issue of military conscription for overseas service, which a majority of French Canadians opposed even while not necessarily being against Canada's participation in the war. Despite some initial enthusiasm for the war in French Canada, proportionately few French Canadians enlisted compared to British-born Canadians and Canadians of British ethnic origin. There existed among French Canadians a tradition of suspicion and even hostility towards the British Empire. While sympathetic to France's plight, few French Canadians were willing to risk their lives in *its* defence either. Public opinion in Québec strongly favoured a vigorous defence of Canadian territory if attacked, but a purely voluntary military effort in the defence of Britain and France. The vast majority of French Canadians viewed compulsory military service as a coercive measure imposed by English Canada in support of nations to which French Canada felt little emotional attachment. These feelings were especially pronounced in Québec. Anti-conscription demonstrations took place regularly in Montreal throughout 1917 and several days of rioting in Québec City in 1918 left several dead. English and French Canadians' views of Canada and definitions of patriotism had never been further apart. Nevertheless, to compensate for heavy losses at the front and to make up for low nation-wide recruitment, the federal government legislated conscription in August 1917.

The LPF's participation at and hearty endorsement of a 1917 pro-conscription "National Unity and Win the War" rally in Montreal could not have endeared it to local anti-conscriptionist opinion. Despite its stance, the LPF made some positive wartime contacts with the French-language community. For example, on August 11, 1916, on receiving information concerning the activities of the LPF (submitted by the LPF itself), Montreal's largest French-language daily newspaper, *La Presse,* published a lengthy and very favourable article on the Fund and its work. *La Presse* expressed pride that it was in Québec that the first organization in the empire devoted to assisting indigent veterans was founded. The goal of honouring in death those who had served loyally in their lifetime "*[se] cadre bien avec la devise de notre province: 'Je me souviens'*". Clearly, the LPF's original goal was laudable; one need not agree with its political views. Although occasionally experiencing difficulty in separating the Fund's practice from its politics, Montreal's French-language press continued to endorse its burial policies. This was extraordinary, especially since many of the LPF's burials were of British immigrants – hardly a group eliciting much sympathy from French Canadians during the war. French Canadian support for the Fund in Montreal, or at least an absence of hostility towards it, stands out as an unusual feature of French Canadians' wartime relationships with English-speaking patriotic groups.

Since religion was a significant social cleavage in Canadian society, the LPF sought to appear strictly non-denominational. It was therefore very pleased when the good offices of executive member W.H. Atherton, a devout Catholic and a history teacher at Loyola College in Montreal, obtained Archbishop Paul Bruchési's agreement in 1916 for the prelate to become a patron of the Fund. Bruchési proved a strong supporter. The LPF's promotional booklets also emphasized the fact that LPF burials would conform to the religious practices of the deceased – a major consideration in strongly Catholic Québec. While the LPF made some well-received gestures to the

French-Canadian community, in general it as yet had little resonance with French Canadians. Its British and imperial nature, coupled with the initial paucity of French-Canadian veterans, denied it social and political access to French Canada. This situation would change somewhat after the war.

In any event, the LPF's wartime stance seems not to have produced any lasting strained relations between it and the French-language press in Montreal. In November 1920, *La Presse* praised the work of the Fund, noting that it *"poursuit son oeuvre sans éclat et sans parade"*. According to *La Presse*, the LPF *"fait disparaître en partie la laideur de la misère. Grâce à cette association la famille du malheureux héros désherité peut aller prier sur la tombe qui lui est réservée…Il ne faut pas oublier que ceux qui meurent ici dans la misère ont combattu et ont fait la gloire du Canada."* This newspaper took particular note when the LPF interred a former member of the famed *22e Bataillon* (the 'Van Doos'). There is no evidence that French Canadians were averse to the Last Post Fund. It was just that French Canadian society only infrequently required its services. This, too, would change.

Seeking Government Help

Significant sources of new funding did not materialize for the LPF during the war, despite the patriotic appeal of its cause. Money remained scarce. Because of the routine need to purchase additional gravesites (at $20 each) and to pay for an ever-increasing number of funerals, the Fund's financial situation remained precarious during the war. From 1910 to 1919, its average annual receipts from all sources averaged $982 a year. Although the period 1917-1919 saw a sharp increase, whatever money was raised was invariably spent on current operations. Costs multiplied and it was difficult for the Fund to stay ahead. The LPF's responsibilities were beginning to outstrip its ability to pay for them.

On July 17, 1916, the Last Post Fund adopted a resolution calling on the government of Québec to express support for its goals and activities and to provide an immediate grant of $10,000 and an annual operating subsidy of $300 – in effect, a guarantee of the LPF's continuity. The Fund needed the $10,000 for the immediate purchase of burial plots in Québec City, Sherbrooke, Trois-Rivières, and elsewhere in the province. Hair dispatched a copy of the resolution to Premier Sir Lomer Gouin, as well as to all members of the Executive Council, the upper house of the legislature. The LPF's petition was endorsed by a strong representation of prominent men and women from varied political, institutional, and religious backgrounds. Also on July 17, an influential LPF delegation met with Gouin to press the organization's case. Hair hoped that, with a war on, it would be difficult for the provincial government to refuse the LPF's patriotic request. This resolution and petition constituted an early call for state intervention in the affairs of needy Canadians – not a popular idea at that time.

But to Hair's consternation, and in a move that fed his growing impatience, the provincial government, after a delay stretching well into 1917, declined to make the requested grants. A meeting between Hair and Gouin in February 1917 failed to resolve the impasse. Like Ottawa, Québec City continued to offer sympathy for the LPF's principles, but no more than that for the time being. Subsequently, Hair sent a copy of the July resolution to dozens of prominent imperial, federal, and provincial military, political, and civic authorities in the hope of obtaining their support for the LPF and its Supplementary Memorial Fund. In Canada, the governor general, the lieutenant-governor of Québec, the prime minister, federal cabinet ministers, and the mayors of Québec's largest cities and towns all received Hair's letter, and virtually all responded positively, including the prime minister, Sir Robert Borden. But few offered more than lip-service.

The executive of the Fund had ulterior motives for soliciting this high-level support. It hoped for "the ultimate nationalisation of the Last Post Fund ideal" and continued to harbour aspirations of widening the LPF into a national institution. Hair, especially, desired official government recognition for the LPF's view that a dignified burial should be the *right* of any veteran, preferably paid for by the government. In August 1916, Sir Hugh Graham's *Montreal Daily Star* stated plainly that "[a] guarantee of six feet of the Empire for every ex-soldier or sailor should he die in indigence" was the LPF's "modest" demand. The newspaper pointed out, perhaps with some exaggeration, that in the United States no ex-soldiers were buried in pauper's graves and that if the LPF's petition to Gouin would only be heeded, Québec's would be the first government in the empire to enact legislation providing for the services thus far offered only by the LPF. *La Presse* echoed its rival newspaper:

> *L'association a contracté certaines obligations dans le passé...et il lui faudra faire de nouveaux achats de terrains et de nouvelles dépenses pour répondre à tous les appels. C'est dire que les autorités provinciales ont le devoir de venir à son secours, en lui accordant volontiers les allocations demandées par la délégation qui s'est présentée devant Sir Lomer Gouin...[N]ous comptons qu'après avoir consulté ses collègues, il en viendra à une décision qui assurera l'avenir du nouveau fonds patriotique...Cette requête nous paraît trop modeste pour que le gouvernement provincial ne songe pas immédiatement à y faire droit...Il existe aux Etats-Unis 83 cimétières nationaux où sont enterrés les militaires. C'est une exemple à imiter.*

The LPF had made some influential friends in Montreal's editorial rooms. Although Hair would have to wait a number of years for a national LPF, the war had made some important circles aware of the need for so devoted an organization. The administrators of the Fund wisely seized the moment to begin the process of obtaining official government recognition.

Hair insisted that one of the primary reasons for the Fund's existence was to "urge the Government to assume a duty it at present ignores – of paying the debt we owe our Defenders should they, by any means, fall by the wayside and become friendless at the hour of death." He made it clear that the LPF was not a charitable body, but rather a "movement" that was supported through public sympathy and voluntary contributions. Still, it was becoming increasingly clear that government funding would be essential for the Fund's postwar survival. The LPF had arranged its 54 indigent burials up to October 1916 without any public monies whatsoever, although "the time is at hand", wrote Hair, "when such will be impossible, and our government must be confronted with its responsibility."

While the war facilitated patriotic fund-raising, the LPF also faced competition for scarce resources from many other public-spirited groups formed in wartime Montreal. Since individuals, groups, or corporate bodies inclined to assist the LPF would also receive requests from the Canadian Patriotic Fund, for example, not all wartime charitable needs could be met. For the over-extended LPF, it was time to expand, with government assistance, or whither away. From overseas, Reverend Almond wrote in a letter published in *The Mail Bag* that he would "oppose with all my might the election of any government that has not for the chief plank in its platform the care of disabled soldiers and fatherless families. The Nation must keep faith with the glorious Army of the Dead." With hundreds of thousands of Canadians serving overseas, government responsibility for soldiers' postwar care, up to and including their burials, was clearly an idea whose time had come.

A Time of Despair

In the meantime, the work of the Last Post Fund continued, though in increasingly distressed circumstances. The Fund sent more petitions seeking funding to the federal government, without success. Since 1909, the LPF had dispatched four separate and strongly endorsed petitions for financial assistance to the Militia Council in Ottawa. All were without result. The LPF's tone was growing more hostile with every passing meeting and each new resolution.

Last Post Fund plot in Mount Royal Cemetery, c. 1919. Note the ornamental 9-pounder field guns.

In the midst of this discouragement, personal tragedies struck the LPF as well. In 1918, Colonel J.J. Creelman, a member of the LPF's executive committee, lost a son killed in action on the Western Front. The assistant secretary-treasurer and chairman of the Grounds Committee, A. Bromley-Smith, lost a brother to the blight of war. That August, in remembrance of his brother, Bromley-Smith organized the erection of an impressive LPF flagstaff at the meeting point of the LPF's Catholic and Protestant burial plots on Mount Royal. The well-attended, moving ceremony was symbolic of the LPF's willingness to struggle on. Not long afterwards, Major George A. Musgrave, an enthusiastic supporter and active member of the LPF, was killed in action in France. In November, A. Bromley-Smith himself succumbed to the influenza epidemic then sweeping the world. The so-called Spanish Flu, killed tens of thousands of Canadians, including thousands of soldiers living in barracks, where the contagion spread easily. Panic spread across the land. Montreal was hard hit, partly because of its congested tenement housing; on October 21, 1918, alone, for example, influenza claimed 201 lives. In the autumn of 1918, as the war finally came to a close, the LPF increased by a third the number of burials to its credit by interring 55 veterans who had died of influenza, thereby almost completely filling up its mountain-side plots. Because of the epidemic, the LPF interred 96 veterans in the fiscal year 1918-19 – eight times the normal volume. Many of these men were buried at the request of the Department of Militia and Defence, which assumed most of the costs. Soon, more cemetery space would have to be purchased, but where would the money be found? This was a bleak period for the Last Post Fund.

In April 1918, the LPF "strongly urged" Ottawa "to consult with those who for years have undertaken from a sense of patriotism a duty which it is becoming daily more obligatory for the Government to assume." During the war, Ottawa had occasionally solicited the knowledge and experience of the LPF, as the federal government prepared to re-establish former soldiers into civilian life. It was painfully obvious that many of these returned men would have difficulty readjusting and that some might soon die penniless. In November 1918, the quartermaster general, General J.L. Biggar, met with the directors of the LPF to discuss planning for veterans' burials. The same year,

Atherton and Hair appeared before a Parliamentary Committee on Soldiers' Civil Re-establishment. But the advice and assistance seemed to flow only in a single direction; the LPF remained in the dark regarding Ottawa's plans. Would the federal government assume the responsibility for veterans' burials? Would it fund the LPF to carry on its work? No one knew.

As Canada began welcoming home hundreds of thousands of men from the battlefields of Europe, the LPF executive, almost in desperation, dispatched Arthur Hair to Ottawa to solicit the aid of high-ranking government officials. The LPF had taken the offensive in a series of four articles written by Hair in his heavy, patriotic prose that appeared in the *Canadian Municipal Journal* between October 1918 and February 1919. These articles were highly critical of the federal government. He claimed that the Canadian Patriotic Fund, while it raised millions of dollars, was "no more worthy of support" than the LPF. Why did the federal government deem the LPF valuable enough to consult yet apparently unworthy of financial aid? There were nearly 200 veterans buried under the Fund's "perpetual care". Did this count for nothing? Hair was losing confidence in Ottawa's willingness to do right by Canada's veteran population. His mood was sombre as he met in February 1919 with Senator Sir James Lougheed, the minister of soldiers' civil re-establishment and Major-General S.C. Mewburn, the minister of militia and defence.

The ministers wanted to know if the Last Post Fund was willing to assume national responsibilities for the burial of indigent veterans and, if so, what the average per capita cost of burial would be. At least they were asking the right questions. Within a month, the LPF drafted a detailed "Canadian Burial and Memorial Scheme", a working plan based on a decade of its experience, addressing the issue of government burial for *all* Canadian veterans, not only those who had fallen on hard times. The Fund sent this outline to federal authorities along with the assurance that the organization was indeed interested in expanding its operations on a national scale. In the draft proposal, Hair provided detailed responses to the ministers' queries about finances. Yet, nothing happened; Hair's doubts had been justified.

The LPF had had enough. The pot boiled over at its annual general meeting, held at Montreal's Ritz-Carlton Hotel in May 1919. There, 24 LPF members unanimously passed the following biting resolution:

That this association known as the "Last Post" Imperial Naval and Military Contingency Fund, on the occasion of its tenth annual meeting, desires to place on record its profound indignation at the deplorable apathy of the Federal Government of Canada, in regard to our soldier and sailor dead, more especially with regard to those who have returned from the recent war to die in our midst, many of whom are in danger of going down to oblivion through the fact that little, if any, systematic arrangement has been made by the Government to keep proper records of their location after decease, despite the further fact that this association has frequently – and especially during the past four years – pointed out this duty to them.

And we further feel that this is a duty calling for the serious and immediate consideration and action of the Government of the Dominion of Canada.

Believing the federal government to be callous, neglectful, and lacking in gratitude, the LPF called on Ottawa at the very least to set aside a special day each year to "perpetuate the memory of our heroic dead". The Fund recommended that the day be known as "National Decoration Day". Regardless of what Ottawa decided, the LPF would still observe a dignified ceremony of remembrance every May 24, at its burial plots on Mount Royal.

But just how long *would* the Last Post Fund survive? Its harsh criticisms and continuing patriotic suggestions masked the fact that it found itself adrift immediately after the war and perhaps even exhausted and overwhelmed. Although the war highlighted in a tragic manner the fact that the need for the services of the Fund was at its peak, it created a perhaps-fatal strain on the LPF's finances. The irony was not lost on the LPF's executive officers.

In September 1919, by its own admission, the LPF faced "insolvency and debt". It had already been forced to use money from the Supplementary Memorial Fund to finance some of its basic commemorative activities. At a discouraging executive committee meeting held on September 11, 1919, the possibility of its folding was seriously discussed. It seems that Hair, tiring of the struggle, had instigated the debate by suggesting that the time had arrived for the organization to "cease active operations" in a dignified manner. It was not that Hair felt the LPF's efforts insignificant – quite the contrary. "It would be impossible", he wrote in a report, "to make any estimate of the national and patriotic value of the work performed, which can only be measured by the heartfelt gratitude of those whose loved ones have been saved from oblivion and honored in death, while the ante-mortem requests of others, to be placed with their comrades in death, have been faithfully adhered to." The secretary-treasurer was also very proud of the fact that "all our accounts have been met promptly, while no special appeal has been made" – no mean feat, given the LPF's lack of resources. Hair also sounded a tone of bitterness when he admitted that the LPF had received "very little interest from the general public". Maybe he had cause for his very great disappointment. After a decade of existence that witnessed a devastating war, he certainly never anticipated the continuing battle for official recognition and sponsorship.

Reverend John Almond, attending his first meeting since his return from the war, spoke passionately, insisting to all present that they must carry on despite the current adverse situation. The work of the LPF was of national significance, and, perhaps once the postwar confusion in Ottawa had settled, the government would officially assist the Fund. This was no time to panic, warned Almond. The other trustees spoke their minds as well. Major-General E. W. Wilson, general officer commanding, Military District (MD) No. 4, headquartered in Montreal, felt that they should carry on and that a public appeal would yield positive results. J. T. Walsh agreed with Hair that waiting on Ottawa seemed fruitless. Yet he could not bring himself to support the demise of the organization that he had helped found. In the end, Walsh endorsed Almond's point of view. Although Hair continued to despair, the decision to soldier on would ultimately prove to have been the right one.

The First World War had been a watershed in world history, as it was for the history of the Last Post Fund. The trial of war allowed the fledgling body to prove its patriotism and the importance of its services to Canada's veterans and their families. The Last Post Fund survived and, in the years following the war, would emerge transformed in organization, scope, and national significance.

3

REORGANIZATION AND MATURITY, 1920–1929

Very often, I have dreams about the war.
In those dreams it is never ending and still goes
on and I remember what a terrible feeling of
disappointment I have.

GENERAL SIR ARTHUR CURRIE, 1927

The Great War was over. But as historians Desmond Morton and Glenn Wright have phrased it, the veterans still had to "win the second battle" – to overcome the trauma of their experiences and to obtain their disability pensions and other assistance on the road to civil re-establishment. The Last Post Fund wanted this "battle" to extend to non-pensioned veterans at the hour of indigent death. Both the federal government and the LPF were soon forced to make some crucial decisions on this matter. Unfortunately, a serious economic downturn took place in Canada from the end of 1918 until the early 1920s. This situation created increasing unemployment, rising poverty, growing social disaffection among many veterans and their organizations, government retrenchment, and a discouraging atmosphere for philanthropic groups such as the LPF. The major problems and preoccupations of the Fund remained financial in character.

At the conclusion of the war, Canada prepared to welcome home the largest group of veterans the nation had ever known. Thousands would return physically maimed or psychologically scarred. Many never recovered and suffered enormous problems readapting to civilian life. For some, the physical strains and painful memories would prove too much, and death would arrive prematurely. The 1920s brought greater needs for the Last Post Fund's services and for the first time most of its burials would involve Canadian-born ex-servicemen. This new demand stretched the Fund's resources to the breaking point.

Despite the LPF's enormous frustrations with Ottawa, the Dominion government was under no illusions concerning the challenges of providing for returned soldiers. The Department of Soldiers' Civil Re-establishment (DSCR) was created in 1918 to deal with these issues. If Ottawa would pay for the burial of indigent veterans, this would allay many of the LPF's problems. In the meantime, the Fund needed to reorganize itself; only then could it adapt and evolve. Accordingly, in 1920 the Last Post Fund took the first steps towards major structural changes. The next decade would see the Fund take on a national presence and solidify its position among Canadian patriotic groups.

Administrative Adjustments

In order for the Last Post Fund to increase its credibility with Ottawa it had to expand its operating horizons – one of Hair's goals since 1909. Already, in 1917, the LPF had appointed district representatives in Québec City, Trois-Rivières, and Sherbrooke. It had empowered these representatives, well known in their communities, to act for the Fund and see to the proper local interment of indigent veterans. The executive hoped, in due course, to set up branches in these and other locations in Québec. More importantly, the LPF looked towards national expansion.

Other administrative changes were in the offing as well. Members of the executive committee decided in April 1920 that the LPF's trustees (originally appointed to ensure the Fund adhered to its founding principles) would no longer act as directors or stand as candidates for executive positions. The administrative burden would be more equitably shared. At the annual meeting held that month, W.H. Atherton was elected president, the first non-trustee to hold this position. Hair was renominated secretary-treasurer; but, in keeping with his pessimistic outlook, he declined to accept, agreeing only to carry on until the May 24 ceremonies, of which he was principal organizer and to which he attached great importance. Although Hair stayed on as a director of the organization and continued to attend executive meetings (although he would shortly resign from the Grounds

Committee, too), an era was ending. The Fund's guiding hand would no longer be at the helm. In July, the executive chose Charles A. Shannon to replace Hair as secretary-treasurer.

There were no hard feelings between Hair and the remainder of the executive. In June 1920, Hair's close collaborator, Lucien Vallée, moved at an executive meeting that the governor general, the Duke of Devonshire, be solicited to recommend some royal recognition for Hair's efforts. No one objected to the idea, although one practical member present, John Munn, suggested rather that a "good position from the Government might be more acceptable to Mr. Hair than a decoration." Although no royal honours were forthcoming (in 1919 Parliament had made Canadians ineligible for such), at a Christmastime meeting in 1920, the executive presented Hair with a suitably engraved wristwatch and $500 collected from members. In a testimonial read into the minutes, members unanimously agreed that the LPF's successes were the result in no small part of Hair's "tireless energy and unselfish work". He had never earned a cent from his LPF work and had often refused honoraria that the executive was prepared to award him.

In August 1920, the LPF decided to seek a federal charter, partly to satisfy Ottawa's requirement that the LPF envelop the entire Dominion before federal monies could be spent on it. But, for the LPF, the more immediate reason was to prevent any new veterans' organizations from using the title "Last Post Fund". The LPF would countenance no competition for a name and reputation that it had spent a decade cultivating throughout Québec and which had become recognized across Canada. The main problem originated with a branch of the Great War Veterans' Association (GWVA) in Regina, which was calling itself the "Last Post Fund" and raising money using that name. This thorny problem would continue for years and cause serious rifts in the LPF's national organization.

The Fund also revised its charter and by-laws to reflect its upcoming federal nature. It adopted a new seal in 1921, prepared under the direction of the College of Arms and for the first time incorporating air force symbolism. The shield would henceforth contain an anchor, a rifle, and a propeller; the mottos remained the same, as did the image of a bugler sounding the "Last Post".

Money remained tight. Operations in the fiscal year 1920–21 had resulted in a deficit of $470, despite contributions from the Army and Navy League and the Knights of Columbus. Since Louis-Alexandre Taschereau had replaced Sir Lomer Gouin as premier of Québec, the LPF decided once again to seek provincial aid. Gouin had assured the LPF of provincial support if and when Ottawa showed the way in what Gouin, quite rightly, pointed out was a federal responsibility. Although Atherton expressed doubts that any good would come of a meeting, the trustees and executive visited Taschereau and requested $20,000 – to no avail. Brigadier-General C.J. Armstrong – who, as the new GOC, MD No. 4, replaced the outgoing General Wilson as a trustee of the Fund – believed the time had come to reject Lord Grey's original insistence that the LPF not publicly canvass for funds. The world had changed dramatically since 1909, and Armstrong felt that the LPF should "put our pride in our pocket". In March 1921, the Last Post Fund dispatched 125 letters to select individuals and organizations, including military units in MD No. 4, appealing for donations to enable it to purchase more gravesites in the plots on Mount Royal. The LPF hoped thereby to raise the $2,000 needed. It failed. The Verdun, Québec branch of the GWVA offered to maintain a local fund-raising program on behalf of the LPF, but the executive rejected this generous offer on the grounds that the LPF was not yet prepared to throw open the Fund to a public appeal. In the years ahead, other branches of the GWVA would not be so kindly disposed towards the LPF.

In April 1921, after a long delay, Ottawa paid the LPF $1,876 to reimburse the Fund for burying some serving soldiers and veterans at the government's request during the previous several years. Ernest H. Scammell, assistant deputy minister in the Department of Soldiers' Civil Re-establishment, helped arrange this payment. Scammell was born in England in 1873 and has been described by Desmond Morton and Glenn Wright as, "one of those officials a wise organiza-tion cherishes" and as a "careful and far-sighted planner". He devoted his civil service career to bettering the lives of Canada's pensioned and non-pensioned veterans. The LPF had great respect for Scammell and he would repeatedly prove his value to the Fund in the years ahead. Atherton felt that the payment of this money signalled a shift in the federal government's attitude towards the LPF and its work, but it may have been the result of pressure on Ottawa from vocal veterans' associations and public opinion to care adequately for the nation's veterans, in life and at death.

Despite Atherton's positive outlook, at the 12th annual meeting of the LPF, held in April 1921, Arthur Hair again sounded a pessimistic, even discordant note when he suggested that members could not continue investing their time, efforts, and even financial resources in an organization lacking government assistance. He proposed a motion advising Ottawa that the LPF's "future responsibilities in this work due to postwar mortality will be such that it cannot with financial security and due decorum continue its operations without some government financial assistance." Hair went on record as wanting to allow Ottawa just one last chance: if no money was forthcoming, Hair again recommended winding up the operations of the LPF. The minutes note laconically that this was "a critical time in the history of the association".

Hair's repeated advice to shut down the Last Post Fund remains puzzling. It seems that the organization was simply not progressing in the manner for which he had hoped. Perhaps he saw his own involvement in the Fund, and its continued existence, as a case of diminishing returns. He never indicated that the goals or ideals that had sparked the LPF's creation were no longer relevant. Nor did he question the value of the Fund's considerable accomplishments, all achieved with minimal funding. Rather, he continued strongly to believe that the indigent veteran, at the moment of death, was owed a decent burial. But for Hair, this obligation was incumbent on the *state*, not on a hard-pressed, voluntary, patriotic organization. One of his avowed purposes in creating the Fund had been for it to act as a conduit to convince Ottawa of its duties in this matter. He felt that he had failed, at the very moment when Canada suddenly was home to by far the greatest number of veterans, and perhaps destitute veterans, in the nation's history. And he refused to agree that the LPF should canvass from the general public. The LPF was a "patriotic society", not a public charity. A founding trustee, J.T. Walsh, agreed with Hair, on this point at least.

Members present were far from unanimous in supporting Hair's recommendations, and a lengthy debate ensued. Colonel J.J. Creelman sympathized with Hair and believed that sending another deputation to Ottawa would prove fruitless. Yet Creelman refused to abandon the Fund or the veterans who might need its services. Showing determination and spirit, the LPF's executive decided to forge ahead and would do so, if need be, without the full support of Arthur Hair, who eventually underwent a change of heart. When Charles Shannon announced that April that he could not continue as secretary-treasurer, Hair agreed once again to step into the breach, *pro tem*. However, he insisted on the right to hire an assistant as required to relieve him of some of the heavy workload. No one objected and Hair returned to the executive committee.

Do or Die

The federal government began to listen to the LPF's pleas in 1921. The Fund reminded Ottawa that of the millions of dollars being expended on veterans' civil re-establishment, none went to post-discharge military burials. "The question of the postwar military dead is one that the Government seems determined to ignore", was the LPF's official opinion. "Not one word [about it] has ever been mentioned on the floor of the House of Commons." It pointed out that following the U.S. Civil War (1861-1865), the American government had set aside 2,500 acres of land for military burials. It was a guiding principle in the United States that no ex-service person should be buried in a pauper's grave. Surely, Canada could do no less?

On April 27, 1921, the Fund was invited to present a brief before a Special Parliamentary Committee on Pensions, Insurance and Re-establishment of Returned Soldiers. Hair and Atherton travelled to Ottawa, and Atherton pleaded the Fund's case for an annual subsidy and presented the LPF's frugal, workable, and sound plan for the continuation of its work under Ottawa's financial tutorship. "You made it known", Atherton reminded the commissioners, "that, to a pensioner who was unable to feel he could get a decent interment...you would grant $100. Now, we have sounded public opinion many years...and we find at the present that everybody is of opinion that you have not gone far enough, and that you ought to bury all ex-service men whether in receipt of a pension or not." Few Canadians and fewer government officials would publicly disagree. In an LPF promotional pamphlet, Hair wrote: "Individual citizens have risen in indignation and exhausted their vocabulary of disgust through the press" at this

Dr. W.H. Atherton, president of the
Last Post Fund, 1920-22

deplorable situation. Perhaps, but it really boiled down to a question of money, not public opinion.

The LPF understood fiscal restraint only too well and guaranteed simple burial arrangements. Atherton returned several times to financial accountability and cost-effectiveness and portrayed the LPF as far more carefully managed than the government's existing inadequate burial plans for pensioned veterans. The average cost of an LPF burial was $56, compared with Ottawa's proposed expenditures of $100 each. Moreover, the LPF knew the burial location of all those interred under its auspices, while the government had few such traces or records for its efforts. Atherton wanted Ottawa to take up its responsibility and relieve the LPF of the burden of maintaining burial plots, to "take them off our shoulders", as he phrased it. He even quoted a letter of February 13, 1919, sent to the LPF by Sir Frederic Kenyon, the director of the British Museum and advisor to the Imperial Graves Registration Commission: "The scale of the recent war makes it impossible to continue such work on the basis of private contributions, and it seems to me eminently right that the State shall undertake the responsibility for its continuance by providing adequate funds." Accordingly, Atherton requested of Ottawa the startling sum of $100,000 to hire staff, acquire burial grounds, and spread the LPF's services throughout Canada. At the very least, Atherton implored, it should arrange *all* veterans' burials, whether pensioners or not. Atherton's strong showing before the committee was a breakthrough of sorts.

On June 22, 1921, the federal government, under the provisions of the Dominion Companies Act, granted a charter to the "Last Post Fund", the LPF's new, shortened official name. This charter allowed the LPF to operate nation-wide, if and when it chose to do so, and recognized it as the sole organization legally authorized to use the name "Last Post Fund". On July 19, 1921, at the Windsor Hotel in downtown Montreal, the final meeting of the 'old' LPF took place. The letters patent had arrived: a new dawn for the organization, and some new hope, were in the offing.

The first Dominion Council of the federally chartered LPF promptly re-elected Atherton as its president. The new organization inherited the poverty of the old, there being but $1,600 cash on hand and dwindling fund-raising opportunities. In addition to charter members, patrons, and trustees, there existed 77 life members and 47 active members, among them prominent men such as Sir George Foster, Lord Shaughnessy, and Canon F.G. Scott. Almost the entire membership was based in Montreal.

It was during this July 19 meeting that Hair was voted a salary of $200 a month "for such duration as [the directors] may see fit especially if the Secretary Treasurer shall devote his entire time to the objects, interests and success of this corporation". In other words, Hair was placed on the LPF's payroll, and he left his accounting job to work full time for the Last Post Fund. It appears that his new position ended any thoughts in his mind of resigning or of recommending dissolution of the LPF – something he had become alarmingly (and perhaps annoyingly) prone to doing. In any event, a $2,400 annual salary was an extremely generous one in 1921, particularly since the LPF's finances were diminishing rapidly. The Fund was down to a mere $1,088 by mid-August. At this rate, unless some major sources of funding were quickly found, Hair's salary alone, much higher than the average Canadian 'white collar' worker, would spell the end of the

LPF. (Although the Fund's archives do not record in what year, Hair's salary was eventually reduced. In the mid 1930s, he earned $150 monthly, though by the end of the Second World War his salary had climbed back to $202.)

One of Hair's first tasks was to recruit members as a means of raising capital. He wrote and distributed promotional literature, "propaganda" he called it. Hair admitted that printing and postage at times cost more than funerals! By September, however, Hair could report only 22 new members, despite his belief that recently demobilized Canadian soldiers would interest themselves in the Fund. His notion that the Fund was slowly but surely "gaining strength" seemed unfounded.

Meanwhile, the work of the Last Post Fund continued. Hair's secretarial reports often detailed burial cases, most involving indigent older veterans not dealt with by Ottawa's burial policies or by other philanthropic organizations. For example, in September 1921 the Canadian Red Cross Society approached the LPF about dealing with a case that neither the Red Cross nor the Canadian Patriotic Fund could handle, according to their constitutions. This particular veteran had served in Canada during the war, unable to pass a physical examination for overseas service. Both he and his wife were seriously ill and destitute. Even the DSCR could do nothing for him. He died not long afterwards, and the LPF arranged his interment. It was a perfect example of the very reasons for the Fund's existence and also highlighted the government's inadequate policy.

The LPF helped in other, perhaps unlikely ways. In 1920, one Private D.M. McNaught died penniless, and the Fund took care of his burial. But McNaught had left behind a dependant: a one-year old baby left "totally unprovided for and parentless". Hair devoted a great deal of time and effort to obtaining for the LPF the legal right of "tutorship" of the child and soon found a good home for the orphan. The whole episode is indicative of the Fund's unheralded, behind-the-scenes work. In a similar occurrence in 1925 an orphaned child was reunited with his grandparents in England.

While the government dithered, the LPF's assets dipped below $1,000. Luckily, burial requests were not as high as had been expected with only a few every month. Hair worked hard to find alternative sources of financing. He organized a war photo and memorabilia display at Montreal's Windsor Hotel in October 1921. But following the traumatic experience of war, the public was weary of things warlike: the exhibit was a dismal failure and ended up running a deficit of $15. Hair found the "apathy of the general public deplorable." On a positive note, that October General Sir Arthur Currie joined the Fund, lending it the strength of his reputation. A good friend of Almond's, Currie was by then principal and vice-chancellor of McGill University, Canada's top institution of higher learning, and a Canadian of great renown. He also had many friends in the military and numerous government contacts in Ottawa.

With this kind of high-profile support, often the result of Hair's continuing recruitment campaign, things began to look up. But time was becoming a critical factor. In January 1922, the Fund could count a mere $435 in cash on hand plus a $400 Victory Bond in reserve, a situation Hair believed to be "urgent" and for which Atherton "felt the responsibility keenly". Since August, Hair's drive had increased membership to only 228, although many of these were "very desirable people", according to Hair. The Supplementary Memorial Fund, which had been used mainly for Decoration Day ceremonies, was nearly exhausted and finally merged with the general account of the LPF in 1921. Something had to give soon.

A Time of Deliverance

On February 14, 1922, the LPF, almost out of cash and desperate, sent a final portentous formal petition to the federal government. It was accompanied by an exceptionally strong showing of support by leading citizens including Governor General Lord Byng of Vimy, the Duke of Connaught, the Duke of Devonshire, the lieutenant-governors of five provinces, General Sir Arthur Currie, top-ranking Montreal ecclesiastical authorities, the mayors and city councils of numerous cities across Canada, dozens of serving and former federal politicians including Sir Robert Borden, many veterans' associations including the Great War Veterans' Association, patriotic groups, social organizations, charitable and philanthropic institutions (especially from Montreal) including the Federation of Jewish Charities and *La Société St-Jean-Baptiste*, many respected and well-known Canadians from all walks of life, and a number of British officials including Sir Frederic Kenyon, Lord Baden

Powell, General Sir Ian Hamilton, and General H.L. Smith-Dorien. The petition was addressed to William Lyon Mackenzie King, the newly-elected prime minister, and the ministers of finance, militia and defence, and of the DSCR. Herbert Marler, Liberal M.P. from the Montreal riding of St. Lawrence-St. George, whom Hair described as "an enthusiastic champion of our cause", agreed to take the petition to the cabinet. Fortuitously, not long after this, Marler became head of a new parliamentary subcommittee to investigate soldiers' civil re-establishment. This was excellent news for the LPF, which had delivered a brief, in vain, to the previous incarnation of this committee in April 1921.

The petition of February 1922 described the primary object of the LPF as "to give honourable sepulchre to any ex-service members of the Empire's Naval, Military and Air Forces, who might at death be in destitute circumstances, friendless, indigent or likely to become a public charge, thus treating their remains with dignity and gratitude." It went on to state that "the principles involved in the foregoing objects of this Association have the unqualified support of all good citizens as evidenced by the attached list of representative Corporate Bodies and individuals, throughout the length and breadth of the Dominion and beyond its borders, supported by the appreciation of parliamentary officialdom in the granting of the Dominion Charter." The LPF sought an initial grant of $15,000 "to help it establish and organize its system of administration throughout the Dominion". It also wanted Parliament to legislate acknowledgment of federal responsibility to pay for the LPF's burial of indigent veterans, disability pensioners or not, up to a maximum of $100 each.

Although several federal statutes touched on the obituary needs of Canada's pensioned veterans, or those under the care or charge of various government departments, there were veterans left out of these programs. Three relevant statutes were in effect in 1922:

- Article 293, Pay and Allowance Regulations: "to meet the contingency of death, while on duty in the Active Militia of Canada".
- Section 7, Chapter 8, clause 7, paragraph (a) of the regulations governing the Department of Soldiers' Civil Re-establishment: "for men and women, who die while on strength of that establishment".

- Chapter 62, Article 32 of the Pension Act of Canada (since 1919): for "pensioners whose estate at death is insufficient to cover the cost of last illness and burial allows a re-imbursement claim to a maximum of $100".

But, as the LPF pointed out, none of these made provision for the "honourably discharged class who, through the adversities of life, may subsequently fall on evil times, and die friendless and in destitution, with no alternative but a pauper's grave." The Fund was not asking for too much, surely, when the additional financial burden to Ottawa would be "insignificant compared with the importance of the national principle involved". As the many influential supporters of the petition believed, "financial responsibility for such work…is a national one and…should not be left to the chance generosity of public charity". On the other hand, government spending on veterans' pensions and civil re-establishment was already high at a time when the economy was weak. Ottawa attempted to balance its responsibilities towards veterans with its perceived need to exercise budgetary restraint.

In the meantime, further changes were taking place that spring and summer within the Last Post Fund. From an average of eight burials annually before the outbreak of war in 1914, the LPF had buried an average of 30 veterans a year since that date. In 1922, A.S. Clarson succeeded Atherton as president. The LPF also elected three women directors – a rarity at this time for any organization not mainly female in composition. One of them, Miss Hay Browne, served as second vice-president and as chair of the new Ladies' Committee (later the Ladies Auxiliary). She proved extraordinarily active and productive throughout the 1920s. Dominion Council meetings were frequently held in rooms provided free of charge by J.C. Wray and Bros., the Montreal funeral home with which the LPF exclusively dealt and which sometimes conducted funerals at a net loss as a patriotic gesture. The "only drawback" to this convenient locale, noted the minutes of a meeting in May 1922, seemed to be that "some people felt there was an air of depression in the surroundings of an undertaking establishment, while others thought it quite appropriate to our work." The fiscal year closed with a balance of $193. That June, the Victory Bond was transferred to the current account of the Fund to meet expenses.

At the Dominion Council meeting of June 19, 1922, just a few days short of the first anniversary of the federal charter, Hair announced the receipt of a communication from Herbert Marler stating that the Special Parliamentary Commission had recommended an annual subsidy of $10,000 for the Last Post Fund. The minutes of this meeting, characteristically understated, reveal only that those present felt that this news "indicated a remarkable point in the history of this organization". In fact, it meant that the principle underlying the Fund's existence had been recognized and its argument won at long last. By helping underwrite the operations of the LPF, the federal government had taken an early small step on the road to greater public involvement in assisting the destitute regain some dignity.

In July, E.H. Scammell, from the Department of Soldiers' Civil Re-establishment, who had worked behind the scenes to secure the financing, attended an LPF meeting to outline the particulars of Ottawa's offer. (He would in fact join the Fund as a director representing his department in December 1922.) DSCR would administer the money, and the LPF would be accountable to Ottawa for burial expenditures. In exchange for this operating grant, and in accordance with Ottawa's terms, the LPF undertook to extend its activities and responsibilities throughout Canada. Scammell strongly recommended that the LPF accept these terms, which the Fund gladly did, although some directors expressed concern that the amount allotted would be insufficient. In any event, Almond, Clarson, and Hair travelled to Ottawa to discuss the implementation of Ottawa's offer with DSCR officials.

Finally, on August 5, 1922, the Committee of the Privy Council passed Order-in-Council P.C. 1581, authorizing the federal grant:

> the Committee has considered the petition received from the Last Post Fund…It is understood that the Fund has carried on excellent work for the past 14 years and is organizing its system throughout the Dominion…The Committee therefore recommends that the Department of Soldiers' Civil Re-establishment be authorised to enter into an agreement with, and to make a grant of $10,000 per annum to the Trustees of the Last Post Fund for the purposes of assisting towards the provision of burial

expenses of former members of the Forces of Canada and her Allies who die in destitute circumstances and for whom no other provision is made...[the grant] shall proportionately be applied for burial of ex-soldiers in all the provinces of Canada.

Accordingly, the Fund grew from a Québec-based organization into a national one. From its inception until the end of 1922 it had provided for the burial of 276 veterans. As sizeable an effort as this number represented, in a few years' time the Last Post Fund would be burying nearly that number annually.

From Coast to Coast

Ottawa's assistance came not a moment too soon: as of August 19, 1922, the LPF had a bank balance of $63! The $10,000 annual grant was meant mainly for burial purposes and did not normally apply to administrative costs or salaries, which the LPF agreed to finance from membership dues and charitable donations. However, Ottawa allowed an administrative appropriation of $1,200 to be deducted from the first year's grant to enable the LPF to extend its system of operations throughout the country. DSCR retained annually a further $300 for disbursement to the LPF as it saw fit. In subsequent years, $1,200 was deducted from the $10,000 specifically to defray part of the secretary-treasurer's expenses and salary, which initially remained a hefty $2,400 per annum.

In most provinces the LPF established a headquarters, usually in the largest city, "under the direction of officers and gentlemen of the highest integrity and social prominence", wrote Hair. Each branch was administered in similar fashion to the Dominion headquarters in Montreal. District or regional sub-branches, in some cases mere committees, were set up to suit local needs. Before a functioning provincial headquarters could be established, something that took longer in the Maritimes, these local committees reported directly to Dominion HQ. Soon, the Fund had official representatives in all of Canada's large cities and most of the secondary ones as well. One pressing early need was to provide for representation in the rural and outlying districts into which increasing numbers of Great War veterans were

moving. In these areas, the LPF organized a network of voluntary representatives, normally men of some standing in their communities, to
carry out the local functions of the Fund.

The man in charge of implementing this new national structure
was none other than Arthur Hair, whose energy and renewed commitment would make him a well-known figure in Canadian patriotic
and philanthropic circles. In November 1922, a laudatory article in
the *Toronto Star* nick-named him "Last Post Hair". It described his
work on behalf of the Last Post Fund as crucial as was "breath to
body", and Hair himself as "the father and apostle"of the LPF. Still, a
hint of Hair's at once reserved and prickly nature appears in another
press comment noting that he "detests the limelight but abhors
ingratitude".Therein lay the essence of a man who moved heaven and
earth to create the Last Post Fund but who, throughout his 38-year
LPF career, was never the association's president and seemingly never
aspired to be.

During the remainder of 1922, Hair embarked, as he phrased it,
on a "vast amount of preliminary and subsequent work" to extend
operations to a national scale. He travelled the country, made presen-
tations to veterans' groups, met with the local media, and almost single-handedly raised the Fund's national profile. Hair would later boast
that within a mere six months the LPF was up and running from
coast to coast. But it was no easy task.

Hair spent four weeks in September and October travelling in
Ontario to Toronto, London, Windsor, Hamilton, Kingston, and
Ottawa to interview prominent individuals interested in the work of
the Fund and to found regional sub-branches or name district repre-
sentatives.The Ontario branch was formed November 10, 1922, during a meeting held at Toronto's King Edward Hotel. Brigadier-
General John A. Gunn, who was to be prominent in the LPF for
decades, was a charter branch trustee.Toronto was selected as the seat
of the provincial headquarters. By his own account, Hair considered
the LPF in Ontario almost immediately to be "very well organised",
especially strong in Toronto and London. The IODE and the
Canadian Red Cross Society helped, and a member of the latter organization's executive assisted by joining the executive of the LPF's
Ontario branch. By 1924, the province's lieutenant-governor had
agreed to his official patronage, and two years later the provincial gov-

ernment granted the Ontario LPF $2,000 per annum and the right to claim back $15 per indigent burial from whatever municipality would otherwise have had to inter the deceased.

In December, Hair travelled to the western provinces, where he met with mixed success. He found Alberta the "most responsive", with Calgary and Edmonton vying with each other to act as provincial headquarters (Calgary won). In December 1928, the LPF set up two separate branches in the province – Northern Alberta and Southern Alberta. The northern branch, based in Edmonton, was responsible for the area north of Red Deer as well as the western Northwest Territories and even regions of northern British Columbia and Saskatchewan too remote from those provinces' provincial headquarters.

While in Alberta, Hair had to overcome a challenge from the Calgary branch of the GWVA, which tried to create its own autonomous "Last Post Fund". Hair invoked the threat of legal action to prevent it from proceeding under that name. Although the GWVA branch agreed to act for the LPF, the seeds of discord remained. In British Columbia, Hair laid the groundwork for a branch in Vancouver, with a sub-branch in Victoria, both becoming operational in 1923.

Matters proceeded satisfactorily in Manitoba, where a solid branch organization emerged. However, as Hair later reported to the Dominion Council: "My efforts in Winnipeg were not effected without a measure of foolish...opposition from certain Soldier Organizations who took the attitude that the government should not have given us any financial assistance to organize". The veterans, the local branch of the GWVA among them, felt that too much of Ottawa's grant money was being "dissipated" on LPF administration. They believed that they could do better with the money themselves. Hair took pains to promote the work of the LPF to a sometimes hostile audience.

On the same trip, a similar and more deeply-rooted problem arose in Saskatchewan, sparking a rivalry that would linger for years. The Regina branch of the GWVA, having used the name "Last Post Fund" since 1918, three years before the LPF obtained its national charter, refused to recognize the LPF's authority in the matter of indigent burials and would not consent to be bound in any way to its constitution or by-laws. Hair had been threatening legal action for a year and this finally forced the GWVA to desist from using the title. This dénouement, however, created hard feelings. Eventually Regina's GWVA officials seemed willing to adhere to the LPF, and a compromise deal was reached, but it was grudging and half-hearted. Indeed, the GWVA repudiated the agreement several months later; it would no longer represent the LPF and, worse, urged DSCR to discontinue its arrangement with the Fund and renew one instead with the GWVA.

The Regina press strongly supported the GWVA. After all, the veterans' group had in fact done excellent work, establishing a fine military plot in a civil cemetery. The *Regina Morning-Leader* viewed Hair as a high-handed intruder who wasted government funds on needless administration and travel. Westerners could care for their own. Hair, too, was aggressive, but despite his unyielding ways, the LPF remained conciliatory (mainly at Scammell's request) and kept the door open to a future resumption of co-operation by agreeing to allow the Regina GWVA branch a nebulous "affiliated" status. The seeds of discord had been planted, however, and the acrimony would last for decades. Things went more smoothly in Saskatoon.

In the winter of 1923, Hair travelled to the Maritimes and parts of Québec to meet with potential LPF representatives. He enjoyed limited success in Halifax and Saint John, although he organized strong sub-branches in Sherbrooke and Québec City. Despite the Maritimers' willingness to co-operate, lasting and comprehensive representation in eastern Canada would take decades to achieve. Even a year later, the best that Hair could say was that the LPF's Maritime representatives were "tardy" in organizing. Only following a further visit by him was a branch headquarters established in Halifax in 1926. Prior to this, a local representative informed Dominion headquarters about the few LPF burials there. A branch was founded in Prince Edward Island the same year, with the island's first burial taking place in 1927.

Ottawa's decision to ensure the Fund's solvency came with clear guidelines governing the manner in which the money could be spent. LPF headquarters was obliged to disburse the grant throughout the country on the basis of calculated provincial wartime enlistments and location of discharges from military service. The grant for burial purposes had to be applied in the following proportions: 42 per cent in Ontario, 13 per cent in Québec, 11 per cent in Manitoba, 10 per cent in British Columbia, 7 per cent in Alberta, 7 per cent in Nova Scotia and Prince Edward Island combined, 6 per cent in Saskatchewan, and 4 per cent in New Brunswick. This was an unscientific and rather arbitrary distribution, and branches in Saskatchewan and Alberta especially felt slighted. The provincial branches were required to supplement their allotment of the grant by local subscription and fund-raising, and they were accordingly allowed to organize events such as concerts, special displays, and sales for this purpose. They submitted quarterly reports to Dominion headquarters, which in turn provided the DSCR with a careful accounting of federal monies spent. Headquarters kept the central registry of burials based on these quarterly reports.

The LPF also benefitted from increasingly friendly links to a widespread network of government and military authorities. Many of the provincial branch headquarters and sub-branches in this early period shared office space with the federal government. The administrative offices of the DSCR in Regina, London, Windsor, Saint John, and Charlottetown doubled as the LPF's regional offices as well. Similarly, in Ottawa, correspondence intended for the LPF was addressed to the Military Records Department; in Kingston, to Militia Headquarters; and in Halifax, to the provincial headquarters of the Red Cross Society. The early involvement of the Red Cross was demonstrative of the non-governmental institutional support for the LPF that had been apparent in varying degrees since its inception. Certain branches of the GWVA also proved keen supporters of the Fund. These offsetting arrangements provided by Ottawa saved the LPF considerable administrative expenses, rental costs, and capital expenditures. As a whole, they constituted a major part of Ottawa's assistance to the Fund in its transition to a national institution. On the other hand, as Hair pointed out, the government was actually saving money by allowing the LPF to operate a veterans' burial system on Ottawa's behalf for what was, in reality, a paltry annual financial outlay. Viewed pragmatically, the LPF and the federal authorities' obligations to each other served the purposes of both parties.

More importantly, Canada's large veteran population would be assured dignified burial in the event of indigent or friendless death.

This is what the Fund had always been about. Nothing in the new Dominion charter altered the primary objective of the LPF. Since the organization had expanded, however, burial policy became somewhat more complicated. Provincial branches had to purchase suitable burial plots and there was to be uniformity of services and ceremony across Canada. Yet, given the country's enormous diversity, the LPF would sometimes have to make special provisions and remain flexible. "In conducting funerals", stated the revised constitution, "careful observance of the customs of the locality in which they are carried out" was essential. Yet, local branches were also to ensure "that the duty undertaken by the Fund may not degenerate into a mere perfunctory avoidance of a pauper funeral." Utmost respect for the deceased and his or her past military services ensured a dignified interment.

LPF burials across Canada rose steadily throughout the 1920s, with Ontario leading the way. The LPF's first official burial outside Québec took place in Toronto in November 1922. Between that time and 1945, the Ontario branch alone averaged 177 burials per year. By the mid-1920s, the Québec branch was burying on average 35 to 40 veterans annually, a figure similar to most western provinces. The Maritime provinces, slower to organize and smaller in population, dealt with far fewer cases. Interesting statistics were beginning to develop regarding the cross-Canada backgrounds of LPF cases. Of 139 burials tabulated by Hair in 1926-27 based on incomplete returns, 113 of those interred were Protestants including only five officers. These early trends would continue until the Second World War. Of 528 burials in Québec to the end of the 1928-29 fiscal year, almost two-thirds were of Protestants. French Canadians accounted for 115 burials. The veterans had served during the Fenian Raids, the Northwest Rebellion, the South African War, and the First World War. Nationally, LPF burials averaged $92 each, including markers.

The BC branch's burials also grew in the 1920s, as did its rather elaborate "Memorial Day" celebrations each June at its Returned Soldiers' Plots in Vancouver's Mountain View Cemetery. Large crowds and strong militia participation distinguished these solemn occasions, as did a large presence from local chapters of the IODE. Because it shared space with Dominion headquarters in Montreal, the Québec branch also organized the annual Decoration Day commemorations at Mount Royal. On May 24, 1921, the ceremony included the spectacular wreath-dropping by aircraft of the Canadian Aero League at the monument to Sir George-Étienne Cartier, Father of Confederation, in Fletcher's Field on Mount Royal. Thousands of gathered onlookers witnessed this event, which received ample coverage in the press. The ceremony the following year was just as impressive. Hundreds of spectators joined large military and veteran contingents at the Cartier monument. An airplane, instructed by signals transmitted by wireless, dropped flowers over the monument and also flew low over the LPF plots on the mountain. It then dropped bouquets in the St. Lawrence River in honour of the naval dead. The Montreal *Herald*, impressed, reminded readers that the well-orchestrated spectacle was the "result of the untiring and practically unaided efforts" of Arthur Hair.

Decoration Day was normally a co-operative venture with other local organizations such as the GWVA, the IODE, and the Boy Scouts. All assisted in cleaning the graves and adorning them with small flags and fresh flowers. The LPF was usually successful in securing the attendance of some prominent personage. Sir Lomer Gouin, former premier of Québec and newly-appointed federal minister of justice and attorney general, attended in 1922 joined by G.P. Graham, the minister of militia and defence, and naval service. Ottawa seemed to be taking the Fund seriously. So did ordinary citizens. "The public of Montreal have come to look upon this annual ceremony of remembrance with much favour", Hair wrote in 1924, in which year 400 graves were decorated with flags. Beginning that year, a second ceremony was inaugurated at the port of Montreal to commemorate the empire's sailors lost during the First World War. A floral wreath was placed in the St. Lawrence River as a symbol of remembrance. The Québec branch also placed floral tributes in all cemeteries containing military burials in the district of Montreal. Only Québec, Manitoba and BC branches annually conducted memorial services at their own plots under their own auspices. Other branches co-operated with veterans' organizations in annual tributes to Canada's dead.

In October 1923, the City of Montreal agreed to pay 25 per cent of the cost of LPF indigent burials (up to a maximum of $25 each), which otherwise the city would have had to assume if the deceased remained a public charge. It was a mutually advantageous agreement. Mayor Médéric Martin had always been an enthusiastic supporter of the LPF. The nearby municipalities of Outremont, Verdun, and

Westmount followed Montreal's lead. Calgary and Regina freely made available city land for veterans' cemeteries. Many cemetery companies across Canada also assisted by offering preferential rates for LPF interments. Steadily, the Fund's financial situation improved, and it could get on with the job for which it existed.

Growing up in the 1920s

In April 1923, General Sir Arthur Currie became a director of the Last Post Fund. One month later Currie became president of the Dominion Council, a position that he would hold for almost nine years. He lent authority and prestige to the Fund and helped build it into a strong, credible, and prominent institution. Currie was an extraordinarily busy man. In addition to the demands of being principal of McGill, he was heavily involved in many other philanthropic causes, often involving veterans' welfare. He was also a director of the Bank of Montreal. Currie, who chaired his first LPF meeting in January 1924, exerted a powerful influence over the Fund's relationships with government and veterans' organizations.

The Dominion Council was comprised of three trustees and 15 directors. The directors were selected by ballot, seven coming from Québec (they doubled as the LPF's Québec branch directors), seven from the other provinces, and one being a representative of DSCR – E.H. Scammell. The executive was chosen from among the directors and consisted of one president, two vice-presidents (one each from Québec and Ontario), and a secretary-treasurer. All directors were well known in LPF circles and men of standing in the community: professionals, business managers, clergymen, and military officers. The three trustees remained Almond, Walsh, and the incumbent GOC, MD No. 4. The trustees continued to hold in trust all moneys and property and maintained a veto power over any financial or legislative decisions that they deemed injurious to the objects of the Fund. Amendments to the Fund's by-laws required a two-thirds' vote of the council, three members present constituting a quorum. The national and Québec annual meetings were held together at Montreal's Ritz-Carlton Hotel, normally with some Ontario branch representatives and government officials present. Other provinces sent delegates from time to time.

Under Currie's stewardship, the LPF remained true to its original purpose – to prevent the pauper burial of veterans. A secondary object was "to act as friend and advisor" to the dependants of deceased veterans. For this purpose it sought: a) to hold as temporary custodian on their behalf the personal effects of the deceased; b) to secure for them as far as possible any pension, rights, or dues to which they may have justifiable claim and to commend them to such other organizations whose function may be to render assistance; c) to trace, if possible, the next of kin. The LPF also had a mandate to "interest itself in the restitution, marking and care of neglected and forgotten graves of deceased naval and military persons and generally interest itself in all matters affecting military obsequies throughout the Dominion of Canada." There were four classes of veterans for whom the Fund was empowered to act: a) indigent male or female veterans receiving no disability pensions, for whom the Fund would pay all or partial burial costs depending on whether any costs could be recovered from the deceased's estate; b) pensioned Canadian veterans, for whom the Fund would arrange burial at veterans' expenses. If this could not be afforded, assistance up to $100 was available from the federal Board of Pension Commissioners; c) Imperial pensioners, for whose burials reimbursement would be sought by the LPF from the Imperial Division of the DSCR; d) ex-service men or women whose relatives desire be interred by the Fund at family expense.

The maximum that the Fund could spend on any funeral, including purchase of the grave and provision of a marker, was $100. Because budgets were tight, the LPF also attempted to recover from or share costs with other veterans' or benevolent societies whose rules allowed them to assist in cases of indigent burial. Moreover, the LPF would not reimburse any individual or group for burial costs after the fact unless the burial took place beyond reach of an LPF representative and was clearly done to prevent a pauper burial. Under no circumstances would reimbursement exceed the amount that would have been expended had the funeral been carried out by the LPF.

Dominion HQ retained no membership rolls, since it acted as an administrative entity to which all branches reported. Branch memberships, however, were open to all, in four categories: active, elected as members and having paid a $5 annual fee; life, a fee of $100; associate, between $1 and $5 (no voting rights); and honorary, or patron, not eligible to vote. In mid-1924, membership passed 400, and it continued to increase throughout the decade. Almost every Dominion Council meeting noted growth in Canada-wide recruitment. The Women's Auxiliary of the LPF (discussed in chapter 4) and the IODE were of immense support in attracting members to the cause. The first foreign membership was granted in September 1923, to a Miss T. Green of Virginia. Although her application elicited some discussion at a Dominion Council meeting, no rules disallowed foreign membership and she was welcomed to the fold.

Problems persisted with certain veterans' groups. As early as 1917, the GWVA, assembled at its founding convention in Winnipeg, and ignoring completely the LPF's primary goal, denounced the LPF as doing the government's work and making it easier for Ottawa to shirk its responsibilities towards veterans. This was a curious attitude given that the Fund existed to assist impoverished veterans. The GWVA raised the alarm again in 1921 over what it perceived as a 'charity' (the LPF) providing services that the GWVA believed the government should recognize as a right. Morton and Wright have correctly pointed out that Ottawa agreed to fund the LPF because this organization undoubtedly could continue its activities in a "wiser and cheaper" manner than could Ottawa. This had been the LPF's view all along. Moreover, until the government acted to assist the LPF, indigent veterans still required dignified burials. Where were the veterans' groups when the LPF was founded? In any event, far from wasting public money on the LPF, as some veterans charged, Ottawa was saving some. This was certainly Hair's argument.

The GWVA remained an occasional thorn in the side of the LPF for several more years. It was a formidable opponent, claiming in 1920 to represent over 800 branches and close to 200,000 members. However, the Army and Navy Veterans, more conservative than the firebrand GWVA, openly supported the LPF and its benevolent work on behalf of destitute members. Currie noted at one LPF annual meeting in the 1920s: "the longer one goes on with this work, the more impressed [one] becomes with the necessity of it. Any other organization which believes that it could carry on this work along with its own would be ill-advised to do so". This was a clear message to the GWVA (and its successor, the Canadian Legion) that the LPF provided vital services to veterans that the LPF alone was uniquely qualified and organized to offer. It was time for all veterans' organizations to recognize this. The DSCR agreed, Scammell noting that "the work is more successful as a separate one, than if made an integral part of any one veterans' society, even though that may be the biggest in Canada." The Fund was not part of the problem, as the GWVA suggested, but part of the solution. Co-operation, not competition, would benefit all veterans and their families.

Despite this, when the Canadian Legion was formed following the amalgamation of several veterans' groups in 1925, it listed as one of its aims: "to perpetuate the memory and deeds of those who have fallen or who die in the future; to promote and care for memorials to their valour and sacrifice; to provide suitable burial; and to keep an annual memorial day." While obviously laudable goals, the Fund had been carrying out these precise activities, on a small scale, since 1909. Nevertheless, the primary *raison d'être* of the Legion was to assist "disabled, dependent, and distressed" veterans and their families, activities the LPF, notwithstanding occasional forays into these areas, could not and was not mandated to undertake.

Some former GWVA members in western Canada who had joined the executive of the Legion were the same persons who had maintained strained relationships with the LPF ever since the Fund expanded to that region. Colonel James McAra led the GWVA in Regina from its inception until the creation of the Legion's Provincial Command in that province in 1926, an event orchestrated under his "vigorous and astute leadership" according to the Legion's first official history, authored by Clifford Bowering in 1960. McAra, who devoted his life to veterans' welfare, was also the grudging local LPF representative, though not for long. In 1927, he was elected the Legion's second national vice-president. Saskatchewan was a Legion stronghold, with one-quarter of all branches located there, which might explain the sometimes-hostile attitude towards the LPF expressed by local veterans. Hair was continually driven to distraction by the Saskatchewan branch's faulty records, inconsistent bookkeeping, and apparent refusal to follow administrative procedures required of all branches.

At the end of 1925, Hair found matters in Saskatchewan "very unsatisfactory" and felt that the branch should be stood down and another reorganized. The next year, he noted a "certain amount of

misunderstanding and trouble" in the province, which he attributed
to the personalities of the LPF representatives in Regina. Hair and
McAra simply could not get along, and Hair's frustrations seem to
have gotten the better of him. He dispatched several blistering letters
to the branch over its failure to administer paperwork properly. One
senses there were two valid sides to the story. McAra, described as
"patient and understanding" in Bowering's later account of the
Legion, a true conciliator who had done much to bring unity to the
veterans' movement in Saskatchewan, was not one to be cowed. Hair,
on the other hand, was a stickler for detail who earned a reputation
as an inflexible, 'by-the-book' administrator. He was blunt and occasionally made matters worse. Visits to western Canada in 1927 and
1929 by Hair and A.H. Abbott, president of the Ontario branch,
helped smooth ruffled feathers, but a hearty dislike of Hair continued
in Saskatchewan, as it did in Manitoba. At the Legion's first national
convention in Winnipeg in 1927, representatives from other veterans'
groups and several government departments were welcomed. No Last
Post Fund representative was invited.

Alberta, too, was a problem for Hair – and *vice-versa*. Following
the resignation of the Southern Alberta branch's secretary-treasurer,
Arthur Wakelyn, after a clash with Hair, Colonel W.B. Ryan, a trustee
of the Southern Alberta branch in Calgary, wrote Hair in 1929: "We
will have no small difficulty in obtaining anyone willing to assume the
unpleasantness and worries of the job of corresponding with the
Dominion Secretary Treasurer as long as that position is held by yourself." Ryan bluntly sought Hair's dismissal. Both Abbott and Currie
felt that Hair was dogmatic and overly critical in his dealings with
branch administrators. When Currie was president of the Fund, for
most of the 1920s and early 1930s, he often read Hair's outgoing correspondence before it was sent, in an attempt to limit the damage
done by the ebullient secretary-treasurer's sarcastic pen. Currie
"insisted" on more tactful correspondence. This seemed to help, but
relations between headquarters and the western branches remained
generally cool.

When the Canadian Legion of the British Empire Service
League was formed in 1925, Sir Arthur Currie was named its honorary president. But his involvement with the Legion was never
overly intimate. Some ex-soldiers considered Currie a distant, some-

times aloof man with whom they felt little affinity. His service to the Legion at such time as he was also president of the Dominion Council of the LPF proved awkward at times. Nevertheless, Currie was a popular figure, perhaps never more so than in 1928 when he won a libel suit against a small-town Ontario newspaper, the Port Hope *Evening Guide*, which had defamed his character in June 1927. In 1928, he was elected Dominion president of the Legion without even attending the annual convention. From 1929 to 1933, he served as grand president of the Legion, a mainly honorific post. Currie exerted influence at Ottawa and fought for the Legion's interests in addition to those of the LPF. His voice mattered, and he was devoted to improving the lot of *his* veterans in life and death. Hundreds of returned soldiers wrote him for help following unsympathetic hearings from DSCR. But Currie was tired, over-worked, and subject to ill health. There were limits to his abilities to carry these organizations' banners, especially simultaneously. Through it all he remained devoted to both the Legion and the LPF, and neither organization could fault his service and his dedication.

Throughout the 1920s, Currie continued to be re-elected as the Fund's president even though the state of his health grew extremely worrying. He missed the 1927 and 1928 annual meetings, and only infrequently attended the rare meetings of the Dominion Council. In March 1928, Currie thanked Hair for "all you have done to make my work as President as light as possible." Currie could not attend the 1928 annual meeting as he was in Cobourg, Ontario, for the libel trial. The gathered directors, supportive of their president, sent him "greetings by night letter". A.H. Abbott, the LPF's able vice-president from Ontario, acted for him at the annual meetings. In 1928, Currie suffered a mild stroke and spent months recovering his strength on an extended visit to Europe. His health was never the same again.

Perhaps Currie's Legion ties had something to do with that organization's finally endorsing the LPF and calling on the federal government to pay for all burials on a basis of need, not merely provide an insufficient, fixed amount. Within a few years of its committing funds to the LPF, there were a number of complaints that the $10,000 allotment was proving insufficient to meet the vastly increased number of cases dealt with on a national scale. In March 1927, Currie and Hair travelled to Ottawa and met with the DSCR's minister, J.H.

General Sir Arthur Currie,
president of the Last Post Fund, 1924-32

King, to request an increase in the annual subsidy. In April, discussions about the annual grant took place in the House of Commons, with even Prime Minister Mackenzie King becoming involved. Liberal M.P. Herbert B. Adshead, from Calgary, claimed that the Alberta branches were running short of cash to carry out their duties. Another Alberta member, E.J. Garland from Bow River, indicated that the previous year he had unsuccessfully "pleaded" with Mackenzie King to increase the LPF's allotment and that some veterans from his province were definitely receiving pauper burials. The prime minister replied that if a need existed to supplement the LPF, money would be found in the next estimates. J.H. King noted that while the LPF had requested additional monies, no destitute veterans should be buried in a potter's field. This was Ottawa's policy. When pressed, however, he claimed that if the LPF ran out of money in the course of the year, additional federal funding "would be impossible", since it was not provided for in departmental budgets.

Despite the minister's apparent inflexibility, and no doubt sensing mounting criticism in the House, the prime minister rose and insisted that "if any cases such as my hon. friend [E.J. Garland] refers to are brought to the attention of the government we will certainly see to it that an appropriate burial is arranged." Mackenzie King further assured the House that while no additional funds would be granted for the time being, the government would ask Parliament to vote "supplementary" financing as necessary. The prime minister's unequivocal pledge "greatly pleased" those present at the LPF's annual meeting that month. It meant that all indigent cases brought to the LPF's attention could be dealt with free from financial constraint. In the future, government financing would be forthcoming to cover costs for burials effected. This was progress.

The LPF's burial policy was growing more complex, and new precedents were established regularly. An estimated 4,000 Native Canadians, who were not subject to conscription, had enlisted during the war, constituting about 30 per cent of males of eligible age. This was twice the national average. In 1928, the Dominion Council unanimously approved placing a standard LPF marker on the many unmarked graves of Native veterans on reservations. This was a goal that the crusading Hair had pursued for a number of years. The Department of Indian Affairs co-operated with the LPF in this matter, which Hair felt "from a financial standpoint is not…serious while the moral effect it will have is beyond computation." Nevertheless, it was not until the 1930s that the first markers were actually erected and that LPF burials were extended to Native Canadian veterans living on reserves; until then Ottawa treated them as "status Indians" falling under authority of the less-than-generous Indian Act rather than as veterans eligible for burial services provided by the Fund.

Yet when the Saskatchewan branch buried a former merchant seaman who had seen war service, Dominion Council would not reimburse the branch for the cost of the marker and warned Saskatchewan against a recurrence of this incident. Merchant seamen would have to wait two generations to be recognized as eligible by the LPF.

Throughout the 1920s and beyond, Hair remained concerned

that too few Canadians knew about the LPF. He took great pains to eliminate from public perception the notion that the LPF was in some official manner linked with veterans' organizations, although he made it clear that it had been set up in the interests of veterans and their families. Although the Fund was receiving at least some recognition in a broad range of government and private publications, Hair himself wrote a number of pamphlets and press releases describing its activities. He also published articles in various journals or newsletters of interest to military officials and veterans, such as the *Canadian Defence Quarterly*, and sent dozens of letters to the editor published in a wide variety of newspapers and other publications, many under the pseudonym "Justicia". His writing style is a reflection of his era and his experiences: lush tones impregnated with patriotic sentiment and stirring with imperial fervour. His words were often a blaze of jingoism and heartfelt admiration and respect for British military tradition. But Hair's "propaganda" was also always full of compassionate lyricism for the past sufferings of British soldiery and the plight of those veterans of all ages finding themselves in less fortunate circumstances, in life and in death. In a public appeal for understanding of their problems, Hair wrote that the penniless veteran had probably been the victim of nothing more evil than the "average weaknesses of humanity" and his condition likely an innocent by-product of the social burdens that afflicted the "industrial masses". At a time when public and government opinion was slow to grasp the effects of modernizing society on the impoverished class, Hair's seemed a voice in the wilderness.

Some of the cases dealt with by the Québec branch of the LPF in 1924 might be mentioned as typical of their kind throughout Canada in the 1920s. Many make sad reading. In July of that year, the case of one J.T. Trotter, formerly of the 60th Battalion, CEF, was brought to the LPF's attention by a clergyman. Trotter, poverty-stricken, left behind a wife and seven children in the care of the Montreal Family Welfare Association. In August, Joseph Morin, formerly of the 6th Field Ambulance, CEF, died of tuberculosis, leaving his wife and three small children a tiny amount of insurance, which she used in moving her family back to St. Eustache, northwest of Montreal. At the Last Post Fund's request, the realty company that acted as her landlord waived the two months' back rent she owed and cancelled the unfortunate woman's lease. Also in August, the LPF buried CEF veterans whose causes of death ranged from heart attacks and accidents to suicide. Indeed, a low but steady percentage of LPF cases involved suicide. One pensioner died while under remand to Montreal's Bordeaux Jail for being in possession of narcotic drugs. He suffered from liver disease and tuberculosis. Owing to his unlawful conduct, the LPF buried him in a civil cemetery rather than on Mount Royal – a seemingly ungenerous decision. More and more, the men dealt with were Canadians, or had seen active service with Canadian units. Yet, in September 1924, the LPF buried an old British veteran of the Zulu War of 1879.

In January 1924, Hair noted in his annual report that the premature deaths of indigent veterans was on the rise from coast to coast. Many succumbed to the "adversities of life, absence of relatives and improvidence". In 1922, *The Toronto Star* described the large number of veterans' deaths since the war as a "pitiful plentitude". "The war's toll", the article continued, "is not measured even by death rolls and the provisions of the pension board. Men's lives have been shortened and their efficiency reduced in ways that pensions do not recognize. As the years extend, the number of veterans who die in absolute poverty will increase." The average wartime age in the CEF had been nearly 30. By the late 1920s there were tens of thousands of veterans in their 40s and even many in their 50s. In 1932, the average age of Canada's First World War veterans was 44. In some cases, advancing middle age compounded war-related health problems, making it difficult for some non-pensioned veterans to find work – and this in an era before national social security measures were in place to assist them. It is not actually known how many of them died in poverty of physical, psychological, or emotional stresses resulting from war service, but many did seem to die relatively young, aged long beyond their years. Even Sir Arthur Currie was prematurely aged and beset with recurrent health problems until his death in November 1933, a week before his 58th birthday. (His funeral cortège through the streets of Montreal was one of the largest in Canadian history.)

Military historian Terry Copp has noted that by 1927, 9000 Canadian veterans were disabled by "shell shock and neurosis" and received pensions for their debilitating conditions. Thousands of other Canadians' claims for similar pensions were rejected by Ottawa for various reasons. Society remained harshly unsympathetic to their plight. However, the federal government came around to recognizing the problem and, in 1930, legislated the War Veterans' Allowance Act, which was meant to redress the imbalance between veterans pensioned for disabilities obviously incurred during the war and those who only came to manifest pensionable conditions in the postwar period. Many veterans in the latter category were men who had "broken down" or "burnt out", and were no longer employable. The War Veterans' Allowance Act provided meagre pensions to impoverished veterans over 60 years of age and those younger who could no longer be reasonably expected to support themselves or their families. The act was passed after several years of persistent pressure on the part of the Canadian Legion. Although the act provided the poorest veterans with at least some financial relief, it probably did little to alleviate the LPF's case load. As Morton and Wright have pointed out, however, what the act did signify was that in the eyes of the government and society, the veteran poor were made different from the civilian poor. This is what Arthur Hair had always suggested should be the case.

Matters would worsen in the 1930s when severe economic depression struck the land and when aging veterans had difficulty finding work: 38,000 of them were unemployed in 1935. The effects of the war remained with many of Canada's veterans still, draining their energy and preventing them from earning a decent wage. Levels of veterans' indigence and the concomitant need for the services of the LPF rose rapidly.

With federal assistance, the LPF had turned a corner at a critical juncture in its young existence. In the process, the Last Post Fund had come of age. When Hair wrote his December 1908 letter to *The Gazette* detailing the sad incident to which he was witness, he had done so in the "hope that it may prevent [its] recurrence". His hope was being fulfilled, and, despite occasional challenges to his optimism, it was in very large part because of his own tireless efforts and firm convictions.

4

TRIUMPHS AND TRIALS, 1930–1939

*No man who served his country in the war should
want for food, shelter or fuel.*

R.B. BENNETT,
PRIME MINISTER OF CANADA, 1931

The 1930s were momentous and successful years for the Last Post
Fund. But they were dismal years for Canada. The Great Depression,
beginning at the end of 1929, wreaked havoc with the economy;
unemployment rose to unprecedented levels; poverty and despair, suffering and helplessness, gripped millions of Canadians.

The Depression was one of the most important economic and
social events in Canadian history and has become a frame of reference against which to measure all subsequent periods of economic
duress. Historians have appropriately termed this decade 'the Dirty
Thirties'. Of all Western industrialized nations (except possibly the
United States), Canada was the hardest hit and the nation in which
the Depression lasted the longest. It was caused by a combination
of factors, including economic over-production, over-investment,
under-consumption, strict international trade barriers, and inept
government fiscal policy. The darkest year was 1933. That winter,
the unemployment rate stood at a staggering 32 per cent, while 20
per cent of all Canadians depended on some form of organized
relief services – whether charitable or municipal. Canada had no
welfare state as yet. Of the major cities, Montreal was worst
affected, and of the regions, the prairies, with Saskatchewan the
poorest place in the country. In the winter of 1933, two-thirds of
the rural population of that province depended on relief. For the
unemployed, underemployed, and unemployable, life became a
struggle to survive. The trauma was severe, and many people no

doubt had their lives shortened by health problems linked to poverty; some of these were veterans.

It is within this discouraging national context that the LPF undertook its second decade of nation-wide operations. While the Fund interred an increasing number of impoverished veterans, it also did more than provide traditional burial services. For example, its Women's Division helped to alleviate the financial and emotional misery of the families of veterans buried by the Fund. Its members' social work during the ravages of the period remains a poignant and proud chapter in the history of the Fund. At the start of this troubled decade, however, the LPF experienced one of the great milestones in its history and took on one of its most enduring and challenging commitments.

The Field of Honour

For the Last Post Fund, though not the nation, the decade began with a flourish. Until 1930, the vast majority of LPF burials in Québec took place in the Fund's plots in Mount Royal and Côte-des-Neiges cemeteries. Other burials were arranged in local cemeteries across the province in separate veterans' plots, whenever possible. LPF branches across the country followed similar practices. But as the LPF's original plots on Mount Royal were becoming nearly filled in the late 1920s, the Québec branch had to decide whether to acquire more plots there or to look elsewhere. The two main factors influencing this choice were cost and independence of burial policy. Civic cemeteries not unnaturally charged market-dictated prices for plots and made the LPF beholden to their regulations. Therefore the directors of the Québec branch decided to purchase a cemetery.

In August 1928, they met to discuss the purchase of land. Not long afterwards, provincial Bill 149 granted the LPF the right to operate a cemetery under authority of the Quebec Cemeteries Act. The LPF found an ideal location about 22 kilometres west of downtown Montreal in Pointe Claire, on the western part of the Island of Montreal. There, on April 10, 1929, the Fund purchased six acres of land adjacent to the Lakeview Cemetery for $8,000. The land was beautifully located on a gentle hill, with distant views of Lac St. Louis and the surrounding countryside. This pastoral location would become the Field of Honour, a distinct, independent military cemetery owned and controlled by the Last Post Fund, which gained far greater flexibility in its funerary arrangements than ever before. The Québec branch held the property, with the understanding that it was ultimately an asset of the national LPF organization, under the authority of which the branch operated.

The branch had secured a bank loan for the purchase price of the Field and repaid it with the help of a generous grant from the government of Québec worth $1,000 per annum for 10 years. Médéric Martin, the mayor of Montreal, and Brigadier-General C.A. Smart, Member of the Legislative Assembly (MLA) for Westmount and a member of the LPF, assisted in obtaining this grant from Premier Taschereau's government. The debt was eliminated in 1934, after only five years. In effect, the Province of Québec had purchased the Field for the LPF. The Field of Honour was the first exclusively military cemetery in Canada since the closing of the old Papineau Avenue cemetery in 1869, following the withdrawal of the British garrison from Montreal.

From the spring of 1929 onward, numerous complicated and costly arrangements had to be made in anticipation of the inauguration of the Field. The ground was surveyed, graded, seeded, and planted. Lawns, trees, shrubs, and flowers were arranged in a manner that would offer visitors tranquillity and an appropriate ambience for reflection. Roads and paths were laid out, with land being carefully set aside for the eventual erection of permanent buildings. Workmen sank an artesian well, laid drains, and put up a massive 73-foot metal flagstaff, formerly a ship's mast – a gift from Canada Steamship Lines, installed at no charge by the Dominion Bridge Company. The LPF removed two cannons and their accompanying pyramids of shot from the Mount Royal plots and placed them on either side of the flagpole to act as solemn sentinels over the burial grounds. It hired caretakers and groundskeepers. Arthur Hair was seemingly always to be found at the Field directing all manner of activity in preparation for the opening. He even gave the cannon balls near the flagpole a fresh coat of black paint. For nearly the next two decades, Hair would devote an enormous amount of time and energy towards the Field.

Finally, one of the proudest moments in the history of the Last Post Fund had arrived. The consecration ceremony and official opening of the Field of Honour took place on the afternoon of Sunday, September 21, 1930, before a very large gathering. The weather was excellent. It was a colourful and very formal affair, with the invited dignitaries wearing either uniforms or morning coats and top hats. Present were all the directors of the Québec branch, including its president, Brigadier-General W.O.H. Dodds. Sir Arthur Currie, the LPF's Dominion president, was also there, as were prominent clerical, military, and government officials and representatives of many charitable and veterans' organizations, including the Legion, the Army and Navy Veterans' Association, French and Belgian veterans' groups, the Overseas Nursing Sisters Association of Canada, the IODE, the Knights of Columbus, and other benevolent organizations. A large number of former and serving military officers, many well-known civilians, and the mayors of the Montreal-area municipalities of Verdun, Westmount, Outremont, Pointe Claire, and Ste-Anne-de-Bellevue also attended the ceremony.

J.H. Dillon, minister without portfolio in the provincial government, gave the opening address and officially declared the Field of Honour open. He stated: "This ground having been legally acquired by the Last Post Fund of Canada as a burial place for active or retired members of His Majesty's naval or military forces and others who by custom, precedent or in virtue of the King's rules and regulations may be accorded the privilege of burial in a naval or military cemetery, including members of His Majesty's allies in the Great War, and having been duly consecrated, I name it Last Post Fund Field of Honour and declare it open for the purpose for which it has been dedicated." Following this pronouncement a military procession filed its way onto the grounds. The band of the Victoria Rifles of Canada led the way, along with buglers and drummers from the Royal Montreal Regiment and trumpeters from the 17th Duke of York's, Royal Canadian Hussars. There then followed a representative group of Canadian veterans and a composite guard of honour drawn from the Canadian Grenadier Guards, the Victoria Rifles of Canada, the Black Watch (Royal Highland Regiment) of Canada, the *Régiment de Maisonneuve*, and the Royal Montreal Regiment.

The Right Reverend J.C. Farthing, Anglican bishop of Montreal, and Mgr. E.A. Deschamps, auxiliary bishop of Montreal, simultaneously consecrated the designated Protestant and Catholic plots, respectively. (A section at the northern end of the Field was reserved for veterans of non-Christian faiths.) E.H. Scammell, of the Department of Pensions of National Health (DPNH), into which the Department of Soldiers' Civil Re-establishment had folded in 1928, then stated: "We are here neither to glory in the exploits of war nor to kindle the martial spirit, but rather to work in the interest of peace." This was an appropriate commentary, given the common view following the First World War that nothing so catastrophic must ever be allowed to happen again. Scammell also drew public attention to the over 20 years of hard work that Arthur Hair and his wife, Janet, had provided on behalf of the LPF. At this point, the "Last Post" was sounded, and, as the spectators "looked on with evident emotion", as one newspaper account described it, Brigadier-General Dodds unfurled a 20-foot Union Jack from the flagstaff.

Official opening of the Field of Honour, Pointe Claire, September 21, 1930, published next day in La Patrie. Top: Brigadier-General W.B.M. King accompanied by Brigadier-General W.O.H. Dodds inspecting guard of honour. Bottom: Monsignor E.A. Deschamps, auxiliary bishop of Montreal, consecrating the cemetery; the Knights of Columbus provided the honour guard.

At twilight, with few people about, Hair lit a hurricane lamp, his own gift to the Field, which he dubbed the 'Lamp of Remembrance'. He then hoisted it to the top of the towering masthead. A caretaker at the Field would repeat this act every evening at sundown. Hair hoped that the light would be seen for miles around and serve as a reminder of the veterans buried below it.

The opening received lavish coverage the next day in the Montreal press, which featured glowing articles and large photo spreads. *The Gazette* especially praised both cemetery and ceremony, describing the events as full of "pomp and ritual", performed in the presence of "reverent spectators". *La Presse* and *La Patrie* published a number of photos and emphasized the participation of senior Catholic clergy. According to all reports, the dedication went by seemingly without hitch or blemish. This moving ceremony symbolized a turning point for the Fund and demonstrated the extent to which it had been accepted and come to be relied on in military, veteran, government, and ecclesiastical circles.

The type of headstone used in the Field of Honour was (and continues to be) a flat rectangular granite marker placed flush with the sod. Before the Second World War, it was the practice to cast the name, unit, and birth and death dates of the deceased in bronze plates and affix these to the markers. This method offered better protection against the eroding effects of Montreal's severe winter weather and produced a more dignified appearance than the plain granite. However, when wartime rationing of raw materials made these bronze tablets unavailable, the LPF adopted a system of carving personal details directly into the granite – a practice continued today. All markers contain the phrase "Lest We Forget". Civil cemeteries often allow families a choice of headstone, even in plots reserved for veterans, and so military historians Herbert Fairlie Wood and John Swettenham have remarked that "nowhere in Canada – with the possible exception of the Field of Honour at Pointe Claire – is there to be found the calm uniformity of the overseas cemeteries." Moreover, like the cemeteries overseas, the Field of Honour does not distinguish between rank or service; grave-marking and perpetual care are the same for all buried there.

Continuing one of its earliest policies, the LPF accepted pre-paid burial reservations for the Field of Honour from any non-indigent veterans desiring to lie alongside their comrades of old. Some spouses also expressed the wish to be interred in the Field, and eventually even unmarried children of veterans became eligible for burial there, all at their own expense. Reservations, made at actual book cost, covered all customary cemetery charges, including a standard marker and perpetual upkeep.

Two veterans were buried in each gravesite, emulating the tradition on Mount Royal. While this policy was a space-saving expedient, Sir Fabian Ware, founder of the Imperial War Graves Commission, established to bury the empire's war dead and to mark their graves, visited the Mount Royal plots in 1925 and was of the opinion that the LPF's practice may have been unique in the British Empire. Ware found it particularly pleasing that veterans from different parts of Canada, the empire, and even beyond, who shared the experience of service and the principles for which they fought, could be interred together in the same ground, united in a bond of comradeship.

The LPF planned for the future upkeep of the cemetery. It set up an Endowment Fund to ensure the perpetual care of the plots. Burial expenses included an automatic contribution to this fund. By 1935, $4.50 per capita was charged on each burial, and any fees received for grave reservations were also credited to this fund. The Women's Division of the LPF contributed its membership dues to the Endowment Fund. The hefty operating expenses for the Field came from the Québec branch's operating budget. In fact, half of its administrative costs went towards maintenance of the Field. Up to May 1931, the LPF had spent $13,000 on the Field all told, and had repaid half of the loan covering the $8,000 purchase cost. This outcome had required sound money management.

With the exception of a small temporary chapel erected by the Women's Division in 1932, the next major addition to the Field of Honour was the Cross of Remembrance, set in a circular mound at the entrance to the cemetery and unveiled during the annual commemoration ceremony on May 24, 1934. Archdeacon (the Venerable) John Almond, president of the Dominion Council, had laid the cornerstone of the five-metre granite cross, which was solemnly dedicated to the memory of Sir Arthur Currie, who had died the previous November. The cross also carried a dedication to "our warrior dead".

The circular path ringing the mound was named Currie Circle. Currie himself was buried not in the Field of Honour, but in Mount Royal Cemetery. A special Cross of Sacrifice, like those found in IWGC cemeteries, marked Currie's final resting place, with his own familiar words, "They served till death – why not we?" carved on the cross. (The Cross of Remembrance unveiled at the Field of Honour was not, strictly speaking, a Cross of Sacrifice according to IWGC stipulations, which describe them as constructed of white Portland stone set upon an elevated hexagonal base.)

In 1937, another significant structure went up at the Field of Honour – an imposing Gate of Remembrance at the entrance in the form of a medieval arch flanked by twin towers. The structure was both commemorative and practical: it provided small lodgings for a permanent caretaker, acted as a repository for the LPF's archives, and contained a public waiting room. Major John H. Molson, president of the Québec branch, had turned the first sod for the gate in the spring of 1937. Archdeacon Almond placed the cornerstone and inside deposited a sealed copper box containing documents, coins of the reigns of George V and George VI, photos, newspapers, and a list containing the names of the directors of the Last Post Fund. It took 13 weeks to build the gate that summer, at a cost of $11,850. The City

Official opening of the Gate of Remembrance, Field of Honour, October 6, 1937.

of Pointe Claire donated $5,000 to the project. The remaining two 9-pounder cannons from the Mount Royal plots were moved to flank the new gateway, giving the cemetery an unmistakably military air. On October 6, the governor general, Lord Tweedsmuir, officially unveiled the structure at a well-attended ceremony that received wide coverage in the local media.

Once a small system of roads and paths in the Field was properly laid out, the LPF named roads were for distinguished Canadian servicemen, such as William Avery "Billy" Bishop, V.C., and well-known Canadian battles, mainly of the Great War, such as Vimy and Amiens. Later, the Fund invoked the Second World War, recalling Victoria Cross winners such as Paul Triquet and Andrew Mynarski, and battle sites such as Falaise. Some visitors' benches were eventually installed, usually donated by Montreal-area branches of the Canadian Legion.

In April 1930, in the Québec branch's annual report, Hair had noted that the Mount Royal plots were to be closed after May 24 and that the Field of Honour would officially open that September. In fact, the first burial at the Field had already taken place and, oddly

Governor General Lord Tweedsmuir inaugurates the Gate of Remembrance. Norman Holland at left, John H. Molson at right, and Arthur Hair immediately above Tweedsmuir's right shoulder.

enough, the veteran in question was a highly decorated Belgian. The final burial at the LPF's plot at Côte-des-Neiges Cemetery took place on April 1, 1930, and the final one at Mount Royal Cemetery not until December 16. Always frugal, the LPF insisted on filling the pre-purchased graves in its plot there. Prior to the opening of the Field of Honour, the Fund had interred more than 600 veterans in its Mount Royal plots and over 1,800 across Canada.

The LPF's May 24 observances continued after the Field of Honour opened. Early-morning ceremonies took place at the old plots in Mount Royal and Côte-des-Neiges cemeteries, followed by a religious service at 11:30 a.m. at the base of the Clock Tower Memorial at the port of Montreal. At noon, a wreath mounted on a lifebuoy was launched overboard from the Harbour Commissioners' tug, normally the *Sir Hugh Allan*. As the lifebuoy floated down river, a rocket salute to the dead was fired, and a white dove released, symbolic of the departed souls of the sailor dead. At 3:00 p.m. the LPF held its major ceremonies at the Field of Honour. These included a brief address in English and French by an invited dignitary, a religious service, and wreath layings. Arthur Hair solemnly read aloud a 'Roll Call' of those the LPF had buried in the previous year. In advance, members decorated each grave with small flags and placed poppy wreaths at prominent locations. Wreaths of fresh flowers adorned the base of the Cross of Remembrance, the focal point of the ceremonies. For most of the decade, simultaneous smaller ceremonies continued to be held at the old military burial grounds on Papineau Avenue in Montreal and in Chambly, south of the city. In 1936, the LPF unveiled two boulders on which were affixed descriptive plaques in each of its Mount Royal and Côte-des-Neiges plots to serve notice to passers-by that the friendless military servants of the empire did not go unrecognized at death. Two years later, the directors of the Québec branch decided to concentrate their remembrance efforts at the Field and river ceremonies and sent only floral tributes to the other sites, including those on Mount Royal. In addition, every Remembrance Day, November 11, a member of the executive placed a wreath on behalf of the Fund at the cenotaph in Dominion Square in downtown Montreal.

Every year since it opened, hundreds of visitors from across Canada and beyond have visited the Field of Honour to pay their respects to relatives and friends who lie buried there. Few fail to remark on its serene, well-tended, and tasteful surroundings. Given their involvement in the Fund from its humble inception and difficult early history, Arthur Hair and John Almond took great pride in the Field of Honour. It was a testament to their determination. The Field of Honour heightened the visibility of the Fund, afforded it greater credibility as a patriotic society, and provided it with a strong sense of identity and permanence. At the start of the twenty-first century, the Field remains a respected LPF presence in the military and veterans' communities. It put the Last Post Fund on the map, literally.

Other Burial Grounds

Following the Last Post Fund's expansion to a Canada-wide organi-zation in 1922, individual branches became responsible for arranging the burial of indigent veterans in their own districts. This normally meant that they acquired plots in existing cemeteries, usually large urban centres. The LPF practice in Montreal of burying veterans two to a grave was not emulated in other cemeteries. Most of the larger ones across the nation already had military or 'soldiers'' sections, many of which were enlarged during and immediately following the First World War. It was natural that LPF branches would seek burial plots in such locations. By the end of the Second World War, the LPF main-tained veterans' sections in nearly 20 municipal cemeteries across the country.

For example, the following Toronto-area cemeteries contain sec-tions reserved for military burials: Beechwood (Downsview), Holy Cross (Thornhill), Pine Hills (Scarborough), and York (Willowdale). York and Pine Hills contain imposing cenotaphs raised by patriotic Toronto citizens in memory of Canada's war dead. Others in the province include Beechwood (Ottawa), Windsor Memorial (Windsor), and Woodland (London). The LPF has used hundreds of cemeteries in Ontario, with and without military sections, since those eligible for LPF services are normally buried at or near the location where they died.

The military plots in western Canada were among the most dis-tinguished. Winnipeg's Brookside Cemetery, for example, in 1915 opened a large and separate military section which has been used by

Impressive entrance to the Soldiers' Cemetery, Regina, c. 1935.

The Soldiers' Cemetery, Regina, c. 1935.

the LPF, other organizations, and individuals. Not long after the Winnipeg headquarters of the Manitoba branch opened in 1922, the LPF obtained some land in this lovely cemetery free of charge. In the first 25 years of the branch's operations, nearly 1,000 LPF burials took place in Brookside Cemetery. The IWGC erected a Cross of Sacrifice in the centre of the original plot following the Great War. In 1960, the Commonwealth War Graves Commission (CWGC) dedicated at this site Canada's only Stone of Remembrance – an altar-like block of stone bearing the inscription "Their Name Liveth For Evermore" – to honour all Commonwealth service men and women who lie buried in Canada. (Stones of Remembrance stand at the entrance to most overseas CWGC cemeteries.) Every year, the Manitoba LPF organized its own "Decoration Day" ceremony, which was attended by thousands.

The Southern Alberta branch, headquartered in Calgary, made use of a burial ground that it too named the 'Field of Honour'. Its original plot, located in the very attractive municipally owned Union Cemetery, rapidly filled up after only 150 military burials; a Cross of Sacrifice was erected on the site (one of 20 throughout Canada). In 1923, the branch opened its spacious 20-acre Field of Honour plot in the large nearby Burnsland Cemetery. Although the LPF believed this plot would be sufficient for the next 100 years, it accommodated nearly 1,000 burials by 1945. The graves there were laid out head to head, which is unusual in Canadian military practice. In 1920, the Edmonton Cemetery Company inaugurated a distinct soldiers' section of 800 gravesites, later enlarged for another 500 graves, which by the 1940s were filling up. A Cross of Sacrifice went up at this site. Because of the rapid increase in military burials, most major Canadian cities have several veterans' burial locations.

Saskatchewan too did justice to the memories of those who served. In 1946, Norman Holland, Dominion president of the LPF, visited the military section of Regina's Municipal Cemetery, opened in 1918, and pronounced it "the most beautiful of all Military (and Last Post) Cemeteries in Canada." It was an "outstanding example", he reported, "of what can be done to make the last resting place of our Soldier Dead not only useful, but beautiful." Its circular form, radiating out from a central Cross of Sacrifice, made it visually very appealing. All former military personnel were eligible for burial there. Nearly

30 years later, more than 700 burials had taken place, many of them LPF cases. In Saskatoon, Woodlawn Municipal Cemetery designated a Soldiers' Plot, officially opened in 1922. It provided the LPF free land, although it charged a minimal fee for opening and closing graves. After 25 years of operation, one-third of the 500 military burials were LPF cases. An unusual Cross of Remembrance graces this burial ground – field stone, with a white cross on top. All LPF graves are inscribed with the customary "Lest We Forget", while the regular military headstones carry the Maple Leaf insignia. The Saskatoon IODE, continuing an enduring bond with the LPF, helped enormously in maintaining the military plot. In Prince Albert, by the 1940s, the Canadian Legion operated a small military cemetery that did not charge any fees at all for LPF burials. Despite the sometimes-strained relations between the LPF's western branches and Dominion headquarters, and between the LPF and the Legion, co-operation in these matters was the norm and the LPF well and truly carried out its tasks.

In Vancouver, municipal authorities co-operated generously with the LPF. In 1924, they gave the Fund the original two and one-half-

Members of the LPF's Women's Auxiliary unveil Vimy Ridge Memorial Cross in the LPF cemetery plot in Mountain View Cemetery, Vancouver, c. 1926.

acre LPF plot known as the "Returned Soldiers' Burial Ground" in Mountain View, a civic cemetery. Ten years later, the city donated an adjacent two-and-one-half acres and assumed costs of upkeep for all five acres, charging only a minimal fee to open and close graves. The number of LPF cases in British Columbia was very high between the wars, second only to Ontario; by 1945, these BC plots were full. Accordingly, in 1941 the city increased the size of the LPF plot to 20 acres. To the end of 1946, the BC branch had buried 2,800 veterans. In that year, the city donated a further 20 acres of land in a nearby but non-contiguous plot, making Vancouver's LPF plot the largest in Canada by far. The beautifully kept grounds contain a splendid eight-sided 'sanctuary' housing four wooden crosses originally erected on or near Vimy Ridge before the end of the First World War to commemorate the fallen of four Vancouver-based infantry battalions – the 7th, 16th, 29th, and 72nd. During the Second World War, a Vancouverite erected a 60-foot flagpole there in honour of his son, who was killed in action over Germany while serving in the Royal Canadian Air Force (RCAF).

Women were largely responsible for the impressive commemorative events held at Mountain View in the interwar period. These attracted wide media attention and rivalled in ceremony and probably exceeded in attendance many of those held in Montreal. In June 1938, for example, 2,600 people gathered to remember Canada's deceased veterans. Nearly 1,000 veterans attended, along with an equal number of civilian friends and relatives and 600 military participants, many from the Seaforth Highlanders, which provided a band and firing party. Members of the Ladies' Auxiliary of the BC LPF placed small Union Jacks on each of the nearly 2,000 LPF graves, and some acted as flag-bearers. The mothers, wives, and widows of the dead laid wreaths – a central part of the ceremonies. Throughout the 1920s and 1930s, these women, and others across Canada, played a significant role in the operations and successes of the LPF.

The Women of the Last Post Fund

For most of its first three decades, the Last Post Fund was able to count on the support and dedication of the Ladies' Auxiliary, known in its later years as the Women's Division. The roots of the Women's

Division extended back to the early 1920s, but the 1930s proved to be both its heyday and the period of its demise. It was during these stressful economic times that the LPF women were able to make the most difference in the lives of the financially and emotionally distressed families of deceased veterans. Unfortunately, by the end of that discouraging decade, the LPF women's organization had become a casualty of changing perceptions and shifting priorities.

Women were present at the Last Post Fund's inaugural meeting in 1909 and always formed part of its membership. The First World War had offered opportunities for the LPF's women members and supporters to display their abilities and patriotism. They organized benefit events and became heavily involved in the Supplementary Memorial Fund. Female LPF members also assisted other benevolent societies, such as the Canadian Patriotic Fund and the Canadian Red Cross Society, with fund-raising and various kinds of war relief work. Tens of thousands of other Canadian women did the same. None of this was unusual since, in the previous two decades, women had become increasingly organized and vocal in social reform issues and in their demands for voting rights. By the outbreak of war, Canadian women had formed high-profile voluntary organizations interested in social, political, cultural, and economic issues. Nevertheless, the LPF women's involvement in the war mirrored socially-accepted gender roles and their efforts did not afford them much influence within their own organization.

Although no formal organization yet existed, in 1917 the LPF's executive made the indefatigable Mrs. Leila Morrison convenor of the Ladies' Auxiliary. She became responsible for attracting and organizing female volunteers to assist the LPF's patriotic undertakings. The executive closely supervised her activities and, despite their hard work and commitment to the principles for which the LPF stood, the female members wielded little power – and this extended even to those women who served as directors in the 1920s. At best, they benefitted from positions of apparent prominence with an increasingly active patriotic organization, but the reality seemed to be that their voices carried less weight than those of the LPF's men, many of whom might be characterized as conservative retired army officers. The revised 1922 constitution of the newly national LPF allowed any branch to authorize a Women's

Auxiliary, complete with its own by-laws, and the branch directors expected the women to assist in the manner requested of them. Many Canadian community, social, and cultural groups had women's auxiliaries at this time, most of which were engaged in fund-raising and promotional activities.

In October 1922, a Ladies' Auxiliary of the Dominion headquarters in Montreal was formed and obtained a sub-charter from the LPF Dominion Council. (Because records of branches' women's auxiliaries do not appear to have survived, the following account relies on the Montreal women's records as being nationally representative. It is known, for example, that BC branch benefitted from an active Ladies' Auxiliary, but no archives have been found to tell its story.) Since Dominion HQ had no membership as such, the Ladies' Auxiliary served mainly the interests of the Québec branch, and this relationship was formalized several years later. It had 17 charter members, including Mrs. Janet Hair and both female members of the LPF executive, Misses Hay Browne and Elsie King. Its avowed purpose was "to assist and co-operate in any way possible to attain the aims and objects of the Last Post Fund". Despite this claim, gender-based differences of opinion emerged as the years passed.

In December 1922, the Ladies' Auxiliary admitted 80 members, each paying annual dues of $5. Most of the women came from English-speaking, upper-middle-class backgrounds, and the vast majority lived in the Montreal area. The wives of virtually all married directors of the Québec branch joined. Many members belonged also to the Imperial Order Daughters of the Empire, and many of its branches joined the LPF Ladies' Auxiliary as associate members. A strong sense of *noblesse oblige* seemed present within the women's group. Mrs. Hair was very active throughout the 1920s, as were Lady Currie, Mrs. Walsh, Mrs. Armstrong, and Mrs. Creelman, wives of long-standing officers of the Fund. Until the mid-1930s, other spouses of later directors would join or replace them. Lady Holt, wife of Sir Herbert Holt, one of Canada's wealthiest men, also joined. Just as the governor general was patron of the LPF, so did succeeding vice-regal spouses became patrons of the women's organization. In addition to grouping together individual members and many IODE branches, the LPF women were also closely allied with the Catholic Women's League and the Overseas Nursing Sisters Association of Canada.

The Ladies' Auxiliary took on important duties, which included raising funds, running membership drives, and volunteering at veterans' hospitals. Its executive met every six weeks on average throughout the 1920s and 1930s, although the frequency gradually declined. It set up a Visiting Committee, led for most of the 1920s by Mrs. Hair, and its members visited the bereaved and often financially troubled families of departed veterans. Many of these poor families needed material assistance, and the Ladies' Auxiliary did what it could to ease their burdens: its members donated or purchased clothing, groceries, and other basic necessities and distributed them to the needy. Their work added a new voluntary dimension to the work of the LPF, one well beyond the Fund's mandate. The women also visited local military hospitals, especially Ste-Anne's (of which John Almond was the chaplain), taking small gifts and cheer to the veterans, mainly of the First World War, confined to these institutions. A Funeral Attendance Committee ensured a presence at all LPF burials, its members sometimes the only mourners present. A women's Ground Committee carefully tended the cemetery plots on Mount Royal.

The Ladies' Auxiliary kept busy. It organized tag days, musical and theatrical shows, tea socials, and dances to raise funds. Already by October 1923, the women had raised $200 for LPF coffers. But this was just the beginning of almost two decades of fund-raising. In 1924, the Québec members – an impressive 180 active and 27 associates – yielded combined dues of over $900. All monies collected went directly to the LPF treasury. In 1926, at an Armistice Ball that they organized, the women raised another $2,667, 40 per cent of which they turned over to Ste-Anne's Military Hospital and the remainder to the Québec branch of the LPF. A similar benefit ball the following year turned a profit of nearly $1,900, divided in the same proportions. As the years wore on, this sort of activity produced diminishing returns. The garrison ball in 1931 earned only $275. Economic conditions were worsening, but the women's organization was also in decline.

By the mid to late 1920s, the always wildly fluctuating membership began to fall off, despite enthusiasm and commitment among remaining members. At the beginning of 1927, the Ladies' Auxiliary was down to 102 active and 24 associate members – a decline of nearly 40 per cent. Certainly the women were annoyed at the LPF

Dominion Council, which showed perfect indifference towards their hard work. A 1924 report from the Ladies' Auxiliary stated that this arrogant attitude "rather discouraged the officers [from] any further effort". The men seemed to prefer the women to follow directives rather than take any initiatives in large fund-raising ventures, and some women felt unappreciated. The intensity of the women's activities was also tied somewhat to the LPF's financial needs. The Ladies' Auxiliary's annual report of 1925 noted that since "the finances of the Fund are in a fairly good condition...the Auxiliary has not felt called upon to make any special effort". By the end of the decade, involuntary inactivity and lack of official encouragement signalled the women's changing status within the organization and led to lessened interest and involvement.

The Ladies' Auxiliary altered its name in May 1927 to the Women's Auxiliary and again in 1931 to the Women's Division – reflecting underlying changes in attitude. Some of the women were tired of being 'ladies' in an 'auxiliary', the dependent wives of male members, and wanted to assert their significant contributions as 'women' constituting a 'division', if not equal in status to the branch, at least increasingly distinct. Not all women felt this way, clearly; a spate of resignations in December 1932 and January 1933 implied that those more traditionally oriented wanted merely to act in a manner dictated by the branch. Tellingly, among those resigning was Edwina Holland, wife of Norman Holland, a director of the Québec branch. Most cited lack of availability or ill health, although the timing of their actions coincided with a growing division between men and women in the LPF. Despite these internal machinations, the women continued to raise money to help defray the cost of branch administration. In 1931, the Women's Division and the IODE were invited to the opening of the large Simpson's department store in downtown Montreal. On this occasion, Charles L. Burton, president of Simpson's, handed over to the LPF women a hefty cheque for $2,000. While the actual reason for the gift remains unclear, it covered a substantial portion of the LPF's administrative budget for the year. The Fund owed much to its women members, perhaps more than was comfortable for some of the men.

In the spring of 1932, the Women's Division organized the building of a small temporary chapel at the new Field of Honour. Its members considered the dedication of this structure the highlight of their activities in this period. They described the chapel as "a small but well-built structure of wood, tiled roof, with one of the windows of stained glass". But arguably more important, at the time of the Great Depression, the Women's Division sought to alleviate the suffering of deceased veterans' families. So much poverty and misery were caused by unemployment that a growing number of Canadians died before their time, many in destitution. The work of the LPF grew as a consequence, and so did that of its Women's Division.

In situations where a deceased veteran had been the family's principal breadwinner, families could be utterly ruined in the absence of government social assistance. Given the economic and social climate of Depression-era Canada, few widowed women beyond middle age, particularly if they had to care for children, could hope to find employment. The province provided widows' allowances in some cases, but these were pitifully low. Members of the Visiting Committee of the Women's Division went to the homes of the deceased veterans' dependants and, if necessary, provided emergency material or financial assistance. For example, in the fiscal year 1932-33, the women made 38 visits to 16 separate families located throughout Montreal. The women provided donations of clothing and footwear, essential home furnishings, medicine (offered through the co-operation of the St. John's Ambulance), and even daily milk supplies to those families with school-age children. The women packaged and delivered special 'Christmas Cheer' baskets with the assistance of the IODE and the Kiwanis Club. The Women's Division also co-operated with the Montreal Family Welfare Association and the ladies' auxiliaries of various Legion branches to ensure that as many families as possible received aid. For the year ending February 1933, the division had disbursed slightly more than $1,000 in charitable aid – a considerable amount in those desperate times.

The Women's Division itself raised money for these acts of kindness. The Montreal Soldiers' Wives' League also generously supported its activities. When the League wound up its operations in the 1920s, it placed a $2,000 bond earning 4 per cent interest ($80 per annum) in trust with the LPF Ladies' Auxiliary. The interest thereby generated was "to be used for the benefit of the widows and families of Canadian soldiers or ex-soldiers who are in difficulties, trouble or distress." In 1931, the money raised for this purpose was deposited in a "Widows and Orphans Emergency Fund". The Women's Division was reinvigorated by its devotion to these unfortunate people, but its insistence on helping was also an underlying cause of its undoing.

On December 3, 1934, Major John H. Molson, president of the Québec branch, sent a letter to Mrs. W. Bovey, president of the Women's Division. At the very height of the LPF women's excellent charitable activities, Molson notified them that the executive of the Québec branch had unanimously decided to withdraw their operating sub-charter. The reason he cited was that the local Red Cross had agreed to assist the surviving family members of deceased veterans. Other organizations such as the *Société St-Vincent-de-Paul* and the Family Welfare Association were available to assist. Therefore, Molson claimed, the need for the Women's Division no longer existed. Following these curt remarks, Molson invited the hard-working LPF women to remain as individual members of the Fund and to continue to take an interest in the organization's affairs. It was quite a slap in the face. The women refused to be cowed, however, for their work in soothing the suffering of veterans' families meant too much to them. They were women helping other women overcome the sort of distress men of privilege like Molson might not have fully comprehended.

Mrs. Bovey hastily convened a well-attended general meeting of members, at which the action of the Québec branch was roundly denounced. In a frank and bitter letter to Molson, Sarah D. Walker, secretary of the Women's Division, reminded him that the LPF women had faithfully and successfully carried out all the Québec branch's requests, including organizing membership drives and raising funds. As a result, the women were "amazed and perturbed" at the men's decision. This was all the more so since, as recently as March 1934, the Québec branch had passed a motion allowing the Women's Division its own discretion in dealing with the emergency relief of dependants of LPF burial cases. A meeting in January 1935 between the two sides was arranged, and the Women's Division survived, on the understanding that all money raised by the women (save the interest on the Soldiers' Wives' League bond) would be placed in the Endowment Fund for the Field of Honour. It was a fund the women were pleased to assist, as they had been since its inception.

But the writing was on the wall. For reasons lost from the official record, the men could not bring themselves to see the continued utility of the women's efforts. Even if a difference of opinion existed over the LPF's role in assisting destitute families, shutting down the women's operations seemed a draconian and regressive response. The 1935 annual report of the Women's Division notes that its work was "much curtailed so that instead of being a body mainly devoted to the help and welfare of the dependants of deceased soldiers, we have passed on that work to the Red Cross Society, at the request of the Men's Division, and are now mainly concerned with the preservation of the Field of Honour and its chapel." Supplementary relief work continued, but it was no longer officially the women's primary *raison d'être*. This was bad news for the fewer than 100 members left, who perhaps alone in the organization understood the value of their charitable deeds.

In June 1935, in the hope of attracting more members, the Women's Division dropped its annual dues from $5 to $3. Even this move displeased the Québec branch directors. In November of that year, John Molson wrote to Mrs. Bovey suggesting that the women's dues would better serve the needs of the LPF if they were assigned to the Field of Honour's Development Fund, to be used to finance repairs, improvements, and additions to the Field. The women preferred the Endowment Fund. Molson "regretted very much" their decision, but the disagreement was typical. The two LPF groups were moving along parallel paths and simply could no longer see eye to eye on most matters. The increased tension contributed to a further loss in women's membership.

The Women's Division continued its relief work, despite the open opposition of several members of the LPF's Québec executive, including its secretary-treasurer, Arthur Hair, who felt that their work should be done by other organizations and the money thus saved turned over to LPF coffers. The women thought otherwise. Mrs. L.E. Hutchison headed the Relief Committee (which was merged with the Visiting Committee in 1933) with great dedication for a number of years. She tired of the disagreements and, at the end of 1935, she turned the job over to two worthy successors, Mrs. Susie Murray and Mrs. Pearl Morgan. These strong-willed women, self-styled "investigators", arranged for the donation of, or used their Relief Fund to pay for, the delivery of milk, medicine, and even cod liver oil to families with children, many of whom were sadly undernourished. They also regularly sent these families children's winter coats, sweaters, mittens, and tuques. These two women worked tirelessly to obtain donations of clothing, bedding, kitchen supplies, curtains, rugs, coal, and furniture for these helpless people. Occasionally, such items had to be purchased. Whenever possible, a wealthier member of the Women's Division would be requested to purchase eyeglasses for a deceased veteran's child or to pay for two weeks of summer camp for disadvantaged orphans. These were activities and items that Murray and Morgan considered worth every minute and every cent. Moreover, such special treats and services were often unavailable through the overburdened Red Cross and other large local charities. In these small ways, the women looked after the dependants of the cases that the LPF handled; they cared for their own.

Susie Murray and Pearl Morgan undertook heart-breaking work. Murray stated that the tragic circumstances in which the families of deceased veterans could find themselves, and which she had personally witnessed, "could fill a book". One particularly sad case – simply "terrible" – they dealt with at Christmas 1937. A 27-year-old widow and her seven children, aged two to nine years, were so destitute that one child was forced to sleep on the floor on a pile of old coats, while a younger boy slept among some newspapers. The Women's Division at once sent food, fuel, and clothing to them. One member, Mrs. G.W. Cook, easily prevailed on her IODE chapter to send additional clothing and arrange for a quart of milk to be delivered to their door every morning for a year. Another case involved a woman with a young child and a working teenaged son living in squalid conditions. When the two investigators arrived to visit her, "the mother was making herself a piece of dry toast for her lunch, and tea without either milk of sugar." Murray and Morgan immediately purchased groceries for them.

In 1937, Susie Murray and Pearl Morgan noted of one penniless widow of a deceased veteran being buried by the Fund that "the poor woman had nothing at all to wear to attend the funeral, not even a pair of stockings. In their final, emotional report, written in February 1939, they applauded the courage of those whom they helped: "the work entrusted to us…has taught us a great deal [about] the silent suffering of many of these poor women, who…without complaining carry on in a world that has little to offer." In four years of dedicated and often distressing work, Murray and Morgan visited and assisted 160 distraught families in the Montreal area – a shocking 80 per cent of all local LPF burial cases. Such was the work which the branch's executive had earlier tried to shut down.

The number of cases investigated by the women had dropped throughout the 1930s. Pearl Morgan regularly telephoned Arthur Hair to inquire if any desperate cases had come to his attention. Hair always replied that the Red Cross would handle such problems or that there were no urgent cases. It is clear that Hair, like the rest of the directors, had ceased endorsing the women's efforts. Perseverance made the women few friends with the directors but won them the undying thanks of those who really mattered – the bereaved and the needy. They received a number of letters of gratitude from the families they assisted. Molson, Hair, and the other directors might have learned something from reading them.

By 1939, the Women's Division was petering out, and so was the Depression. Many women had 'dropped out' in the previous year, and only 21 members remained, including institutional members. The division had less than $30 in its various funds combined, and, since the chapel at the Field was completed and no further projects would be forthcoming, in March 1939 the women disbanded. On March 10, Molson sent a restrained letter to Mrs. E.B. Creelman-Savage, the last president, thanking her for the women's assistance in years past and appending two resolutions passed by the Québec branch two days earlier requesting that the women return to the LPF their sub-charter and all funds and also remit the $2,000 bond from the Soldiers' Wives' League. (The LPF returned the bond to the League when the latter reformed on the outbreak of the Second World War.) Given the help that the women had extended to hundreds of poor and despondent Montrealers, the coolness of Molson's tone and the crispness of the resolutions should have made the directors of the Québec branch blush.

So ended a spirited chapter in the history of giving that stands as a sterling example of the work of the Last Post Fund. Through the tireless and at times emotionally distressing labours of these women, the LPF was able not only to care for the dead, but to assist the living.

"Devoid of glamour, extremely exacting and distinctly depressing"

Throughout the 1930s, the Last Post Fund continued to bury mostly former army privates or non-commissioned officers who had served in the Canadian Expeditionary Force or with British forces during the First World War. Exceptions were few: of 291 cases in 1930 there were only seven officers and four naval ratings. All the veterans were Christians (mainly Protestants) save for a single Muslim. Of over 300 burials the next year, there were but six officers, one man of the Jewish faith, and several Allied veterans, including an American, a Belgian, and two Italians. Of the 428 cases in 1932, 307 had been on Canadian service, 86 were 'Imperials', and 13 had seen action with the Royal Navy and one with the Royal Air Force. Only five of the deceased were officers, and all were Christians except for one Jew and one Buddhist. From that year onward the LPF was burying an average of more than one veteran a day; before the decade was out, the average would be almost three a day. About 80 per cent of LPF burials were of Canadian-born veterans, 80 per cent were Protestant, and Ontario accounted for about one-third of cases. This trend continued through the 1930s, with the numbers of officers, naval ratings, and Allied veterans rising only very marginally. In each of 1936 and 1938, the LPF buried four former nursing sisters of the Great War.

Burials had been more numerous than expected in Québec and western Canada (especially in British Columbia), about 20 per cent lower in Ontario and 50 per cent lower in the Maritimes. This factor helps explain the problems of budget administration in the west and the smooth functioning of the Ontario branch. The average age of those buried by the LPF across Canada in the fiscal year 1931-32 was only 40 – a telling statistic. Many of these men were in their early or mid-30s and had finally succumbed to the physical or psychological hardships imposed on them by the war; suicide, as noted earlier, was not an unknown cause of death among LPF cases. The Fund recorded a heavy increase in caseloads beginning in 1933, at least partly because of the increasing hardship brought on that winter by the Depression.

In the early 1930s, the Fund was still able to bury veterans for an average of less than $100 per case, including undertaking ($50 maximum), grave preparation ($25), and a grave marker ($25). Hair estimated that this was only one-third of normal market costs. Average expenditures varied by province. The Québec average was $91 whereas the west hovered around $100. At the end of its first year of operation (1909-10), the LPF had spent $500 on funerals. Twenty-five years later it was incurring annual costs of $60,000. Every year, Ottawa liquidated the LPF's funeral account deficit and overall paid about 80 per cent of its expenses. The remainder of the money was raised by the LPF itself or obtained through cost recovery from estates. To the end of 1937, the LPF had buried over 6,500 veterans, including 100 in the United States, three in Britain, and one in Newfoundland. The LPF interred over 800 people in 1937, for an average of 393 a year since the Great War. Administrative costs of $7,000-$8,000 per annum never exceeded 11.74 per cent of the annual funeral costs – an acceptable ratio.

In 1932, Ottawa organized unemployment relief and labour camps in some rather remote areas of Canada, where single, unemployed men cleared land, built aircraft landing strips, extended roads, erected public buildings, and performed other useful and less useful work – all for the painfully low sum of 20 cents a day. Until they closed in 1936, the camps were administered by the Department of National Defence – somewhat ominously since many of the thousands of men attracted to these sites were considered potential left-wing "agitators" by the government of R.B. Bennett.

Among the over 170,000 men who participated in this program were many down-on-their-luck First World War veterans, including a number who died in these relief camps as a result of natural causes or accidents. They were buried in the locations where they died, and the LPF took it upon itself to provide standard grave markers for them. In the spring of 1936, Ottawa acquiesced to the Fund's insistent demands, and the markers were erected. While these men were not, strictly speaking, the responsibility of the LPF, the Fund was committed in a wider sense to commemorating their service and marking their passing; indeed, this was an extension of the principle on which it had been founded. Similarly, following a seemingly endless exchange of correspondence between Hair, E.H. Scammell at the Department of Pensions and National Health, and the Department of Indian Affairs, in 1936 the LPF placed markers on the graves of Native veterans of the First World War located in Native burial grounds or reservations. Between the relief camps and the reservations, the LPF erected 40 markers over graves that otherwise would have gone unidentified as those of veterans.

The LPF dealt with some odd cases. In 1930 Hair recounted the bizarre story of a veteran whose body was retrieved by the LPF, in the nick of time, from Montreal's anatomical research laboratory, where it had been scheduled for dissection. The man was unidentified except for a regimental insignia with a number alongside tattooed on his body. The LPF investigated and, learning that the number was a service number, was able positively to identify the man. It transpired that the unfortunate veteran had left behind a widow and three small children. Solving this mystery was all in a day's work for Arthur Hair.

As a result of its impressive record, the LPF increased its profile with an appreciative veterans' community. The Fund's reputation grew. In 1932, one old ex-soldier in Montreal, on his deathbed, sent for Hair to obtain the latter's personal assurances that the LPF would bury him alongside his former comrades-in-arms. Another terminally ill veteran approached the Fund to assist him with properly planning his funeral, at his own expense. In that year, three widows of LPF cases were buried in the Field, as were two soldiers whose remains were transferred there from other cemeteries at their families' request and expense. In 1938, a 57-year-old Hamilton veteran of the South African War and the First World War wrote an angry letter to *The Hamilton Spectator* complaining of his chronic unemployment: "The only thing that an ex-service man is sure of is that the generous Last Post Fund will cheerfully bury him and only then will he cease to be a burden on his family instead of a help." The LPF was able to offer the satisfaction in death that dismal economic conditions and government policies were unable to provide in life.

Hair was generally satisfied with the functioning of the LPF on a national scale. Still, some branches continued to be the source of concern and difficulty for the Dominion Council, and for Hair in particular. In New Brunswick, there were altogether too many resignations and too few burials. In 1930, the branch's sub-charter was revoked, and it was replaced by a "local committee"; the few LPF burials there (none in the previous year and only one the year following) would be handled directly by Dominion headquarters.

Hair complained throughout the decade about the western

branches' habitual problems in relaying proper financial returns to headquarters. But, despite the occasional flare-up over procedures, Hair really had little about which to complain. The western provinces were well-organized and very active. In November 1930, however, the Dominion Council seriously considered withdrawing Manitoba's sub-charter because of its persistent and serious difficulties in filing its quarterly returns. Moreover, that branch was apparently far too lax in verifying the deceased's service record, information that Hair was normally able to ascertain accurately within 48 hours. Although HQ did not revoke their sub-charter, problems with the administrators in Winnipeg would persist. In 1939, Hair travelled to Manitoba to settle what had become a very serious problem. That branch was extremely delinquent in submitting its returns to Dominion Headquarters – a situation that was causing the Fund difficulties with DPNH, which administered the federal grant. The Dominion Council at one point even considered legal action to seize the books of the Manitoba branch. Personnel changes seemed to help, and the issue was eventually resolved. At the end of 1931, Hair reported chronic problems in Saskatchewan, too. That branch was apparently overspending, failing to raise funds (a persistent problem in Depression-plagued western Canada), and disorganized.

Perhaps these charges were true, but it became apparent to many individuals having to deal with Hair that he was an inflexible administrator and a difficult task master. Hair, of course, handled Québec's finances adeptly and knew perfectly well what was involved in being a branch treasurer. This helps explain his impatience with other provinces' failures to provide accurate and timely reports employing established forms and procedures. Hair's insistence on applying the letter of the LPF law occasionally involved him in personal antagonisms that only magnified differences. This had been the case in the 1920s, and so it was in the 1930s.

In 1935, Hair noted the need to strengthen the bonds linking the LPF branches with Dominion HQ. By the middle of the decade the western branches were growing annoyed that annual meetings were always held in Montreal. Travelling to these events was expensive and time consuming for western representatives, and few undertook the journey. Partly to accommodate the branches, in 1934 the timing of the LPF annual meetings was changed from April to October, a less busy time of the year administratively, making it easier for branches to prepare their reports for auditing. In March 1936, the LPF Dominion Council met outside Montreal for the first time. Archdeacon Almond and Norman Holland, president and vice-president, respectively, travelled to Toronto's Royal York Hotel and were joined there for a meeting by the Ontario branch directors. This did little to allay western grievances in the matter of travel, but it was symbolic of the council's esteem for the Ontario organization. In any event, some members from Ontario had travelled to the Montreal meetings regularly and it was perhaps time to repay the favour. The BC branch partly solved its travel dilemma by having Hair act as its proxy at Dominion Council meetings – an ironic choice in a sense, since Hair constantly complained about the branch's tardiness in processing claims.

There was also increasing interest in the services of the Fund among Canadian veterans residing in the United States. Many inquiries were received about burial policy for indigent Canadians passing away there and also for grave marking for Canadian veterans generally. The issue was a delicate and complicated one, and the Dominion Council dealt with it only on an ad hoc basis. Headquarters worried about setting a precedent that would end up costing the LPF inordinate sums of money. Many questions arose over cost, procedure, and uniformity of grave markers. Sustained operations, or even a major presence in the United States, were difficult to achieve. Nevertheless, the Canadian Club in New York represented the LPF between 1926 and 1930 and dealt with several cases. Until 1936, there was no blanket coverage for Canadian or imperial veterans passing away in indigence in the United States. That year, revisions to the order-in-council governing the federal grant to the LPF allowed the Fund to arrange for the indigent burial of Canadian veterans dying outside Canada.

By the end of the decade, the Québec branch was suffering from a lack of membership and increased expenses associated with maintaining the Field of Honour. Too few new members were joining, and a shortage of dues resulted in insufficient income to pay for general administration. The branch's directors decided to launch personal appeals to some 1,500 individuals targeted as being "interested in matters military". They included military officers, members of veterans' and regimental associations, politicians, government officials, and prominent citizens. Each was sent a leaflet describing the work of the LPF and soliciting membership. But contributions were more difficult to come by during the Depression and this special appeal met with "very disappointing results". It is ironic that the underappreciated Women's Division was more or less pressed into winding up its activities at this time, given that fund-raising had been one of its traditional and principal functions. Most Montreal-area military units continued their tradition of helping. For example, in early 1939 the officers' messes of the Black Watch, Canadian Grenadier Guards, and the Victoria Rifles all donated small amounts. Little did they know that in years not very distant many more of their members, having taken part in the Second World War, would be buried by the Fund.

Relations between the LPF and the Canadian Legion gradually improved in the 1930s. However, problems arose with a number of Legion branches in western Canada. From time to time, they would seek reimbursement from the Fund for veterans' burials, which Dominion headquarters, after careful investigation, deemed outside the mandate of the LPF to underwrite. Unfortunately, LPF branches in western Canada also suffered from a tendency to pay for after-the-fact requests of this nature, for which Dominion HQ refused them reimbursement. This situation caused friction not only between the LPF and the Legion, but between western branches and headquarters. It seems that the westerners staffing LPF and Legion branches on the prairies and in British Columbia had more in common with each other than with their respective headquarters in central Canada, for the Dominion Command of the Legion and the Dominion Council of the LPF co-operated fully with each other. The westerners wanted to bury veterans in need without being overly concerned about bureaucracy; headquarters, while sympathetic to the patriotic impulses stimulating this view, yet had to account to Ottawa for all expenditures. Reconciling these competing imperatives was never easy.

Some Legion officials in the west viewed the LPF as a convenient source of burial cost-recovery and often displayed ignorance of the LPF's goals and its ultimate accountability to Ottawa. At the end of 1931, the LPF sent to all Legion branches in Canada a detailed information sheet intended for posting in each branch to promote understanding of the LPF's operations. This helped, but not sufficiently to prevent a Legion branch in Calgary from spreading false information among local veterans regarding the costs and quality of LPF burial services.

In June 1934, the Provincial Command of the BC Legion officially complained to DPNH that the BC branch of the LPF was slow in processing Legion invoices for burials for which it sought reimbursement. Hair strongly supported the local LPF branch, even though he expressed dismay over western accounting and reporting practices and must have suspected that there was some merit in the Legion's accusations. There was. But Hair was livid over the Legion's actions, since it constituted the first complaint ever lodged against the LPF.

Not all in the LPF–Legion relationship was acrimony and misunderstanding. In Ontario, the two bodies assisted one another in a spirit of utmost cordiality and with the best interests of the province's veterans, living and dead, at heart. The North Bay Legion branch wrote Hair a letter of appreciation in June 1932 following the LPF's provision of a grave marker for one William Edwards, a deceased veteran. After receiving the marker, the Legion explained that its members "took it out to the cemetery and placed it on the grave. It certainly is a very nice thing that we have a Fund of this sort which looks after the burial of an ex-serviceman who has no relatives in this country." The Legion and the LPF in Ontario combined to ensure that veterans' graves in more than 215 locales throughout the province were properly maintained.

In April 1938, following further instances of Legion confusion over the LPF's role and services, all Legion Provincial Command presidents were invited to sit in as non-voting members at executive meetings of LPF branches in their respective provinces so that they might better acquaint themselves with the work of the LPF. While Legion officials only infrequently accepted the offer, the relationship between the two groups across Canada entered a new, more understanding phase as the decade came to a close.

Other events occupied the LPF in these years. In July 1936, Canada unveiled the spectacular Vimy Memorial atop the famous ridge in northern France where, on Easter Monday, April 9, 1917, Canadian troops achieved one of their most spectacular successes of the Great War. King Edward VIII officially unveiled the memorial during an impressive and colourful ceremony. The crowd numbered over 50,000, including nearly 7,000 Canadian veterans and their families (the 'Vimy Pilgrims'), whose presence was organized with much hard work by the Canadian Legion. The LPF participated in this historic and moving event by sending "a fitting tribute" of evergreens and maple leaves from the Field of Honour in the care of Major J.M. Humphrey, a director of the Québec branch. Humphrey brought back some soil from Vimy as well as poppy seeds from the site, which were planted at the Field of Honour. (The poppies did not do well in Montreal.)

In 1936, Arthur Hair dourly, though perhaps realistically, termed the work of the LPF "devoid of glamour, extremely exacting and distinctly depressing", requiring "a combination of human sympathy and business acumen." For Hair, the "economic depression such as has never before been experienced in the world" was a contributing factor in the much-increased workload of the Fund. He admitted that in these difficult circumstances, the LPF's work was truly "pathetic". Despite the social upheavals caused by the Depression, the routine, and not so-routine, work of the LPF carried on.

In August of that year Hair gave an address over CFCF radio in Montreal on the Last Post Fund. The text of his rather convoluted broadcast survives and is evidence of his strong personal convictions regarding such matters as the need to uphold national honour, to protect military tradition, to promote patriotism, and to reward personal valour. In these matters, Hair was very much a man of the nineteenth century, espousing lofty and noble sentiments no longer so much in vogue. The widespread social disillusionment occasioned by the appalling losses of the First World War, followed by the economic catastrophe of the 1930s, made many Canadians, veterans included, less willing to indulge in a potentially dangerous martial spirit. Public opinion was perhaps divided on the question of whether the indigents buried by the Fund were legitimate national heroes or mere victims of government policy. If the LPF was to remain relevant in a changing world and successfully promote its ideals, Hair's outmoded broadcast indicated the need for an updated image.

Nevertheless, Hair's major point was that the LPF was a living, evolving, and useful war memorial. He insisted that the public should think of the LPF *as* a war memorial, not merely as a vague organization fitting in somewhere with the government's general plans for veterans' civil re-establishment. Enormous sums had been spent across Canada on "sculptural" memorials; perhaps more could be found for a memorial that actually *did* something. He reminded listeners that the widely publicized Vimy Pilgrimage had fixed the nation's gaze on a breathtaking war memorial in France. But what of that long-established 'memorial' in existence on this side of the Atlantic? "Too little is known" about the LPF, he complained, not for the first or the last time. While monuments commemorated the glorious dead, the LPF served the survivors of war who might slip into poverty and pass away without leaving the resources to care properly for their remains. Invalided soldiers found to be indigent at the moment of death were buried at the government's expense; not so the man or woman discharged as apparently 'fit'. The LPF was devoted to serving the material interests of the dead, those no longer capable of offering gratitude. According to Hair, this made the LPF one of Canada's "most honourable institutions". People familiar with the works of the Fund would have agreed.

Faces New and Old

The 1930s turned out to be a period of transition for the leadership of the Fund. Long-standing members left or passed away and were replaced by younger men. As these changes were taking place, Arthur Hair continued as secretary-treasurer and provided continuity into the 1940s.

At the annual meetings of 1930 and 1931, the directors of the LPF again acclaimed Sir Arthur Currie as president of the Dominion Council. However, in April 1932, in a letter to Hair, an exhausted Currie made official his desire to retire as the Fund's president. He was overburdened and thought it best to allow someone else the opportunity of leading the LPF. Currie chaired his last annual meeting on April 29, 1932. In his address he especially thanked Scammell and Hair for their faithful services. This famed Canadian nevertheless retained an association with the Fund as he accepted the specially created position of honorary vice-president. The Duke of Connaught, former governor general (1911–1916), was honorary president until his death in 1942.

In his Dominion secretary's report of May 15, 1932, Hair

recorded his "profound regret" at Currie's resignation and remarked: "In the performance of my duties as Secretary-Treasurer I have never found Sir Arthur too busy in the midst of his many duties to give wholehearted and interested audience to the requirements and cause of this work…I shall miss Sir Arthur's most kindly and courteous counsel." The LPF's association with Currie is one of which the Fund is unabashedly proud.

To replace Currie as president, Archdeacon Almond retired as a trustee of the LPF. Almond had returned to Trinity Church after the war and, in the 1920s, began the task of building a new Trinity Memorial Church in Montreal's west-end district of Notre-Dame-de-Grâce. Because of his own service in two wars, Almond insisted that the word "memorial" be included in the official name of the church. In 1932, he was named an archdeacon, and throughout the interwar period he was an honoured guest at countless religious and patriotic services in Canada and the United States. He, too, was an extraordinarily busy man, who would serve as the LPF's national president until his death. He was replaced as a trustee by Brigadier-General W.O.H. Dodds, formerly president of the Québec branch.

In 1929, J.T. Walsh had passed away, and his place as a trustee had gone to Brigadier-General E. de B. Panet. There were then only four founding members of the Last Post Fund still alive: Almond, Hair, Alexander Mackay, and Lucien C. Vallée. The 1930s took their toll on long-serving LPF members. In 1934, Dr. A.H. Abbott of Ontario passed away, to be replaced by Major-General J.A. Gunn as Ontario president and as vice-president of the Dominion Council. Gunn was also an executive member of the Legion's Dominion Command, and this no doubt helped solidify relations between the two organizations in Ontario. Two Fund trustees also died in 1934: Dodds and Major-General C.J. Armstrong. Panet was soon joined by replacement trustees Colonel C.B. Price and Brigadier-General G.E. McCuaig, both very active in the Canadian Legion.

In many ways, the aging Hair remained the bedrock of the organization, and the Fund began to recognize him and his achievements. The work of the Fund grew constantly, and in 1938 the LPF took on an assistant to help Hair. Miss Kathleen Cobbett, at first hired as a stenographer, soon became an indispensable asset to the office organization and administration of the LPF. At the 25th annual meeting in

October 1934, the 61-year-old Hair received a round of applause for a quarter-century of service to the LPF and in particular for his sound financial stewardship. Norman Holland, a director from the Québec branch, strongly endorsed Hair's work for the organization.

Québec branch president John H. Molson opened the 1935 annual meeting by announcing that Buckingham Palace had awarded Hair the King's Jubilee Medal, issued for the silver anniversary of the reign of George V to honour meritorious service by British subjects. It was the only such medal awarded to the Last Post Fund. Archdeacon Almond proudly presented the medal to Hair. Almond and Molson were both of the opinion that the award marked not only Hair's ceaseless dedication but also the work of the LPF across the country. Said Almond, "I don't know anyone in Canada, or any organization in Canada, that deserves recognition more after 26 years…than Mr. Hair." In accepting the Jubilee Medal, Hair replied, "I am extremely honoured to wear this decoration and I feel very, very pleased to know that this work, which we all have so much at heart, has at last been recognized. I would like to say that in asking me to accept this honour, I do so also in the name of my beloved wife and family, because Mrs. Hair and my children have had a great share in anything I have tried to do." It was a memorable occasion, one that Hair would cherish.

Near the end of the decade, two stalwarts of the Last Post Fund went to their final calling. In 1938, E.H. Scammell died. Scammell had been instrumental in the negotiations that led to his department's (at that time Soldiers' Civil Re-establishment) funding the LPF in 1922. Ever since, he had faithfully attended virtually all council meetings as a sympathetic and helpful representative of the federal government. Scammell was replaced at Dominion Council meetings by successive appointees from DPNH. At the October 1938 annual meeting, LPF president Almond remarked that, over the previous 30 years, many outstanding and devoted men and women had worked for the LPF and had departed. In fact, this would be Almond's own last annual meeting.

On September 17, 1939, Colonel (the Venerable) Archdeacon John MacPherson Almond, C.M.G., C.B.E., V.D., M.A., D.C.L., died suddenly in his sleep. He was 68. The next day, in a front-page obituary, *The Gazette* described him as "one of the best-known clergymen in the Dominion" and one of Montreal's most respected citizens. Advancing age had not prevented the patriotic Almond from volunteering his services to Ottawa on the recent outbreak of yet another war to assist in organizing a chaplain service for overseas. The offer was under consideration at the time of his death. Although the minutes of the LPF's annual meeting on October 19 are strangely muted, merely noting a resolution of sympathy extended to Almond's family, John Molson, who replaced him as president, noted that his death signified that a "phase in the history of the LPF has come and gone". It was true; September 1939 ushered in a new era both for the LPF and for Canada.

In April 1939, Hair reported that the "peak" of LPF cases arising out of the First World War had not yet been reached. He anticipated that demands for the services of the LPF would accelerate in the 1940s. He was only too right, but not for the reason he expected.

5

THE SECOND WORLD WAR AND THE END OF AN ERA, 1939–1947

All these were honoured in their generations and were the glory of their time.

ECCLESIASTICUS 44:7

The Second World War and the years that followed proved a watershed for the Last Post Fund. The onset of a new war highlighted the organization's role and the Fund's benevolent services touched an ever-growing number of Canadians and others. These years also marked the ascendency of the incomparable Norman Holland as president of the LPF. He would steer the Fund for more than a decade through some of its, and the nation's, most dramatic years. This period also witnessed one of the LPF's greatest losses: Arthur Hair, founder and inspiration of the Last Post Fund, passed away.

Canada's War

Canada's status as an international actor had undergone significant change in the interwar period. Constitutionally, Britain's Balfour Report of 1926 and the Statute of Westminster in 1931 had made Canada a fully independent nation with the right of discretion in matters of war and peace – a power that it had lacked in 1914. The British Empire had evolved into the British Commonwealth of Nations, in which member states remained voluntarily bound by allegiance to the same monarch. British foreign policy nevertheless heavily influenced all members of the Commonwealth. As the world lurched from crisis to crisis in the 1930s, it grew increasingly obvious to all but the most hopeful observers that the First World War, supposedly the 'war to end all wars', would prove only the opening round of a continuing conflict.

In the late spring of 1939, as King George VI and Queen Elizabeth undertook a wildly successful Canadian tour, instilling pride and loyalty everywhere they travelled, the world teetered on the brink of catastrophe. There was no doubt as to what Canada's position would be: in the event of war between Britain and any combination of enemies threatening the survival of the 'Mother Country', Canada would support Britain. When the time came, Canada quickly offered its aid, not with wild enthusiasm as in 1914, but with grim determination.

In August 1939, Nazi Germany concluded a non-aggression pact with the Soviet Union and prepared to invade Poland, whose security Britain and France had pledged to uphold. On September 1, Germany struck; two days later Britain and France declared war on Germany. One week later, on September 10, Canada, acting in its own right, declared war on Germany. The Second World War had begun.

From a population of only 11.5 million, slightly more than one million Canadians were in uniform during the conflict. Overseas, following the tragedies of Hong Kong and Dieppe, Canada's army distinguished itself in Sicily, Italy, and the invasion of Normandy, and throughout the campaign to liberate northwest Europe until victory in 1945. The Royal Canadian Navy (RCN) grew 50-fold to a force of nearly 100,000 and played a crucial role in winning the Battle of the Atlantic and maintaining open the vital sea lanes to Britain in the face of a determined German submarine offensive. From a meagre force of largely obsolete aircraft in 1939, the Royal Canadian Air Force, which enlisted almost 250,000 men and women during the war, came to be an essential player in the Allies' gaining air superiority in Europe and in mounting devastating bomber raids against enemy targets. The RCAF also operated the Canada-based British Commonwealth Air Training Plan, which trained over 131,000 Commonwealth and Allied aircrew to carry the war into Germany and German-held territory. These military contributions helped win the war, but the cost was high: more than 42,000 Canadians lost their lives, and another 55,000 were wounded.

On the home front, industry produced massively to support the war effort. Canada produced warships, merchant vessels, bombers, fighters, tanks, vehicles of all kinds, artillery pieces, and all sorts of military equipment and munitions, employing millions of people directly or indirectly. Farms produced immense amounts of meat, grain, and other produce to help keep Canada, Britain, and the Allies fed and fighting. It was a phenomenal accomplishment. Through it all, the Last Post Fund persevered, its members knowing perfectly well that the shattered lives resulting from the war would, in the not-too-distant future, produce large numbers of the sad cases and circumstances that they had come to know on a daily basis.

The Norman Holland Years

If Arthur Hair and John Almond had dominated the affairs of the Last Post Fund in the interwar period, another man would fill that role in the 1940s and 1950s. Norman Holland was a chemical engineer, successful businessman, and self-made millionaire. He was born in Montreal in 1880. Married, with one son, he retired from his business interests in 1928 after selling at considerable profit a varnish company that he had founded. He then devoted five years principally to charity, assisting a variety of hospitals and organizations promoting children's welfare. Holland became involved in nearly a dozen charities and philanthropic organizations, of which the LPF was only one. In the 1930s, he gave the Montreal Shriner's Hospital $50,000 in government bonds. Most of the money came from the sales of his book, *Southern Sky Trails*, a folksy account of his air travels throughout Latin America, which he published himself. He then cajoled 14,000 Shriners into purchasing copies for $3 each, all the funds being turned over to the hospital. His philanthropy was such that, in 1948, he employed a staff of nine wrapping the 2,100 Christmas presents that he distributed that year. Each month in the years 1947 and 1948, he dispatched a ton (!) of food parcels to economically hard-pressed Britain.

After being managing director of Brandram-Henderson, a well-known Montreal paint company for four years, he purchased control of it in 1937, when it was debt-ridden because of the Depression, and built it up into Canada's largest domestically-owned paint manufacturer. Holland was a capable administrator, an energetic workaholic who neither smoked nor drank and slept only about four and one-half hours a night. He left for the office at 5:30 every morning, seven days a week. He paid a great deal of attention to detail and asked a lot from his employees, but no less than he demanded of himself. He sold his interests in Brandram-Henderson in 1951 but, owing to his outstanding managerial skills, stayed on as executive director and principal advisor until 1953, at which time he established his own business office to handle his charitable work.

Holland was devoted to the cause of the Last Post Fund. During his tenure as president he helped revive its fortunes and propel it onto the national stage. No one could have better handled the Fund's dealings with Ottawa. Although Holland's active interest in the LPF's affairs went back to the First World War, he is mentioned first in the Fund's records in March 1922 as having given an unspecified "illustrated address" at the Ritz-Carlton Hotel, with the proceeds accruing to the LPF. In 1929, he was named a director of the Québec branch. By 1938, he was vice-president, and the next year, president. In 1942, in addition to leading the Québec branch, he became Dominion president, a post that he held for over a decade.

Norman Holland was a colourful, well-known figure in Montreal. He was an authority on the evolution of humour through the ages and enjoyed giving humourous talks to service clubs and association meetings. He also collected jokes and had over 3,000 of them listed on card files. His office at Brandram-Henderson resembled a joke shop: it was full of gadgets and gags, including exploding chewing gum and rubber peanuts that he routinely offered to visitors.

He was an invaluable asset in obtaining frequent and favourable press publicity for the Fund and its activities. In 1948, the *Montreal Standard* claimed that "in the past two decades, much of the Fund's phenomenal rise and nation-wide public approbation has been due to Norman Holland". Later that year the Canadian edition of *Time* magazine described the short, heavy-set Holland as "a dapper little man with a sinister droop to his left eyelid". He was sometimes accused of seeking publicity for his firm with his ostentatious philanthropy. His retort was clear: "I don't give a damn about front pages. I've had good health, a good home and a good business all my life. I figure I owe something." The Last Post Fund was lucky to have piqued his interest.

The other members of the Dominion Council appreciated his no-nonsense approach, and they often referred to his ability to get matters settled. They also often remarked on his generosity and hospitality in hosting meetings of the LPF council over dinner at the posh Mount Stephen Club in downtown Montreal. Holland's relationship with Arthur Hair is difficult to assess. Throughout the 1930s, Holland had regularly been Hair's champion at council or annual meetings, often singling him out for his hard work and praising his dedication. But these men possessed vastly different personalities: Holland was jovial and outgoing, Hair quiet and retiring, with a dry, even sarcastic sense of humour. Perhaps they complemented each other well. In any event, their relationship does not appear to have been especially close.

Holland manifested enormous respect for the past patriotic services rendered by the men and women interred by the LPF. Indeed, so reverential of their final resting places was he that throughout the 1940s and 1950s he retained near complete control over the Field of Honour. He organized much of the business related to the cemetery and spent countless hours supervising the groundskeepers and staff and ironing out personnel difficulties. He and Hair insisted on maintaining the Field in a state appropriate to commemorating the services of the men and women reposing there. With tight budgets, this was not always easy.

Holland left his imprint on these years in the LPF's history. His high-energy 'can-do' approach got things done, and he did not mince words with Ottawa over issues of major concern to the LPF. He was the right person in the right job at the right time.

Wartime

For the second time in barely 20 years, the Last Post Fund undertook its patriotic and benevolent activities within the grim context of Canada's involvement in another world war. But the LPF carried on throughout the war much as it always had. At its first wartime meeting, Arthur Hair prefaced his secretary's report of October 1939 with the following observation: "In submitting my report…I regret to do so in the atmosphere of another war, the ultimate magnitude and disaster of which it is impossible to predict…However, there is one thing we can predict and that is an increase, rather than a decrease, of the causes which brought this institution into being." Beyond this and other minor such remarks, the war is strangely absent from the minutes of the period, although it must often have been foremost in the minds of those present.

The greatest immediate effect on the LPF was the enlistment or mobilization for active service of a number of its trustees, directors, employees and volunteers across Canada. In 1943, Holland estimated that 64 per cent of the LPF's (admittedly small) pre-war male staff members were on active service or involved full time with civilian auxiliary services such as the Canadian Legion and the Red Cross – a situation that caused administrative difficulties in some branches, especially Manitoba's.

In June 1941, the Dominion president, John H. Molson, by that time in his 40s, went overseas on active service as a lieutenant in the Royal Canadian Naval Volunteer Reserve (RCNVR). Molson had served in the Black Watch during the First World War. His friends at the LPF presented him with a gold and silver cigarette case embossed with his family crest. Molson resigned the presidency (as John Almond had done during the Great War), agreeing that Norman Holland would act as president during his absence. In May 1942, Molson wrote the Dominion Council announcing his permanent resignation. The council promptly acclaimed Holland president and named Molson honorary vice-president – a post that had stood vacant since the death of Sir Arthur Currie nearly a decade earlier. At the October 1942 annual meeting, Holland paid tribute to the "well-known patriotism and generosity" of the Molson family. Of course, Holland himself rivalled the Molsons in these matters.

Other prominent LPF members served during the war. Major-General J.A. Gunn, president of the Ontario branch, vice-president of the Dominion Council, and a long-standing Legion executive, presided over the extensive and extremely successful Canadian Legion War Services. Québec branch vice-president J.M. Humphrey also served overseas with the civilian auxiliary services to the Canadian military. LPF trustee Major-General C. Basil Price was away on war service for the duration. A First World War veteran thrice wounded, Price was a dairy executive in Montreal and had long been active in promoting veterans' rights. He was elected a vice-president of the Legion in 1938 and was mobilized in December 1939. The LPF had difficulty replacing men of this calibre.

Last Post Fund 1941

PATRON-IN-CHIEF
FIELD-MARSHALL H.R.H. THE DUKE OF CONNAUGHT, K.G., K.T.

HONORARY PRESIDENT
HIS EXCELLENCY, THE RT. HON. THE EARL OF ATHLONE, K.G.

EXECUTIVE COMMITTEE

LT. COL. JOHN H.
MOLSON, E.D.
President

MR. NORMAN
HOLLAND
1st Vice-President

MAJ.-GEN. J. A. GUNN
C.M.G., D.S.O. V.D.
2nd Vice-President

MR. ARTHUR H. D. HAIR
General Organizing Secretary-Treasurer

CHARTER TRUSTEES

BRIG.-GEN.
G. E. McCUAIG
C.M.G., D.S.O.

BRIG.-GEN. E. de B.
PANET, C.M.G., D.S.O.

MAJ.-GEN.
C. B. PRICE
D.S.O., D.C.M., V.D.

LAST POST FUND - 19

Illustration in LPF booklet, 1941.

Still, the Fund's work continued. The Dominion Council met two or three times a year, and annual meetings took place every October, until these reverted to April, beginning in 1945. Representatives from a number of veterans' or regimental associations, such as the *Fusiliers Mont-Royal,* the Polish War Veterans, and the South African Veterans Association, attended the wartime annual meetings to express their thanks to and support for the LPF during those difficult days. The LPF still formally met at the Ritz-Carlton Hotel, since its offices in the Red Cross building could not properly accommodate a full Dominion Council meeting. Since the 1930s, the Canadian Red Cross Society, always a strong supporter of the LPF, had provided the Fund with two basement rooms, rent free, at its headquarters on McTavish Street in downtown Montreal. The rooms were sufficient to meet the basic office needs of Dominion headquarters as well as the Québec branch. In 1945, the Red Cross made two additional small rooms available to the LPF.

By the outbreak of the Second World War the LPF had buried over 8,000 veterans, whose service spanned virtually every conflict, large or small, involving the British Empire from the Crimean to First World War. Arthur Hair reported in October 1939 that in the year

Major-General C.B. Price, long-time director and trustee of the Last Post Fund.

previous the LPF had buried 856 people (including several women): 802 of them in Canada, 53 in the United States, and one in Britain. Ontario led the way, as it did every year during this period, with 283 burials, followed by British Columbia (143), Manitoba (101), Québec (99), and Alberta (91). The vast majority of these burials were of CEF veterans. Surprisingly perhaps, the number of LPF cases across Canada dropped during the war, and Hair believed that this was the result of booming economic conditions, which allowed even aging veterans with few skills to find work and lead healthier, happier lives. But the war assured the LPF a future heavy workload.

In October 1941, Holland noted that the LPF's operations had grown continent-wide, and he felt that the burials were being carried out "in a systematic manner by the smallest paid staff of any organization covering such a wide area." No funeral took place without a representative from the Fund and a clergyman present. In 1942, the LPF recorded its 10,000th burial and its expenditures since 1909 surpassed $1 million.

Burials in the United States increased considerably as Canadian veterans emigrated or retired there. The graves of virtually all the several score buried in that country to 1939 remained unmarked, since

This 'war trophy' was in the LPF's Mount Royal plot until 1930. The Montreal Daily Star, *December 28, 1940. Norman Holland at left, Arthur Hair at right.*

unfavourable currency exchange rates rendered erection of markers prohibitively expensive. Because of the war, Hair worried that it would be some time before the rates returned to a level permitting this important task. Moreover, because of the many and varied cemetery regulations across the United States, it was not always possible to place standard LPF granite markers. This matter bothered the LPF's secretary-treasurer. As late as February 1947, Hair, seriously ill, expressed frustration at the ongoing delays in installing the markers in many American burial grounds caused by their strict rules and the Fund's financial limitations. Hair was "desperately anxious" to see as many markers as possible erected quickly in the U.S. He even appealed to the cemeteries there to "consider a very patriotic international gesture" in agreeing to erect the LPF's markers, even though he would never have stood for such a breach of regulations in the Field of Honour. Not surprisingly, few American cemeteries proved as accommodating as Hair had hoped.

In February 1944, the LPF dealt with one especially unusual case. It seems that one Minnie Oram, the deceased wife of Private H. Oram, had expressed a wish to be cremated and have her ashes spread from an airplane. Accordingly, the LPF co-ordinated a special memorial service with an RCAF aircraft from which an air force chaplain officiated. Holland described this incident as "something entirely new in our long experience". The LPF's president could hardly oppose the woman's wishes, for, as he later wrote to Flight-Lieutenant R. Pinkerton, who had arranged the RCAF's participation: "I have flown more than 650,000 miles in some 47 countries and it is my intention to be cremated and to have my ashes scattered over Montreal." Holland and Mrs. Oram were kindred spirits.

Throughout the war years, Holland did what he could for veterans in financial difficulty or physical discomfort. He often sent cigarettes or other gifts – in the name of the LPF – to men too poor or ill to obtain these things for themselves. For example, at Christmas 1943, Hair brought to his attention the case of ex-sergeant F. Whatling, a Verdun veteran of the First World War, originally from Kent, England, who had spent 16 Christmases in bed "in untold pain", though without regrets, as he was "thankful" to have had the opportunity of doing his duty. Holland sent Whatling cigarettes and asked Hair to keep in touch with this "helpless invalid". Similar stories of Holland's and the LPF's compassion were commonplace during the war.

One wartime policy issue for the LPF concerned the burial status of men dying in indigent circumstances while on strength of the Canadian Active Service Force (CASF), Canada's Second World War all-volunteer army on duty at home and overseas. By the winter of 1940, there already had been several cases of penniless CASF men dying in Ontario. Some had passed away mere weeks after volunteering for active service. The problem was that the Department of National Defence (DND) allowed only $50 for their burial, while the LPF spent approximately $100 per interment. If the deceased had no family or friends to assist with costs, LPF branches were unable to absorb the balance themselves. Strictly speaking, these men were Ottawa's responsibility, not the LPF's. The Fund felt that the government allowance for CASF burials was "totally inadequate", and much confusion developed within the LPF's ranks about whether or not it should take on these cases.

A visit to Ottawa by Hair in March 1940 procured no clarification from DND officials. But action had to be taken quickly, and the Dominion Council decided to accept CASF cases until Ottawa made a definitive ruling. In August 1940, the Fund asked the minister of national defence to arrange an order-in-council to augment the $50 allowable expenditure so that the LPF could bury these men properly and respectfully. The LPF "humbly and urgently" beseeched the minister for an increase to $100, but without immediate success. At the heart of the matter was a bureaucratic tussle: the Fund could not contribute to what was essentially a DND responsibility by using funds made available by another government department – namely the Department of Pensions and National Health. And DPNH insisted on the LPF's observing this practice. In the meantime, some impoverished CASF members were buried with dignity in properly marked graves, while others were not. Even as late as May 1942, there remained some interdepartmental confusion over these matters. Underfunded, the LPF found its hands tied.

The issue of eligibility for members of the Veterans Guard of Canada also arose. Since this home-defence guard force, established in May 1940 and made up of First World War veterans, was employed by the Royal Canadian Mounted Police (RCMP), which had its own burial program, the LPF could not pay for the Veterans Guard either. Moreover, the RCMP fully expected the Department of Justice to meet the basic $100 burial allotment that DND did not offer its own men on active service. Nevertheless, some of these older volunteers fell through the cracks as well. One Ontario Veterans Guard named Beauchamp was buried in a pauper's grave through the apparently "callous indifference" of his wife and the LPF's bureaucratic inability to see to the case. For Holland, Hair, and all the members of the Fund, this was tantamount to a rejection in death of the ideals that the CASF and Veterans Guard volunteers had sought to defend with their lives. But the LPF could not undertake all burials by itself.

During the war, the LPF was forced to determine burial policies regarding indigent deserters from military service, former military personnel not honourably discharged, conscripts, and other classes of men and women who had seen military service. In the spring of 1945, with the war in Europe drawing to a close, Hair canvassed all branches to determine their opinions on these issues. The results were an interesting and diverse mix of views. British Columbia adopted the most conservative and hard-line approach arguing that the LPF should withhold its services not only from all those not honourably discharged, but also from home defence conscripts mobilized under the provisions of the National Resources Mobilization Act (NRMA). Ontario and Saskatchewan were the most lenient branches, willing to alter the LPF's constitution in order to remove the legal constraints that prevented the Fund from burying certain classes of veterans. They felt that the LPF should not be a judge of character in these matters, but merely an organization respectfully marking the passing of individuals who at one time served their country.

In 1941, the Ontario branch buried a deserter and received a rap on the knuckles from Dominion HQ for its troubles. Most provinces wanted no amendments to the official policy of denying privileges to those not honourably discharged. The patriotic intensity fuelled by the war, and the heartache caused across the land by the war's casualties, no doubt contributed to this sentiment. In the end, no change was made. In 1951, a further review upheld this position, with the Dominion Council ruling that "discretion must supplant...sentimentality". LPF unity was more important than a fully inclusive burial policy. Many members felt that most veterans would not want to lie eternally in the same burial plots as those whom the veterans might consider guilty of dishonourable conduct.

Wartime had the effect of making most veterans' and patriotic organizations close ranks and co-operate for the benefit of those whom they professed to serve and assist. Closer ties emerged between the Last Post Fund and the Canadian Legion in the 1940s. Personal relationships and friendships linking men of both organizations went a long way towards easing the sporadic tensions of previous decades. A new war perhaps reminded leaders of both groups that the goals of each were separate and allied, not overlapping or competitive.

Still, in 1939 Hair remained extremely proud of the LPF's successes and was annoyed that another patriotic organization, namely the Legion, often received public credit for the Fund's services and activities. "The LPF, which has hoed a single furrow in hard ground, and made a success of it", he wrote, "is confused with other societies whose...success...waned while ours persisted." He added that "frequently...the credit goes to others while we have made the work possible and pay the bills." Part of the problem lay, in Hair's view, in the Fund's modesty and "unostentatious" ways. Even when the Legion and the LPF attempted to co-operate, some confusion occurred. In April 1943, the Dominion Council expressed disapproval because publicity on behalf of the LPF in the Legion's own magazine, the *Legionary*, left the impression that that group actually paid for the funerals.

Some LPF directors wondered whether the Legion was trying too hard to become interested in the LPF. In May 1939, the Québec branch felt obliged to modify slightly an ambiguous by-law so that the Legion could not try to exercise as many votes at a branch annual meeting as it had individual branches as members of the LPF. Every institutional member, such as the Legion, was to have but a single vote, no matter how many of its branches contributed to the LPF. The revised by-law read: "Any Society contributing will only be allowed one vote and must declare its properly accredited representative who must be present in person to exercise his or her vote." This wording stemmed from a legal opinion that the Fund had obtained. In 1948, it obtained similar opinions from Judge Gerald Almond, John Almond's son. Only members of Legion branches who took out individual memberships in the LPF would be eligible to vote at annual meetings, where reports were presented and directors selected, even though no business was specifically discussed and no major decisions were made.

In October 1940, perhaps the most pressing issue affecting relations between the two organizations came to light. The Los Angeles branch of the Canadian Legion had incorporated itself in California as the "Southern Area Last Post Fund Inc., the Canadian Legion of the British Empire Service League", and was raising funds under that name to carry out local burials of Canadian or imperial veterans. The LPF's Dominion Council considered this an unauthorized usurpation of its name without the California Legion branch's formally adhering to the Fund's administrative hierarchy or constitution. Hair had visited Los Angeles in 1936 to iron out this problem and achieved a compromise: the Legion would apply for an LPF branch or local committee sub-charter; but it never did. Still, the Los Angeles Legion continued to seek reimbursement for local burials from the Fund's Dominion HQ, which paid the costs for all legitimate cases that the Fund would otherwise have assumed. But the LPF considered this arrangement with the Legion branch informal. Once the Legion actually began using the LPF's name, the issue had to be resolved.

Hair wrote to the State of California and to the Dominion Command of the Canadian Legion stating that he was prepared to seek an injunction against the Los Angeles Legion. Hair had always been prickly and territorial about use of the LPF name. When Major-General J.A. Gunn, president of the Fund's Ontario branch (and honorary president of the Canadian Legion), suggested in a telegram to Dominion Council that he felt that the LPF was not about names but about burying indigent veterans, Hair protested vigorously and vehemently. Too closely tied to both organizations to be a useful arbiter, Gunn stayed out of the matter thereafter.

In January 1941, representatives of the Dominion Command of the Legion, the Los Angeles Legion branch, and the LPF met in Montreal to iron out their differences. They agreed, after difficult and sometimes strained discussions, that the name of the Los Angeles branch would become "Southern Area Last Post Fund and the Canadian Legion" and that the branch would formally apply for an LPF sub-charter. It took until October 1942 for the matter to be finally settled, and only after the LPF refused to reimburse any more burial cases paid for by the California Legion. In 1943, Hair travelled to Washington, DC and formally incorporated the LPF (at considerable trouble) in the United States.

In October 1942, a similar and long-festering issue arose in Regina, where the Legion was using the LPF's name for its own purposes. Lieutenant-Colonel James McAra of the Regina Legion was at it again, as he had been intermittently for almost two decades: holding tag days to raise funds to bury indigent veterans, citing the LPF in the process, and collecting nearly $1,000 without sending the LPF a cent of it. In April 1943, both Holland and Hair wrote friendly letters to the Regina Legion to inquire about the whereabouts of the money that had been raised illegally using the Fund's name. No replies were forthcoming, although a subsequent legal letter from the LPF seems to have ended the problem.

Despite these incidents, co-operation was the hallmark of wartime and postwar LPF–Legion relations. For example, the Fund's Ontario branch co-operated closely with the Legion in locating unmarked graves of service people throughout the province. The goal was to ensure the proper identification and marking of veterans' burial sites. In the years ahead, S.G. Olsen, secretary-treasurer of the LPF's Ontario branch would refer to the "kind and efficient co-operation" that existed between his organization and the Ontario Command of the Legion. Moreover, as of July 1946 there were between 50 and 60 cemeteries across Canada in which local Legion branches maintained veterans' graves. Despite this encouraging start, there remained thousands of unmarked veterans' graves throughout the country.

A new departure in relations between the Fund and the Legion took place in November 1946. Holland spent several days in Ottawa meeting with Legion officials at the invitation of Major-General C. Basil Price, a trustee of the LPF and recently elected Dominion president of the Legion. The two men, united in common purpose, overcame at an executive level many of the minor irritants that in the past had crept into bilateral relations. From this point on, the complementary goals of each group would benefit from an enhanced mutual understanding of each other's functions and services. The minutes of an LPF Dominion Council meeting on November 29, 1946, refer to Holland's visit to Ottawa as "the first opportunity there has been of forming that closer contact" for the "greater good" of both groups and, more particularly, of veterans.

Holland and Price had begun a thaw. Being a devoted member of both organizations, Price would not countenance silly turf wars. Holland was the guest of honour at a dinner hosted by the Legion for the governor general, Field Marshal Viscount Alexander of Tunis. A Legion representative attended the 1947 annual meeting – a first. An LPF pamphlet intended to prompt Legion members to reserve their burial spaces in the Field of Honour noted that the Legion in Québec was "supporting most generously the work of the LPF". In 1949, Holland felt comfortable enough to refer to the Legion as "one of our very active supporters, and we are deeply grateful to them". He was right; this was a new departure indeed.

Relations between the Dominion Council and the Fund's branches and local committees, most of which were operating soundly, were generally very good. In 1939, Hair travelled to western Canada to establish contact with LPF representatives and to facilitate local administration and co-operation with Dominion HQ. (Holland would do the same in 1946.) By 1940, Hair was able to report that, for once, Manitoba was "functioning excellently" following a reorganization. The Alberta branches were working well, as usual, and those in Saskatchewan and British Columbia were proceeding satisfactorily.

Lack of volume in the Maritimes had led Dominion HQ in the 1930s to downgrade the LPF's presence in eastern Canada to the status of local representatives, not branches. The Nova Scotia representatives kept functioning despite their secretary's being called to war service. There continued to be few LPF burial cases in the east, although Hair had logically anticipated an increase in cases with so many military personnel concentrating there on their way overseas or actually being stationed there. New Brunswick and Prince Edward Island were doing fine with their local committees. Notwithstanding these optimistic reports, by the end of 1940 both Nova Scotia and Manitoba were short of personnel and Hair once again travelled there to straighten things out. Manitoba was obliged temporarily to revert to a local committee, with funeral arrangements handled directly from Montreal. There were plenty of cases, but not enough staff in place to handle them.

Many branches wanted to send representatives to Dominion Council meetings in Montreal, but there was little money available for this purpose. In October 1940, the council agreed that the costs incurred by an Ontario representative could be absorbed from the Dominion Council's administrative budget and that other branches could also attend meetings at HQ's expense, but only on a rotating basis. British Columbia was the first branch invited to send its representative – the much-respected Lieutenant-Colonel H. St. J. Montizambert, in November 1940. Montizambert had had a long affiliation with the LPF. Hair was convinced that this participation from the branches would offer "great encouragement" to those toiling on behalf of the LPF in the field. He was right. These small gestures helped create a closer atmosphere in the organization and improved working relationships. In April 1943, Colonel J.Y. Reid of Manitoba found a meeting of the Dominion Council "an eye opener", for he previously "had not the faintest idea" of the national extent of LPF activities. Reid admitted that only those provincial representatives who attended the Montreal meetings could understand the full scope of the work. Reid's words seemed welcome praise to the Dominion Council workhorses present, especially Arthur Hair.

Perhaps the "great encouragement" that Hair mentioned prompted the Fund's largest branch to begin making greater demands of Dominion HQ. In November 1940, Ontario insisted on greater representation on Dominion Council, given that one-third of all LPF burials originated in that province. The next year, it sought three council seats and funding from Dominion HQ for the travel costs of at least two representatives sent to council meetings. Hair pointed out that satisfying these requests would require a constitutional change, and nothing was done. On another matter, the Ontario branch wanted permission (and funding) to transport the remains of indigent veterans passing away in remote locations to a more conveniently located burial ground. Headquarters would rebuff Ontario once again: there was no mandate or money for this additional expense.

A third rejection came in 1944. For 11 years the second vice-president of the LPF had been the Ontario head (the first vice-president was the head of the Québec branch). Then, in the interest of sharing some executive power, it was decided to rotate this position with other provinces. Ontario wanted its permanent vice-presidency back, but the council (consisting mainly of Québec members) said no; Ontario would have to wait its turn. The Ontario branch apparently took these decisions well enough: the minutes and archives of Dominion headquarters show no evident recriminations, although the Ontarians' disappointment would be understandable. Notwithstanding these setbacks, the Ontario branch was doing very well. Overall, however, the finances of the Last Post Fund were being stretched to their limit.

More Money Woes

In July 1941, so as to be able to assist more surviving families, the LPF broadened its definition of a pauper to one whose estate, including life insurance benefits, did not exceed $500 and who had no additional assets. On occasion, the LPF still buried a veteran if the estate was slightly larger, particularly if there were children. The idea was to offer services as inclusively as possible and prevent potentially crippling burial expenses for impoverished families. This was crucial during the war years, as funeral costs rose dramatically across the country, especially in Montreal. The LPF's maximum rates of $50 for undertaking and total funeral expenses of $100 were no longer realistic, especially since the Department of Pensions and National Health allowed itself $135 for veterans' burials. It was almost impossible to arrange for undertaking services in the United States for the amount allowed, especially in U.S. funds. In April 1944, the Dominion Council urgently petitioned DPNH to raise allowable undertaking expenses to $65.

In 1944, the LPF's burial budget came under the administration of the Department of Veterans Affairs (DVA), created June 30 that year. The Dominion Council immediately requested an augmentation in its total burial allotment from $100 to $115 per case. This increase was authorized in 1945, but not before a number of funeral directors across Canada had threatened to cease handling LPF cases as not worth their while. Concerned with their businesses, they had a point. Patriotism had its limits.

Other financial changes were in the offing during the war. In April 1943, Ottawa set up a fixed imprest account for the LPF, as opposed to financing the Fund against burials effected. It replenished this account regularly in exactly the amount expended. To start with, slightly more than $25,000 was distributed proportionately between the branches and local committees. Ontario received $7,700, followed by British Columbia $6,300, and Québec $3,000. An imprest system ended the need for the annoying quarterly returns from branches to Dominion HQ. In the long run, the new arrangements saved personnel time and administrative expenses. Before they went into effect, and because of a growing financial crisis, at a Dominion Council meeting in May 1942 Hair had shockingly proposed some sort of administrative affiliation, even merger, with the Canadian Red Cross Society in order to keep costs lower. A.J. Dixon, representing DPNH, would not hear of it, insisting that Ottawa would go to the LPF's aid if a serious financial difficulty arose and that, in any case, the LPF should be careful to maintain its own strong and independent identity. It was indeed a curious suggestion, especially coming from Hair, who had always led the fight against any encroachments on the Fund's operating independence.

The benefits of the imprest account took time to filter through, however. In April 1944, LPF headquarters experienced a serious budget crunch: Dominion Council suspended paying branch representatives' travel costs to council meetings in Montreal and even had to borrow $500 from the Québec branch to make ends meet, as it did again the following year. Earlier in 1944, some of the Fund's oldest friends in Montreal had tried to ease its financial problems. Henry Birks, of the famous family of jewellers, paid $100 to become a life member as a result of Colonel P.P. Hutchinson's membership and fund-raising drive at the Black Watch (Royal Highland Regiment) of Canada armoury. The drive raised a total of $137. The Victoria Rifles of Canada's Sergeants' Mess sent $25 a year to the LPF. Since its inception in 1909 the LPF had counted on the support of the same donors doing what little they could to help.

Holland was growing tired of Ottawa's parsimony towards the Fund, especially when federal spending was higher than ever and wartime seemed a logical opportunity to increase funding for veterans' burials. The situation was reminiscent of Atherton and Hair's struggles of more than 20 years' earlier. In February 1944, Holland wrote to Colonel E.G.M. Cape of the Montreal Poppy Day Relief Fund, who had sent the LPF a cheque for $250: "It isn't always easy to carry on, because I am sorry to say that the average citizen doesn't take any particular interest in the soldier who passes out of the picture. We don't find it an easy matter to raise the necessary funds for administrative work. The Government does see that we always have enough funds for the actual burials, but are not overly generous with funds for administrative purposes."

Holland made it a top priority of his presidency to obtain greater administrative funding from the Department of Veterans Affairs. He was insistent and hoped that DVA would not make a "mountain out of a molehill" over the issue. Indeed, considerable debate about this increase took place in the department in late 1945 and early 1946. Lieutenant-Colonel G.S. Macfarlane, since April 1945 DVA's representative on the Dominion Council, was accommodating and sympathetic, but Holland was growing impatient. Dominion headquarters (and most branches) were starved of funds on a fixed budget while costs were growing rapidly. As a sign of their needs, in April 1946 the Québec branch, which spent thousands of dollars annually maintaining the Field of Honour, sent a letter seeking financial assistance to 16 service clubs. Only three replied favourably: the Kiwanis Club, the Lion's Club, and the Rotary Club. The total yield was $400, which the branch felt was "not too encouraging". The war had imposed great sacrifices on Canadians, and special appeals, whether governmental or private, had made ceaseless demands on their generosity; people were tired of giving.

By 1946, salaries alone (for Hair and his assistant, Kathleen Cobbett) were eating up most of the approximately $5,000 provided by Ottawa to cover administration expenses at headquarters. The remainder of their salaries came from the limited funds raised by Dominion HQ. The LPF desired $10,000 annually from Ottawa to pay for its administration. It needed new and permanent quarters, and it literally required rent money (estimated at $1,200 a year). Holland felt that even if the LPF did not immediately leave the Red Cross building, this latter organization was "entitled to something". Moreover, there were a wide variety of administrative costs for which no official provision was made and for which Holland often paid from his own pocket. But he grew tired of doing so, not because he hesitated about personally assisting the LPF, but rather because he strongly felt that Ottawa should be funding *all* administrative costs. As far as Holland was concerned, his generosity constituted a form of windfall to the federal government. As he bluntly reminded a Dominion Council meeting in January 1946, perhaps directing his remarks especially to MacFarlane, "it is not likely that this organization will forever have a president that happens to be well off and is head of a company that can do work for the Last Post Fund such as painting, carpentry, etc. for nothing." Holland's own personal staff undertook much of the clerical and other work of both Dominion HQ and the Québec branch, and "the government has had a great deal of work for nothing". He had had it.

At that meeting, Macfarlane bore the brunt of Holland's displeasure. While delighted that Ottawa recently had authorized the requested burial ceiling of $115 (which was barely sufficient), Holland thought it only logical to allow the Fund an amount equal to what decent funeral services cost in the market-place, especially since DVA was paying up to $175 per burial of pensioned veterans. Macfarlane hastened to point out, however, that Ottawa was legally responsible only to its pensioned veterans and that it funded the burial of indigent veterans through the LPF out of a sense of decency, not, strictly speaking, out of obligation. Such talk made Holland angry, and some of the exchanges at the meeting were rather heated, with Hair remaining discreet. Holland wanted Ottawa to pay the salaries of new staff, which he felt the LPF desperately needed, including a stenographer and a general office manager to work with Hair, who was not getting any younger. In fact, Holland was planning to hire a successor to Hair, who by this point in time earned $202 a month from Dominion HQ and a further, smaller salary as the Québec branch's secretary-treasurer. The Fund needed office furniture and supplies, and Holland thundered that "the government has never paid a nickel" for any of these and that "for 21 years we have not asked for anything, but that is a thing of the past." Simply put, the LPF could no longer count on the generosity or charity of its friends and supporters. Membership had fallen off considerably, and the Depression and the war had exhausted the giving spirit of patriotically motivated people on whom the LPF's headquarters and branches had traditionally depended to help pay for their administration. The LPF needed more from Ottawa. But, understandably, the federal government's priority was to care for living veterans, not the dead, and it did so generously. In 1946, it published a 300-page volume commonly known as the Veterans Charter. It contained all the legislation passed up to that point, most of it in 1944 and 1945, dealing with the civil re-establishment of Canada's hundreds of thousands of veterans. The cost would be enormous. While Holland and all members of the Fund no doubt agreed that postwar Canada should be a 'land fit for heroes' it was somewhat disheartening to them that Ottawa could find no additional funding for the LPF.

The beleaguered Macfarlane, a true friend to the Fund, agreed with Holland in principle but insisted that the LPF, in order to convince Ottawa to up the ante, would have to submit a carefully considered business plan justifying its request for additional funding. He promised to promote the interests of the LPF with his own department. The greater problem lay with Treasury Board. But, after initial refusal, in January 1948 the cabinet ministers making up this body relented – somewhat. Holland's wishes were granted that month with the promulgation of P.C. 178, an order-in-council that he termed "the most important event in Last Post Fund history". The Department of Veterans Affairs agreed to cover the Fund's administrative expenses up to $8,500 annually. While this was less than the $10,000 that Holland had requested, it was a result that the Dominion Council found acceptable. In November 1948, DVA granted an additional $300 for office furniture. Holland was proving that strong leadership obtained good results.

The Field of Honour Matures

The Field of Honour took on greater symbolic importance in the veterans' and military communities during the war and its immediate aftermath. It increasingly became a recognized focal point for commemorative activities in the Montreal area, and its reputation grew. In May 1944, *Le Petit Journal* (Montreal) described the Field as "*l'un des plus beaux de l'Empire britannique.*" This is what the LPF believed too.

Even before the war ended, more and more veterans of both world wars arranged for burials there. In November 1944, Hair reported to the executive of the Québec branch that he had "a most interesting call from an English officer, Captain Roland Stewart, who is alone in this country, and wanted to make arrangements for [his] inevitable end…He paid for the reservation of a single grave in the Field of Honour, with the understanding 'it may used for some soldier who may not be able to pay…' In other words…he wishes a double grave, so that another soldier may be interred with him. I am impelled to say that it is a very patriotic and worthy gesture, and once again bears out the wisdom of our provision in the Field of Honour for other than those who have no one to look after them."

While this particular case was remarkable, in the postwar period the LPF achieved some moderate success from its efforts to sell plots to recent veterans. It published a pamphlet reminding demobilized veterans that gravesites in the Field of Honour were reserved not solely for indigent veterans but for any veteran desiring to make the necessary arrangements prior to his or her death. Veterans could prepay for themselves and their spouses (or one child). The Québec Command of the Canadian Legion fully endorsed the idea of veterans' burials at the Field, but, despite the availability of LPF printed material in Legion branches, former service people remained generally unaware of the Fund's services and activities. Perhaps as still relatively young men and women, most did not feel any immediate need to plan their funerals. The LPF's pamphlet noted that "the Field of

Ian Mackenzie, minister of pensions and national health, third from right, inspects Cross of Remembrance, September 10, 1941. Arthur Hair second from left; Norman Holland third from left.

Honour…offers advantages to veterans which the great majority of them do not seem to realize." Costs were kept low: single burials were set at $125, burials in a joint plot with another veteran (including a single marker with two inscriptions) were $100, and a double burial including a spouse or child cost $200. The inscription on a veteran's marker listed the date of birth, date of death, military rank, and unit; for a spouse it showed date of birth, death, maiden name (if applicable), and "wife [or husband] of…". This was in keeping with LPF grave-marking traditions.

By October 1943, the Wartime Prices and Trade Board, which administered Canada's rationing of foods and materials, had established various restrictive regulations that affected the Field of Honour. For example, bronze was rationed, and the LPF could no longer obtain inscription plaques made of this material to mount on its grave markers. Earlier, in 1940, branches in British Columbia and Saskatchewan had sought a waiver on government-imposed war taxes for grave markers, but Ottawa had refused to grant one. In addition, a number of basic materials needed for the Field, including lumber and plumbing supplies, were difficult to find. Hair took the matter up with officials in Ottawa and was at least successful in obtaining priority status for the Fund regarding the disposition of rationed supplies. In 1946, Holland was becoming disenchanted with the quality of the Field's upkeep (and the workers responsible). Part of the problem was the lack of a power mower, which, even by 1946, had been on order for two years but could not be delivered as a result of war restrictions and pent-up consumer demand. The LPF would just have to wait.

The ceremonies at the Field seemed to take on a special solemnity in wartime. In 1941, the guest of honour was the lieutenant-governor of Québec, Sir Eugène Fiset (a veteran of the South African War). By 1944, the press considered these events sufficiently meaningful and newsworthy that CBC radio in Montreal carried them live. The speaker that year, Major-General L.R. Laflèche, minister of national war services, invoked the memory of deceased comrades and also commented on the improving military situation overseas, to which Canadians were contributing mightily on land, at sea, and in the air. Canadian military and government officials were well represented at every wartime ceremony at the Field. So too were a military guard of honour (often from the Victoria Rifles of Canada),

Major-General L.R. LaFlèche, minister of national war services, inspecting guard of honour with Norman Holland at the Field of Honour, May 24, 1944.

diplomatic representatives of Allied governments, representatives of the Canadian Legion, of the American Legion, and of the South African War Veterans Association; nursing sisters from Ste. Anne's military hospital; and civic officials from interested municipalities, including Mayor Edward Wilson of Verdun and Mayor W. John Kenna of Pointe Claire. Local clergy officiated at the religious services. These ceremonies were poignant and meaningful for all present, held as they were while Canadians were dying in the struggle against tyranny and in the knowledge that many of those same men and women, serving overseas or at home, would eventually be interred by the LPF.

The ceremonies in 1946 marked the first time since the creation of the Last Post Fund in 1909 that Arthur Hair did not read aloud the names of all those buried by the Québec branch in the course of the previous year. Serious illness prevented him from attending. Instead, his replacement as secretary-treasurer of the Québec branch, Lieutenant S.J. Smith, read the 120 names for the previous year. By May 1946, over 1,300 veterans had been buried at the Field of

Honour, and a further 555 lay at the old LPF plots on Mount Royal. They included not only Canadians and Britons, but Americans, Australians, Belgians, Frenchmen, Poles, Russians, South Africans, and other Allied nationalities of all ranks.

In 1947, Air Vice-Marshal C.M. McEwen, C.B, M.C., D.F.C., was guest of honour at the Field. He recounted the following anecdote: "On one occasion a mother, separated from her son by time and great distance, came to Montreal to seek her loved one's resting place. The Last Post Fund was able to take her to his grave which was within their care. Imagine the joy in the mother's heart in knowing that in his loneliness her loved one was among friends forever." It was for rea-

Air Vice-Marshal Clifford M. McEwen, famed fighter pilot of First World War and commander of No. 6 Group (RCAF), Bomber Command, during the Second. A director of the LPF, he was buried in the Field of Honour in 1967.

sons such as this that the LPF and the Field of Honour existed. As a representative of the RCAF, McEwen also recited the moving poem "High Flight" by John Gillespie Magee, killed during the Second World War while serving with the RCAF. McEwen became devoted to the Fund, served as a director, and, twenty years later, in 1967, was himself interred in the Field of Honour.

The Transfer from Papineau Avenue Military Cemetery

One of the long-standing mandates of the Last Post Fund was "to interest itself in the restitution, marking, and care of neglected graves of…military persons, and generally…in all matters affecting military obsequies throughout the Dominion of Canada." Even by the time of its founding in 1909, military graves or entire military cemeteries in the Montreal area had fallen into disrepair and even near-oblivion. These sites often had been prey to acts of vandalism and desecration. Arthur Hair and Lucien C.Vallée, in particular, took very seriously the LPF's pledge to improve the conditions of military burial grounds and to re-establish them as places of respect and dignity. Accordingly, for the first 40 years of its existence the Fund variously maintained, refurbished, or rededicated sites at the 19th-century British military burial grounds on St. Helen's Island and at Fort Chambly, east of Montreal.

However, one of the signal events in the history of the LPF during the Second World War was the transfer of soldiers' remains from Papineau Avenue Military Cemetery in Montreal to the Field of Honour in Pointe Claire. From 1814 to 1869, British military authorities in Montreal had used the Papineau Avenue grounds for the burial of troops from the local garrison. In 1849, Lieutenant-General Sir Benjamin D'Urban, commander-in-chief of British forces in North America, died in Montreal and was buried there. A large memorial – a tapering obelisk mounted on a square base over his grave – formed the centrepiece and largest monument in the cemetery. Many of those buried alongside him were veterans of the Napoleonic wars (including several from Waterloo) and the War of 1812. Ironically, the City of Montreal later named the street passing the cemetery in honour of *patriote* leader Louis-Joseph Papineau, against whose forces some of the interred British troops had fought and died. In May 1944, *Le Petit*

Journal stated of the cemetery that *"là dorment depuis plus de 100 ans des héros de l'armée britannique et des pionniers de l'empire colonial de la Grande-Bretagne"*.

Following the departure of British troops in 1869, the cemetery rapidly fell into neglect, and in May 1912 it was badly vandalized, necessitating costly repairs by the Department of Militia, which had inherited maintenance obligations for the site from the British. Montreal's English-language press was incensed at this vandalism, but no more so than Hair, who called the act "preconceived", hinting that perhaps land developers or even municipal interests had been behind it. As the city expanded, the old burial ground was increasingly coveted for redevelopment, and Hair and Vallée correctly feared civic attempts at expropriation. The first such effort in fact dated back to 1876. Following the desecrations of 1912, the Department of Militia replaced the old fence surrounding the property and thereafter provided a small annual operating budget of $20 a month to the LPF to maintain the cemetery. Hair and Vallée were frequent visitors.

The burst of patriotism brought on by the First World War rekindled interest in the old burial ground. The Department of Militia decided to overhaul the site, and not a moment too soon: the LPF's W.H. Atherton described the grave markers there as "time-worn and crumbling", with "undecipherable" names. In 1916, Reverend Robert Campbell, a concerned and patriotic Protestant clergyman, claimed that the authorities acted "mainly due to the agitation maintained by the Last Post Fund from 1912 to 1914". In April 1915, the cemetery was rededicated, and D'Urban's memorial refurbished. The governor general, HRH the Duke of Connaught, patron-in-chief of the LPF, unveiled a new memorial tablet. As a young officer in the 1860s, Connaught had been stationed in Montreal, and he knew the cemetery well. Things were looking up.

There matters stood until May 1922, at which time the LPF protested vigorously against a recent motion in Montreal city council to bisect the small, 125 x 50-metre cemetery to allow a road extension to run through it. The city eventually dropped the idea, and, justifiably or not, Hair claimed that the Fund alone had saved the site from a form of official "desecration". On five more occasions between 1923 and 1931, the LPF successfully fought off the city's persistent attempts to split the cemetery, convert it into a public park, or redevelop the land. The LPF remained the first line of defence and its strong stance on the matter became common public knowledge. The Montreal press correctly considered Arthur Hair an authority on local military burial history and regularly interviewed him on the subject. The LPF reinforced its proprietary interest in the matter every May 24, when it laid a wreath at the D'Urban memorial as part of its city-wide commemorative activities.

The LPF had friends in high places and sought their help in protecting the cemetery. The premier of Québec, Louis-Alexandre Taschereau, much interested in the Fund's work and largely responsible for its acquisition of the Field of Honour, firmly opposed expropriation. Moreover, since the site was under the administration of the Department of National Defence, the city could do little without Ottawa's consent. However, with the completion of the Harbour Bridge in 1930 (renamed the Jacques Cartier Bridge not long afterwards), and given that the cemetery was virtually in its shadow, it was perhaps inevitable that the burial ground would be disturbed for street extension to facilitate access to the bridge. Since the Field of Honour also opened in 1930, city officials viewed the transfer there of the remains from Papineau Avenue as the best solution to an increasingly urgent problem.

In 1939, DND made the Fund the official caretaker of Papineau Avenue. This made sense, since the LPF was the group most concerned with its preservation. Nevertheless, municipal authorities applied growing pressure on provincial and federal officials to allow the city to take over the grounds. In an attempt to mobilize public opinion, Holland announced to the Montreal press in 1941 that it would be "most regrettable" if, during wartime no less, a decision was taken to redevelop or even eliminate a military cemetery. He also admitted that $1,000 was needed immediately for repairs. But, given the site's uncertain future, there was little inclination from any source to provide this sort of funding. The LPF's fight was running out of time.

In 1942, DND announced that the city would purchase the grounds from the federal government for $35,000, with the LPF to use the money to transport, refurbish, and rededicate the grave sites, including physical remains, headstones, and monuments, to the Field of Honour, which would require considerable landscaping. DND eventually provided an additional $4,200. There were precedents for such a transfer. In 1917 and 1929, the LPF had moved to its plot on

Mount Royal some soldiers' remains found by workmen in a public park in downtown Montreal. They had been buried prior to 1814 in the long-forgotten Dufferin Square Cemetery.

Complicated and time-consuming planning for the transfer began in 1943 and occupied an immense amount of the directors' energies – especially Hair and Holland. While the Papineau excavations were under way, a simultaneous operation prepared the Field of Honour to receive the remains, markers, and monuments. By 1944, Holland was splitting all his available time between the Field and Papineau Avenue. Hair, too, was frequently at Papineau Avenue, cleaning it and, with the help of a Montreal-based detachment from the Royal Canadian Engineers, repairing the low fence along the boundaries. Although he knew that the cemetery's fate was settled, he was particularly upset that vandalism, perpetrated mainly by juveniles, continued to desecrate it, despite augmented police patrols and his own vigils at the site. In early May 1944, Hair, who was 71, even went so far as to test a police motorcycle patrolman by hopping over the dilapidated fence to see if the officer, who clearly had seen Hair,

Transferring remains of Lieutenant-General Sir Benjamin D'Urban from Papineau Avenue Military Cemetery to the Field of Honour, July 22, 1944. Mixed honour guard of South African War veterans (honorary pall bearers) and detachment of the Royal Canadian Engineers. Arthur Hair stands at head of casket.

would stop and order him from the grounds! To Hair's dismay, he did not. It was time to move the remains to prevent further desecration.

The transfer was difficult partly because the LPF was unable immediately to identify the soldiers' resting places, let alone the human remains interred there. Most of the original headstones had disappeared or crumbled; most of the old bones could not be matched to individuals known to have been buried there. However, in May 1944, Sydney Ham, a man apparently without employment and living at the YMCA in downtown Montreal, became so moved by the Fund's work that he offered his services on a purely voluntary basis. Following a meeting with Hair, it was agreed that Ham would obtain or compile a complete list of burials at the site. To this end, Ham enthusiastically undertook extensive research at the Court House, local churches, and other archival sources. He also copied the information from all the headstones before their removal – crucial for the future layout at the Field. Following, in Hair's words, "many months of most careful and painstaking research", offered as a "labour of love", Ham produced a complete record of the 1,797 burials (and burial locations) at Papineau Avenue. In this way, illegible gravestones were identified and could be re-cut for their transfer to Pointe Claire. Hair and Holland were delighted with Ham's efforts, and Holland sent him some small gifts of appreciation. Ham remained involved with the LPF for several years thereafter.

The removal of the remains from Papineau for re-interment in the Field began on July 17, 1944, and took five days. All bodies and monuments were moved with full military honours. Present at the transfer ceremony at Papineau on July 22 were representatives of the governor general, the lieutenant-governor of Québec, DND, veterans' groups, and the diplomatic corps. Montreal mayor Adhémar Raynault was also in attendance. The DOC, MD No. 4, Major-General E.J. Renaud, placed a gun carriage and a firing party at the disposal of the LPF for the ceremony. The body of Sir Benjamin D'Urban, and the memorial towering above it, were the first items to be transferred. The monument was massive but, for reasons of sentiment, history, and art, was worth the expense of moving; it was taken apart and transported to the Field of Honour, where it was reassembled. D'Urban's body rested inside a lead coffin in a concrete vault directly below the centre of the monument and was returned to this position in the Field.

Norman Holland reading proclamation at rededication of Papineau Avenue
Military Cemetery in the Field of Honour, September 22, 1945.

It had taken months for everything at the Field to be readied and
a suitable area landscaped to provide dignified surroundings for its
new arrivals. The D'Urban monument was finally rededicated on
September 22, 1945, in the presence of most of the Québec-based
members of the Dominion Council of the LPF and many other local
dignitaries. The special speaker at the ceremony was Colonel H.C.
Osborne, secretary general of the Imperial War Graves Commission

(Canada). There was a guard of honour from MD No. 4, a religious service was held, and Holland read a solemn Dedicatory Proclamation: "For the purpose of historical record and in memoriam of the many Soldiers originally buried in the Papineau Avenue Military Cemetery, we dedicate this sacred spot to the glory of God. It shall ever remain in memory of those Imperial officers, rank and file, and their families who died while on service in the City of Montreal during the years 1814-1869. It shall be known in future as the D'Urban Circle." The honour guard fired three volleys, the "Last Post" was sounded, and the ceremony ended with the singing of "God Save the King". The D'Urban Circle was a special site several hundred metres directly across from the Currie Circle, which was at the entrance to the cemetery, near the Gate of Remembrance. The 54 old stones removed from Papineau were arranged in a circle surrounding the D'Urban memorial. While some were severely worn, at least they were salvaged. Beneath them were re-interred the remains of hundreds of British soldiers and their families.

With this new arrangement, the Field of Honour gained greater symmetry and even majesty. But it also needed to expand. In 1945, the Québec branch of the LPF purchased six acres of adjacent land, doubling its size. John Molson, former president of the branch still away on active service, donated $1,000 towards the purchase. Given the enormous increase in demand for the Fund's services after 1918, it seemed clear that an even greater volume would follow the Second World War. The Field would be ready to accommodate the demand.

D'Urban Monument at the Field of Honour, 1999.

Department of National Defense

The Death of Arthur Hair

On March 13, 1946, Holland convened an emergency meeting of the LPF's executive to discuss an urgent and sad matter: Arthur Hair was seriously, perhaps terminally, ill in hospital and likely to remain there for a long time. For over 35 years Hair had been such a key and valuable member of the Fund's administration that his loss would leave an enormous void. In fact, Holland had called the meeting to develop an immediate strategy to ensure continued smooth functioning during Hair's anticipated prolonged absence. Accordingly, Kathleen Cobbett, Hair's office assistant for nearly a decade, was unanimously selected to replace Hair on an interim basis, with the title of assistant secretary-treasurer – a role that she had been assuming for some time in any case.

Hair was too ill to attend the 37th annual meeting of the Last Post Fund, held the following month. The members unanimously passed a motion "expressing to Mr. Hair their deep regret that he was unable to be present for the first time in all the years since the Last Post Fund was formed. They wish him to know that his presence has been very much missed." Nevertheless, Hair was represented at the meeting by his two daughters, Ruby and Jessie. Hair also remained on the slate of candidates for executive positions, more out of the Fund's sense of respect than out of practicality. Indeed, from this point on, and until his death, the Dominion Council could no longer count on Hair as a fully active administrator. It was obvious that the organization's founder would never again be able to devote the energy to his tasks that had become his hallmark and which would form his legacy. Hair was duly re-elected Dominion secretary-treasurer, although it was understood that Cobbett, in whom Hair and Holland had great confidence, would assume his responsibilities. The succession was being planned.

It was also time to split the duties and responsibilities of Dominion and Québec treasurers, a dual task held by Hair for nearly 25 years. The administration and budget of the offices of the headquarters and of this branch had existed jointly since 1921, embodied in the person of Arthur Hair. This was no longer feasible. That April 1946 meeting formally separated the two tasks and appointed S.J. Smith Québec branch secretary-treasurer. This move was perhaps overdue.

According to Hair, being secretary-treasurer was an onerous responsibility: investigating cases, making funeral preparations, keep-

Arthur Hair at the Field of Honour, May 24, 1945, reading aloud names of those interred in previous year. Norman Holland in centre, wearing bow-tie.

ing records, paying for accounts, conducting meetings, and being ready every day to deal with cases and burial arrangements that could not wait. Hair wrote: "Our system of operation is necessarily exacting in detail, and entails much correspondence, careful investigation, bookkeeping, preparation of lists for erection of grave markers, recovering claims where possible, and making returns to Dominion Headquarters, all of which is done with remuneration as a secondary consideration." Hair's devotion would be difficult to replace.

Hair attended a Dominion Council meeting held November 29,

1946; it would be his last. While there, he strongly endorsed the work of Kathleen Cobbett and supported her request for an increase in monthly salary from $125 to $150. She was quite a bargain for the LPF. Hair was too sick to be present at the Fund's 38th annual meeting on April 25, 1947. His illness had reached a terminal stage, and Holland solemnly reported that Hair lay very weak but that "despite the handicaps under which he has been operating…he has still continued to give a very great deal of his time and effort to the carrying out of [his] work, to which he has now given a long lifetime. Nothing that the Last Post Fund can say or do would adequately express the debt of gratitude that we owe him." Cobbett also paid a warm tribute to Hair, admitting that times were "trying" at Dominion headquarters without Hair's passionate energy and "guiding influence". In recognition of his service, in September 1946 the president and directors sponsored a bid to have Hair made an Officer of the Order of the British Empire (OBE). Unfortunately, Hair's name did not appear on Buckingham Palace's New Year's honours list for 1947. He would have been a good choice.

Hair's name was left on the ballot for the Dominion Council elections held during this September meeting, and, while he was unanimously elected, it was understood that he would never again be well enough to assume any duties. The gathering passed another resolution of gratitude, and he and his son Douglas were made honorary life members. To help his family pay for his medical expenses the Fund also sent Hair $500 – a considerable sum for a cash-strapped organization, but an even more substantial amount for Mrs. Hair. Colonel Macfarlane, the DVA representative to Dominion HQ, told the meeting that he had seen Hair that afternoon and found him to be in "bright spirits, considering his physical condition and the outlook he had". The end was near.

On the afternoon of June 27, 1947, Arthur Hair died at his Westmount home. He was 74. He was survived by his wife, the former Janet MacIntyre, and their four children, Jessie, Ruby, Douglas, and Arthur. The Montreal press praised his life's work and his accomplishments. *The Gazette* noted that "he brought to his work an approach based on sympathetic understanding of veterans and their problems and his disposition to decide matters on compassionate grounds endeared him to all who sought recourse." In an editorial of

July 3, the same newspaper reminded readers that Hair, despite numerous obstacles, had guided the Last Post Fund to national prominence. His life was one worth honouring. Appropriately, the South African War Veterans Association paid him tribute in a statement released to the press: "Our association, being one of the senior veterans' associations, has received a great deal of sympathy and service from [the Fund]. Mr. Hair was a gentleman, always ready to serve in the cause of taking care of the remains of the old soldier. A man unselfish in every respect, he was always sympathetic and kind and we are sure, if the truth was heard, made many a sacrifice for the noble cause of the Last Post Fund...The Field of Honour is a monument to this brave gentleman." Arthur Harold Douglas Hair was laid to rest on June 30 at the Field of Honour, in grave No. 1 of the Directors' Circle that surrounds the Cross of Remembrance. He became the first director of the Fund to be buried in this section of the Field reserved for active officials of the organization. "Now, with his work done", stated *The Gazette*, "Arthur Hair has lain down with his comrades...duly honored himself by the company of those whose honorable rest he himself assured." *The Montreal Daily Star* appropriately echoed the ancient epitaph: "if you would seek his monument look about you".

In addition to his family and friends, mourners at the funeral included all the officers of the Fund, numerous representatives from veterans' organizations, veterans from both world wars, and representatives from DVA, DND, the Red Cross Society, and various philanthropic and patriotic organizations, along with many others. While individual Legion branches were represented at the funeral, J.C.G. Herwig, the general secretary of the Dominion Command wrote Holland on July 10, expressing his disappointment at not learning sooner of Hair's death. "We saw nothing of this in our Ottawa papers and feel very much upset that Dominion Command was not represented at the funeral or able to even send a wreath." Disagreements with the Legion were a thing of the past.

Dozens of letters and telegrams poured into LPF headquarters remembering Hair's patriotic contributions to veterans' causes. One came to Holland from Brenda Chillas, director of the Red Cross Social Service: "As one who worked closely with him during the past 18½ years, I could well appreciate the wonderful contribution he made to the veterans and their families at the time of their passing and

Burial of Arthur Hair in Directors' Circle, Field of Honour, June 30, 1947.

trouble. His unfailing patience, courtesy, and personal sympathetic attention, given in every instance was most outstanding...He will surely be very much missed but has left behind him a marvellous structure." R.W. Walker, president of the Army, Navy and Air Force Veterans in Canada, observed: "We have had...many occasions to meet Mr. Hair in connection with the interment of many of our own members and have always found him extremely co-operative and obliging. Our unit feels that it has lost a very good friend." A.J. Morris, secretary of the LPF's Southern Alberta branch, wrote Holland that "the number of grave markers scattered throughout this country will forever be testimonial to his work." Hair had made a difference.

Arthur Hair was the last active original member of the Last Post Fund. It was the end of an era.

6

RENEWAL AND GROWTH, 1948–1969

O, wither'd is the garland of the war.

WILLIAM SHAKESPEARE,
ANTONY AND CLEOPATRA, IV. xv. 64

Arthur Hair's death had left a void in the administration of the Last Post Fund. But perhaps his greatest legacy was his role in creating a strong Canada-wide organization able to withstand the passing of its founder and move on to even greater challenges. In the 25 years following the end of the Second World War, other men and women accepted the challenges of steering the LPF into a new, more complex era. In addition to Hair's death, these years saw the passing or retirement of many key players in the early development of the Fund. A new Last Post Fund emerged, shaped by the influences of new members and the existence of one million Canadian veterans.

Canada, too, was experiencing major changes. By the 1950s and 1960s, economic depression and world war had yielded to massive economic growth, a vastly increased standard of living for most Canadians, and the uneasy peace of the Cold War. The Korean War broke out in June 1950, and not long afterwards Canadians were again fighting overseas. Before the conflict ended in stalemate in July 1953, about 25,000 Canadians had served; 516 were killed or died while on active service. Korea produced a whole new crop of veterans just a few years after the last ones had returned home from an earlier war.

Because of the military threat posed by the Soviet Union in Europe, in 1949 the former western Allies of the Second World War formed the North Atlantic Treaty Organization (NATO), a defensive military alliance aimed at deterring Soviet aggression. Canada was a charter member of NATO. With the proliferation of nuclear weapons in the 1950s, the next major war risked being a thermonuclear exchange, resulting in global Armageddon. The post-1945 world was rife with tension. In 1951, in a dramatic peacetime policy shift, Canada decided to station troops and combat aircraft in western Europe to help protect the weakened democracies of that continent against the hostility of the Soviet Union. This necessitated an enormous growth in Canada's armed forces, which peaked at over 120,000 in 1963. But veteran status would elude the men, and later women, serving Canada and the world on NATO duty, which, while occasionally tense, was hardly a 'shooting' war.

At home, Canada was a structurally altered country. In the 1950s, the economy was booming, population growth was phenomenal, and, across the country, hundreds of thousands of new dwellings were built, as was the infrastructure required to service them. Canada also developed, in stages, a so-called welfare state, in which Ottawa promised a basic minimum standard of living to all citizens through a host of public programs designed to prevent destitution. These emerging policies, such as unemployment insurance, children's allowances, seniors' pensions, the Canada Pension Plan, universal health care, and welfare payments to the poorest became available to all Canadians as a matter of right, or entitlement, and not only to those society deemed impoverished. As historian James Struthers has noted, this helped eliminate the stigma of receiving charitable aid and meant that fewer moral judgements would be passed before aid was dispensed. Ottawa spent enormous sums on these programs. By 1952, expenditures on only family allowances and old age security exceeded the amount of the entire federal budget for any given year in the late 1930s. These initiatives would have a major effect on the Last Post Fund. If government programs and economic growth improved the deplorable standard of living with which the nation's most impoverished families had to contend, then it stood to reason that many poor veterans' families would also benefit materially. This helps to explain why the number of LPF cases grew more slowly during these years than after 1918. Government adjustments to the war pension allowance regulations in the 1930s provided minimal income to a greater number of veterans whom the pension board determined would be unlikely to ever again be self supportive. These interventionist policies, too, helped to lessen the LPF's caseload.

Massive immigration from all over the world transformed the

social and cultural composition of Canada. Canadians of British ethnic origin made up a smaller percentage of the population with each passing decade. By the 1960s, the political and emotional ties that bound Canada to Britain had diminished considerably. Even the British Empire had become a thing of the past, replaced by a more loosely bound Commonwealth of Nations of uncertain meaning to many Canadians. In any event, Canada's security interests and defence policies were more in step with those of Washington than those of London. More than ever, Canada was a North American nation.

In 1952, amid a burgeoning sense of nationalism, Ottawa appointed the country's first Canadian-born governor general, Vincent Massey. In 1965, Canada adopted the maple leaf flag, relegating the old Red Ensign, with its emblematic Union Jack, to the dustbin of history. The structure of Canadian federalism was also increasingly being called into question, especially by the growth of *Québécois* nationalism and the rise of regionalism, which imposed severe strains on Confederation.

Through it all, despite the shifts, changes, and modifications to the country and its society, Canada's veteran population, in excess of one million persons, continued to be served by the Last Post Fund. The twenty years following Hair's death would continue to highlight the great need for the services that the Fund had traditionally offered.

Leadership Changes

In early July 1947, the Dominion Council of the Last Post Fund named Kathleen M. Cobbett to replace Hair as secretary-treasurer. Cobbett, who had originally joined the LPF in 1935 as a volunteer worker, and later assisted Hair as a salaried employee, would carry out her predecessor's work in a manner of which he would have heartily approved. In fact, in the next 15 years Cobbett would go on to become an 'institution' in the LPF. Norman Holland, who was president of both the Québec branch and Dominion Council, praised her for "the manner in which [she] carried on the work during Mr. Hair's illness and also for the great amount of extra work which it was necessary for her to do. Her experience under Mr. Hair, both in dealing with provincial matters and those connected with the nation-wide work of the Last Post Fund, will amply qualify her for the important position to which she has been appointed." Cobbett also made very favourable impressions on branch directors across Canada, who would certainly have echoed Holland's boast that Cobbett "practically lived at the office". Her salary was raised to $200 a month, the same paid to S.J. Smith, the Québec secretary-treasurer. The Dominion secretary-treasurership was arguably the most critical position in the LPF hierarchy, in effect determining the degree to which the organization functioned as it was intended. As a measure of the trust that Holland placed in Cobbett, it was then uncommon for a woman to hold a position of such responsibility in an organization mainly comprised of men. Cobbett was more than equal to the task, but, unexpectedly, she was obliged to wait several years before adequately displaying her considerable talents.

In October 1947, the Red Cross reluctantly asked the LPF to vacate the premises on McTavish Street that it had made available to the Fund free of charge. The LPF scrambled to find a suitable location, and, in the end, the Red Cross generously made available some of its office space in another downtown building on Inspector Street. In November, on her very first day at the new site, Kathleen Cobbett fell down a steep flight of stairs and was taken to hospital suffering from serious injuries. She would spend the next nine weeks in hospital and would not be fully healthy again for years to come.

Given the Fund's lack of an LPF employee health plan, Cobbett suffered a serious loss of income, and the Dominion Council voted her a $300 bonus for the immense amount of overtime she had contributed during Hair's illness. (In 1950, Dominion headquarters awarded Cobbett another $125 towards her medical expenses.) No doubt spurred by what had happened to Cobbett, in 1949 the national organization and the Québec branch each adopted Blue Cross health insurance plans for their permanent employees. The LPF paid half the costs, and the employees half.

By February 1948, Cobbett's progress had been very slow, and her doctors advised her that she was months away from a full work schedule. In the meantime, and indeed since Hair's illness, Holland (and some of his staff at Brandram-Henderson) had toiled long and hard to carry on the work of the Fund. In the previous year alone, Holland had taken a leading role in organizing the LPF's move to its new location, supervised its response to P.C. 178, by which Ottawa subsidized

*Kathleen Cobbett, secretary-treasurer general of the
Last Post Fund, 1947 and 1951-63.*

the LFP's administrative costs, and personally handled much of the
work that Cobbett otherwise would have done. But the aging
Holland could not do it all; it was time to get some help.

In March 1948, a special meeting of the Dominion Council took
place, with all three trustees in attendance. The directors felt that a
new secretary-treasurer should be appointed, and they already had
someone in mind: Lieutenant-Colonel D.E. Macintyre, D.S.O., M.C.,
five times mentioned in dispatches, and an expert on veterans' issues.
Macintyre agreed to manage the affairs of the LPF, effective March
15, 1948. The council members decided that once Cobbett was
healthy enough, she could return as Macintyre's assistant. This she did
later that year, although it must have been humbling.

Macintyre came to the LPF with strong credentials: he was a distinguished soldier of the First World War and a well-known public
figure. Many LPF directors knew him personally. In 1936, he had
been the principal organizer of the Legion's Vimy Pilgrimage, and
from 1939 to 1946 he had directed the Canadian Legion's War
Services Fund. But Macintyre did not come cheaply. His salary was a

very hefty $4,800 for the first year and $5,100 for the next. This was more than twice what Cobbett would have received, but was in line with Macintyre's pre-LPF income.

Despite accomplishing some excellent work and earning the respect of his colleagues, by the end of 1950 Macintyre had had enough of commuting to work in Montreal while maintaining his residence in Ottawa. He resigned. Replacing him was no easy matter, notwithstanding the attractive salary of $4,000 offered prospective candidates. The Fund sought a veteran under 55 years of age, who had "executive ability, a knowledge of accounting and a pleasing personality". In the end, despite having received 131 applications and hiring a man (who did not work out) for three months on a trial basis, on February 13, 1951, Holland named Kathleen Cobbett as the 'new' secretary-treasurer general (as the position became known). It had been a long road for Cobbett, but it was a choice that no one would regret. Indeed, following Macintyre's resignation, it was silly not simply to have offered her the job in the first place.

All this seemed too much for S.J. Smith, who had long wanted the Dominion position. He quit abruptly in September 1951, leaving Cobbett holding the bag as the Québec branch's secretary-treasurer as well. No replacement for Smith was named until November 1952, when P. Ackerly took over the job, and he quit in April 1953, leaving Cobbett in the lurch for organizing the annual May 24 ceremonies. But she was made of stern stuff. More than ever, Holland considered Cobbett an invaluable asset to the Fund. In 1953, Cobbett received the Coronation Medal in recognition of her meritorious service to the LPF and to Canada's veterans. One suspects that Holland had a lot to do with securing her nomination for this prestigious and well-deserved award. In 1954, he told those gathered for the LPF's annual meeting that he "could not visualize the office without her". Dominion headquarters ran very smoothly under her influence.

The Fund hired an assistant for Cobbett – the first in a long line of female office help, rarely exceeding two persons, that Dominion HQ would hire in the next two decades. Because of this employee turnover, throughout the 1950s Cobbett spent an inordinate amount of time training and supervising staff. Although some employees stayed for eight or ten years, it was difficult for the LPF to attract and retain outstanding people because of its inability to offer 'fringe benefits'. Its employees were not civil servants and did not benefit from government pension or health plans. Accordingly, no obvious successor to Cobbett was ever groomed from the 'inside', as had been the case with her.

On April 20, 1955, several members of the Dominion Council met for a brief emergency meeting. The only item on the agenda was a letter to the Fund dated April 12, 1955 which Cobbett read aloud. It was from Eva Slattery, Norman Holland's personal secretary at Brandram-Henderson. The letter read in part: "Mr. Holland has been advised by his doctors that he must divorce himself from practically all outside activities and, much to his regret, this letter will constitute his immediate resignation from such offices as he holds in Last Post Fund." Holland was 74 years old and ailing. He had joined the LPF in 1922 and served as president of the Québec branch since 1939 and as national president since 1942. He had been a guiding influence during some of the organization's most critical years. The council accepted his resignation, although Holland became an honorary vice-president, replacing John H. Molson, who returned to the LPF as a director.

The directors present at that April 20 meeting asked Molson to be president, but he declined, citing his many other commitments. Finally, Commodore Paul Earl, C.B.E., the naval-officer-in-charge, Montreal, and a member of the Dominion Council for only two years, agreed to serve as president, the first sailor to head the LPF since J.T. Walsh in 1920. Earl, aged 60, was a well-known Montreal businessman, veteran of both world wars, and past president of the Navy League of Canada. He strongly believed in community service and was heavily involved with a number of benevolent organizations. Several years later, while still a director of the Fund, but no longer president, Earl entered provincial politics and, in 1960, was elected Liberal MLA from the Montreal riding of Notre-Dame-de-Grâce. The new premier, Jean Lesage, promptly named him minister of mines. From 1961 until his death in May 1963, Earl served as minister of provincial revenue. Like all his predecessors, Earl proved a high-profile and much-respected president of the Last Post Fund.

Paul Earl chaired his first meeting as president in May 1955, at the Fund's 46th annual general meeting. Cobbett used the occasion to pay tribute to Holland, who was not in attendance, thanking him for his "unfailing assistance" over the previous 15 years. "His excellent business acumen [and] his guidance eliminated many problems", she said. At the subsequent meeting of the Dominion Council, the directors voted to award Holland a scroll and a framed photo of the Field of Honour, which he had helped obtain in the late 1920s, "in recognition of the achievement and success of the Last Post Fund under his leadership". Holland's resignation proved the end of another era in the history of the LPF; he died in 1956.

Although Earl's interest in the Fund was very great, in 1957 he relinquished the presidency after only two years, believing that others should have a chance of holding that office. In May 1957, Lieutenant-Colonel Stuart Rolland, a long-time LPF stalwart, became president. Rolland's six years in office were complicated by a series of health problems. When he spent two months in hospital in 1958-59, Cobbett handled day-to-day operations and, when necessary, would visit Rolland at home during his convalescence, taking him material to read or sign. The president wondered aloud at the May 1961 annual meeting whether the LPF could get along without her. The Fund would soon find out.

NAC PA-142588.

Commodore Paul Earl, president of the Last Post Fund, 1955-57

In the interval between the 1962 and 1963 annual meetings, Cobbett married a man named Eric Garrett. She also made known her intention to resign. For a well-deserved going-away present, the Dominion Council awarded Cobbett $1,528 – the surplus left over prior to the closing out of the books on March 31, 1963. Moreover, several LPF members of the Dominion Council and from two western branches donated a combined total of $305, for an overall cash bonus of $1,833. This money was basically offered in *lieu* of a pension plan. The executive also presented her with a silver cigarette box marked with the LPF's crest. Cobbett received dozens of letters of thanks, congratulations, and appreciation for her more than 25 years of service to the Fund. The Southern California Branch of the Canadian Legion awarded her its Certificate of Merit. She had been an excellent administrator, and all who knew her were aware that the LPF was losing an outstanding worker and passionate supporter.

Cobbett was replaced by V.M.C. Webb, from the DVA's office in Montreal. Webb, a gunner during the First World War and a veteran of the RCAF during the Second, passed away in 1966. Miss Monique Millette was then in charge of the office pending appointment of a new secretary-treasurer, who turned out to be Lieutenant-Colonel A.G. Edward, M.C., D.F.C., who took over on June 15, 1966.

Stuart Rolland resigned in 1963 and was replaced by Romuald Bourque, 74, an Ottawa-born former newspaper publisher and mayor of the affluent Montreal suburb of Outremont from 1947 to 1964. Bourque had also been Member of Parliament for Outremont from 1952 to 1962. In 1963, he was appointed to the Senate. His interest in the LPF went back to 1934, and he had been a director since 1941. Notwithstanding his many other duties, Bourque, the first French-Canadian head of the Last Post Fund, would prove a very hard-working president, even well into his 80s.

Relations between the Last Post Fund and the Canadian Legion (which gained the prefix "Royal" in 1960) continued to be harmonious and co-operative in the 25 years following the end of the Second World War. Nevertheless, the LPF, the senior though much smaller society, jealously guarded its area of jurisdiction against Legion encroachment. The Fund's leaders were responsible for upholding the LPF's distinct role in the community of organizations assisting veterans. In January 1952, Major-General W.W.P. Gibsone, a trustee of the

Senator Romuald Bourque,
president of the Last Post Fund, 1963-74.

LPF, remarked that "the Legion has been trying to take over our job". Others felt the same way.

In 1948, a concerned D.E. Macintyre, himself a long-time Legion supporter, had written to Holland about a noticeable increase in Legion members in LPF ranks. Macintyre felt it was possible, though unlikely, for the Legion to "pack" a branch directors' meeting and take over the whole proceedings. Although this subject arose from time to time, Holland felt that "there was nothing we could do about it" and that, in the absence of any firm evidence, it was simply best to "drop the matter". Still, in August 1951, Holland wrote to Cobbett to the effect that this situation, while not really urgent, was one that she should "keep in mind". Cobbett believed that "the only threat appears to be if a branch had on its Directorate a majority of members belonging to an organization; in other words if the Directors of the Québec branch were predominantly Legion members then their vote might force an issue." At the time, approximately 41 Québec branches of the Legion were members of the Québec branch of the LPF (yielding $550 in dues). In 1960, when Dominion Council replacements had to be found for Howard Stutchbury (Alberta) and F.W. Marshall (Newfoundland), the council was careful not to choose prominent Legion members. The directors felt very strongly that the Fund and the Legion had to remain visibly separate entities, even though council members recognized that many individuals were active in both organizations.

Beyond this underlying sense of suspicion of Legion motives, some LPF members felt that there was also evidence of Legion meddling in the Fund's affairs. For example, it had long been the LPF's practice to erect grave markers engraved with the words "Lest We Forget", from Kipling's poem, "The Recessional". In June 1956, delegates at the Canadian Legion's Dominion convention formally issued a resolution asking the LPF to cease adding this phrase to its markers on the grounds that it distinguished those buried in LPF plots as indigent at the time of death – a stigma that the Legion felt the veterans did not merit. The Fund's directors were highly indignant. To begin with, not all LPF burials were of indigent veterans. Moreover, because the words by themselves could not in any way suggest the possible poverty of those buried beneath them, and in fact were a moving testament to their military service, perhaps something else lay behind the Legion's resolution. Namely, the Legion, which also used this phrase in its promotional literature and on ceremonial occasions, sought to be the only organization associated with it. The Fund had been using these words as its motto, and on its seal, crest, insignia, letterhead, forms, *and* grave markers, since its inception in 1909. It had no intention of ending this tradition just because another group requested it do so: "Lest We Forget", an appropriate message to grace LPF grave markers, continued as its signature imprint.

Relations between the LPF and the Canadian Corps Association (CCA) were close throughout the 1950s. Major-General J.A. Gunn, prominent in the LPF's Ontario organization since the 1930s, was an honorary president of the CCA. In May 1958, *Torch*, the CCA's magazine, published an editorial lauding the LPF's work. This is not surprising, since the material for the editorial had been provided by George McRae, the Ontario branch's secretary-treasurer. "The work of the Last Post Fund", exclaimed *Torch*, "has brought comfort to the relatives of thousands of the Empire's fighting men. Its services appeal particularly to the Canadian Corps Association, because every loyal veteran wants to see every needy veteran assured of a burial fit for a warrior, in a last resting place made secure to him and his kin for all time." This had been the LPF's message for half a century.

The LPF generally benefitted from strong leaders in these years, and their competence and force of character enabled the Fund to solidify and enhance its role as the caretaker of Canada's indigent veterans at the moment of death.

Paying the Bills

In one important respect, the postwar period seemed hardly different from previous eras in the Fund's history. Its administrative costs continued to be greater than its ability to pay for them. It was seemingly in constant negotiation with the Department of Veterans' Affairs to increase administrative funding and raise the allowable costs of funerals.

Money was available from another source, however. Across Canada from 1937 to 1947, LPF 'reclaims' from estates, and reimbursements for funerals, had averaged $18,000 per annum. All of this money was returned to the federal government, whose funding had actually paid for the funerals. But the Fund increasingly eyed these reclaims as an essential source of self-financing, since Ottawa's allotment for administration was simply insufficient to meet expanding operations.

Finally, in January 1948, P.C. 178 allowed Dominion headquarters to keep branch reclaims and apply this money towards administrative costs – a decision that Norman Holland believed the "most important clause in the whole order-in-council". With this new proviso in hand, Dominion Council resolved that if branches encountered unavoidable operating deficits, LPF HQ would make these good. All that was required was an audited branch statement identifying the need for reimbursement.

Lieutenant-Colonel G.S. Macfarlane and A.J. Dixon, of DVA, had been instrumental in convincing their department to allow the Fund to use these reclaims. After all, they argued, government monies to pay for funeral expenses had already been budgeted and spent; any reclaims amounted to bonus money for federal coffers. Government generosity prevailed. By 1950, Holland believed, perhaps with some exaggeration, that the LPF's finances as a result were "in better condition than they have been for a long time". This was due in large measure to Macfarlane, who proved a valuable LPF asset in his role as

DVA's representative on Dominion Council. His ardent support was reminiscent of the strong backing that E.H. Scammell had provided the Fund in the same capacity a generation earlier.

While P.C. 178 was welcomed by the LPF across the country, its implementation also touched off some quarrelling in the LPF family. Major-General John Gunn, first vice-president representing Ontario, was hesitant about this arrangement. He would have preferred keeping Ontario's hefty reclaim amounts for his branch's own administration, contrary to the stipulations of the order-in-council. His stance led to stormy relations between the Ontario branch and the rest of the LPF.

A major rift was developing. Perhaps seeking to avoid open censure, the Ontario branch boycotted a Dominion Council meeting in February 1949, even though Holland had "pleaded" with Gunn to be present. All the other branches attended and unanimously endorsed Dominion HQ, which argued that Ontario's position was difficult to understand, since the Dominion Council was on record as promising to make good any branch shortfalls. Major R.H. Tupper, the BC representative, strongly objected to Ontario's maverick behaviour and reminded the meeting that British Columbia, too, had funding problems, although it would never consider contravening an order-in-council. Howard Stutchbury of Alberta reinforced this view by adding that his branch funded itself by working hard to obtain office space and other administrative requirements free of charge. Why could Ontario not do the same?

The LPF's Ontario branch was an excellent one, accomplishing some outstanding work. Still, its record in submitting reclaim money to Dominion HQ was spotty. For example, in the previous 11 years, the Québec branch had collected over $32,000 in reclaims from veterans' estates, government departments, British pension authorities, and other sources, and it had sent the entire amount to Dominion HQ. In the same period, Ontario had reclaimed over $35,000 but had only slowly and grudgingly sent HQ $19,000, or barely half. It had transferred virtually nothing since 1946, even at a time when the LPF was obliged to return this money to the federal government. Moreover, the Québec branch collected an average of $30 in reclaims per funeral, while Ontario collected only $13. Dominion Council felt that Ontario could do a lot better.

There was more to this episode than meets the eye. Ontario was protesting more than its need to keep reclaim money. The branch wanted greater representation on Dominion Council, especially since it accounted for nearly one-third of LPF burials. But the minutes of this February 1949 meeting show very clearly that all branch delegates and regional representatives rejected Ontario's demand. Dominion HQ's Montreal-centred composition was "as it should be", state the minutes. "Last Post Fund was founded in *Montreal* by *Montrealers,* and the burden and cost of operating it has *always* been borne by Montrealers." Ontario needed its wings clipped.

So annoyed was the rest of the LPF with Gunn and his branch that Dominion Council gave serious consideration to withdrawing Ontario's sub-charter and reorganizing the branch. The council gave Holland *carte blanche* to deal with the matter in any manner he saw fit. In the end, Holland's 'quiet diplomacy' paid off. Under siege, Gunn backed off. By April, Gunn was singing the praises of Dominion HQ and thanking the council for its "patience and assistance". For its part, Dominion Council congratulated Holland for his "strenuous efforts to arrive at an amical solution". There is no record of what inducement Holland offered along with his threats, but it does seem that Ontario was allowed greater flexibility in spending money for the transportation of bodies for burial and in other matters of particular concern to that branch. While the Fund was normally a happy family, sometimes there were instances of sibling rivalry and adolescent rebellion. Whether Gunn's recalcitrant ways and willingness to argue his branch's position forcefully exerted any influence, Montreal HQ proved generous with the branches: by mid-1951, 70 per cent of reclaims were being returned to them as financial assistance.

Funeral costs rose steadily in the postwar period. At the end of the fiscal year 1948-49 they had risen 13 per cent over the previous year. Undertakers, cemeteries, and manufacturers of grave markers from coast to coast demanded an increase in the LPF's allowable fees for their services. The situation had reached an intolerable stage when, on December 28, 1950, Ottawa passed an order-in-council increasing acceptable undertakers' charges to $110 per burial, exclusive of grave markers. The next month, Holland told members of the Québec branch that "it was not necessary to broadcast this" to all funeral directors, as there might be a natural inclination on their part to charge the

LPF the maximum allowable fee as a matter of course. Branches across Canada still had a responsibility to keep costs as low as possible. "The amount of the payment", wrote Holland, "must depend absolutely on circumstances, and there are plenty of occasions in the smaller places where a payment of even $75 will be quite sufficient."

By 1956, funeral directors were again clamouring for more money, with those in Toronto insisting that the Fund was paying less than a municipally-arranged pauper's burial. The issue of under-funding became a constant, frustrating struggle involving DVA, the LPF, and Canadian undertakers. DVA insisted on obtaining evidence from the Fund that an increase in allowable expenses was absolutely necessary. This demand met with a frosty reception, since DVA consistently allowed itself more to bury its pensioned veterans than the LPF's allotment. Obviously, DVA was aware how expensive it was to inter a veteran. Finally, in November 1958, Ottawa allowed the Fund to pay undertaking costs up to $175, which was a very great relief to Dominion HQ. This increase was critical to the continued success of LPF operations in large Canadian cities and anywhere in the United States.

Equally important, Ottawa almost doubled the LPF's administrative budget to $15,000 per annum. But this last item was a case of 'give and take', since the Fund was again to turn over burial reclaims to the federal government. Ottawa also increased the LPF's annual capital account from $40,000 to $58,000, which made life "much easier" for everyone at the Fund. Since operating expenses rose in proportion to Ottawa's financial commitment, the LPF was obliged to continue its careful, thrifty ways.

Ottawa's budgetary policies were always reactive, in response to a crying need on the part of the LPF. The delays in enacting sensible financial legislation regularly stretched the Fund to its financial limits. Despite continually rising costs, Ottawa next authorized a burial increase only in 1965, when allowable undertakers' expenses rose to $240. In exchange, however, undertakers were obliged to provide LPF cases with a better-quality, rounded casket instead of the square, box-like coffins traditionally employed. This brought LPF caskets in line with those used in DVA burials. Slowly but surely, DVA was beginning to accept the notion that LPF burials should be in no way inferior to those of destitute veterans under DVA care. But Ottawa carefully audited the LPF's funding and expenditures, and financial disagreements often increased tension between the two parties during this period.

The Fund continued throughout the 1950s and early 1960s to benefit from the largesse of friends and supporters. In 1961, it received an unusual donation from the trustees of a fund established in 1917 by the officers of the 148th Battalion, CEF, for the benefit of members of the battalion or their dependants fallen on hard times. The trustees decided that since no calls had been made on their fund since 1954, they would donate the amount remaining – almost $2,300 – to the LPF, which they considered a most appropriate beneficiary. The money could just as easily have been left to the Legion.

From the late 1940s until 1954 (at which point a new policy stifled its generosity), the Québec Branch of the Canadian Red Cross made annual donations to the Fund. Other groups that regularly made small gifts included the Canadian Legion, the City of Montreal, the Khaki League, the Kiwanis Club, and the Montreal Police War Veterans Association. A fund-raising campaign in 1950 yielded $2,000 from about 250 donors. The Québec government intermittently gave $1,000 annually. It was all just barely enough.

Plus ça change, plus c'est la même chose

Despite the wrangling with Ottawa over funding, and a series of personnel changes within its executive, the Fund's routine business remained the same: burying Canada's deceased veterans and establishing criteria of eligibility for its services. In any era, this was what the LPF did.

One order of business that D.E. Macintyre considered a top priority on becoming secretary-treasurer in 1948 was the erection of markers over LPF graves in the United States. Since 1937, at least 169 unmarked burials had taken place. The major issue had always been cost, which was magnified during the war by unfavourable exchange rates. As well, U.S. cemeteries insisted on concrete foundations for headstones, the laying of which exceeded the LPF's authorized budget for markers.

During his first year with the Fund, Macintyre dealt with this persistent problem in a very thorough manner. Armed with a meagre budget of $25 per marker and dogged determination, he obtained the co-operation of most of the American cemeteries concerned, many of which erected foundations and markers for free, something that Hair had been unable to achieve. At the end of a year, only thirteen LPF graves in the United States remained unmarked, the result of excessive costs demanded by unyielding administrators. Overall, Macintyre accomplished his complicated and time-consuming task by spending only several hundred dollars more than allotted – a result that greatly satisfied the Dominion Council. In February 1949, Holland noted appreciatively that this bothersome situation had been "cleared up" for the first time in 30 years.

In 1949, the Dominion Council once again debated what "military service" meant vis-à-vis LPF burial. P.C. 178 clearly specified that eligibility was limited to "active service" during the period of hostilities or post-hostilities demobilization, as set out by Ottawa. In other words, the LPF existed for war veterans, not military personnel who had experienced only peacetime military service. The following periods qualified: October 11, 1899 to May 31, 1902 (the South African War); August 4, 1914 to August 1, 1921 (the First World War); and September 1, 1939 to September 30, 1947 (the Second World War). Ottawa later added July 5, 1950 to October 31, 1953 (the Korean War).

LPF benefits did not cover service in the merchant navy. Ironically, although thousands of merchant navy veterans received military campaign medals, such as the 1939-1945 Star and the War Medal 1939-1945, they were civilian participants in the war and not on strength of His Majesty's Forces. As such, they remained ineligible; no military discharge certificate, no LPF-sponsored burial. By the mid-1960s, the Fund agreed that it could inter those merchant seamen dying while under government care according to the provisions of the Civilian War Pensions and Allowances Act. In 1965, there were 1,140 such merchant marine pensioners alive and the LPF estimated that only a handful of cases a year would be in need of LPF services. By 1968, however, the government was paying allowances to approximately 20,000 merchant seamen and 3,500 Newfoundland foresters. The LPF expected some 1,000 of these people eventually to die in indigent circumstances and be buried by the LPF. The eligibility pool was widening.

During the fiscal year 1953-54, the LPF recorded its first burial of a veteran of the Korean War. However, only those who actually served in the 'theatre of operations' during the official period of hostilities were eligible. Accordingly, in 1954 the Fund was obliged to reject the case of a veteran of the Princess Patricia's Canadian Light Infantry who had volunteered for service in Korea but who was posted in Canada only. Similar cases arose from time to time. But the LPF's hands were tied; this ruling came directly from Ottawa. A similar situation affected South African War veterans: they had to have actually served in South Africa, not merely have been in the Dominion's military forces during the period of hostilities.

In February 1955, the Dominion Council debated the definition of "veteran" yet again. Some members objected to the interpretation of "active service" in P.C. 178 (a definition repeated in P.C. 1954-1932). Lieutenant-Colonel Stuart Rolland, arguing forcefully for inclusiveness, opposed retention of this phrase, since he believed that any person who had served in wartime, whether at home or overseas, in whatever service and under whatever circumstances, should be eligible for the Fund's benefits. He sought simple, blanket coverage. Commodore Paul Earl agreed. Major-General C. Basil Price, who had commanded the 3rd Canadian Infantry Division in Britain until 1942, in which year he became head of the Canadian Red Cross overseas, felt that inclusion of the words "active service" defeated the Fund's original purpose and left out many people who had faithfully volunteered for duty. Although Lieutenant-Colonel G.S. Macfarlane, representing DVA, was sympathetic to this broad interpretation, the department was not interested in changing the rules defining those men and women it was willing to inter at its expense. The LPF was free to bury whomever it saw fit, but at the Fund's own expense if the cases did not conform to DVA parameters. In any event, there was no unanimity among LPF members on eligibility.

At a December 1955 council meeting, Rolland again raised the matter. He reminded those present that, at that very moment, thousands of Canadians were stationed in Europe on duty with NATO, serving on the front lines against possible Soviet expansionism. Though not combat veterans, they were all voluntarily in the armed forces at a time of high international tension. Should they not be eligible for LPF services? However, the Fund's mandate, constitution, and by-laws, and its formal arrangements with Ottawa, as stipulated in a series of ordersin-council, were all clear: these former military personnel (not veterans) were ineligible. There the matter stood for over a decade.

Canadians deployed abroad on United Nations (UN) peacekeeping duties fared no better. In 1969, Lieutenant-Colonel C. Fred Black, DVA's representative to Dominion Council during the late 1960s, and a man much admired by the LPF directors, re-iterated DVA's traditional eligibility policy. Black insisted that Canadian military personnel who had served on UN-sponsored peacekeeping missions did not qualify, since Canada was not at war during these deployments and these military personnel were not on active service, despite the dangers many faced. The federal government's, and therefore the LPF's, funeral services would extend to British, Commonwealth, and Allied veterans residing in Canada and included British veterans of various military campaigns throughout the empire, but it would not include Canadians serving in peacetime, no matter what their duties.

In the 1950s, the council clarified another LPF burial regulation, this one regarding dishonourable discharges. If a soldier who had seen active service was awaiting criminal trial before a military court, and died penniless before he was sentenced, he was eligible for the services of the Fund. However, once convicted he or she was thereafter ineligible. The directors' perceptions of morality and honour continued to override any sense of obligation to a service person's war record. There were examples to the contrary, however. In 1947, an honourably discharged veteran was shot and killed while attempting a hold-up at Sparling, Manitoba. He was buried by the LPF just the same. The 'morality' policy was subjective and could be inconsistent. In 1969, S.H. Daines, the Dominion Council's representative from the Southern Alberta branch, suggested that the time had come for the LPF to assume burial responsibility for all cases of indigent veterans, notwithstanding the nature of their discharge from the armed forces. Since there might have been mitigating circumstances surrounding a dishonourable discharge, circumstances with which the Fund might even find itself in sympathy, there was no longer any justification for this 60-year-old discriminatory regulation. After considerable discussion, a consensus emerged that the Fund should apply no moral distinctions to veterans. All veterans would henceforth be considered of equal status at the time of their deaths and thus eligible for LPF burial services. Times had changed dramatically from the honour-bound and perhaps less flexible days of Arthur Hair.

Still, the basic operating procedures governing the Fund's work would have been recognizable to Hair two decades after his death. As ever, a burial case to be assumed by the LPF still required proof of active service, usually in the form of a discharge certificate. In the absence of such a document, the next-of-kin or some other responsible person who had known the deceased could swear out an affidavit to this effect. Then, it had to be demonstrated that neither the deceased's estate nor any immediate relatives could provide for the burial and that no friend or other organization would bear the costs of the funeral. Proving indigence could be a humiliating experience for the deceased's survivors. The necessary documentation having been provided, the LPF then authorized undertaking services to proceed within the financial limitations of its regulations. These regulations clearly outlined the allowable costs and procedures for the removal and transport of the remains, allowable casket types, public viewing of the remains for one day before interment, funeral services including a hearse and the use of a car for family members, a flag to drape the coffin, the opening of a grave, and the burial service, including, wherever possible, the voluntary services of a military chaplain or clergyman. Strict adherence to these rules enabled branches to apply the Fund's funeral services uniformly and consistently across Canada.

There was some flexibility allowed in the decision to accept cases, however. Indigence was proven by a simple means test. In 1954, the allowable estate was still fixed at up to $500, but, with a sense of compassion growing in the organization (not to mention inflation in the economy), the Dominion Council persuaded Ottawa to raise this amount to $1,000 if there were medical bills outstanding or if children were left in poverty. It was also possible for LPF branches to accept a case and then seek full or partial reimbursement from surviving families later. The unmistakable trend was towards ever-increasing inclusiveness.

In December 1954, P.C. 1954-1932 replaced P.C. 178, raising the maximum estate to $1,000 and recognizing a common-law spouse, "if publicly presented as the veteran's wife", as next-of-kin. (The wording assumed the veteran to be male.) As usual, G.S. Macfarlane had been behind this shift. On his retirement from DVA in 1955, the LPF granted him an honorary life membership. It was richly deserved, since he had worked on behalf of the Fund with such conviction and sense of commitment that at times his DVA colleagues must have thought that he was the LPF's representative in Ottawa!

In 1961, the federal government raised the waiver to $1,000 plus the cost of the funeral to the LPF – in effect a total of about $1,200. If the deceased was survived by a widow or children, then the allowable waiver was $1,500. Ottawa was recognizing that, if a widow was left with an estate exceeding $1,000 (even by a few dollars), she had to pay for the funeral. In this case her cash balance dropped to below $800 – an amount that the LPF considered barely sufficient to sustain a family. Also, the Fund had to consider remaining family debts, such as health care bills or back rent, and other variables, including the need to purchase clothing or basic furniture, before deciding whether or not to assume the costs of a funeral. In 1963, Ottawa further increased the maximum estate to $1,250.

In general, it was LPF policy to be generous and not unnecessarily frugal. Because of the need to consider all aspects of a situation, the onus was more than ever on the branches to determine the eligibility of each case and to recover costs, if possible, from estates larger than the allowable maximum. More discretion in the hands of individuals in the branches sometimes meant that uniformity was lost in application of the increasingly elastic LPF regulations. Branch secretary-treasurers were given wider interpretive powers. Their decisions to accept cases, while bound to a set of regulations and guidelines, were also based on common sense and humanitarian principles. This was as it should be.

Burying the Dead

The LPF averaged between 700 and 800 burials a year in the first decade following the Second World War. Surprisingly, from 1948 to 1953 British Columbia led the country in burials, before Ontario reclaimed that distinction. The Fund conducted about 20 funerals a year in the United States during the postwar period. Most burials continued to be of Great War veterans, although many Second World War veterans were already passing away in indigent circumstances. In 1952, the LPF buried an aged and destitute veteran of the 1885 Northwest Rebellion, one of Canada's last survivors of this campaign.

Canada's South African War veterans were also fast disappearing. The LPF buried 28 of them in the fiscal year ending in March 1952, and 15 the next year. In 1966-67, the Fund interred a mere five. Only a few survived the decade.

By the summer of 1955, the LPF had buried more than 20,000 men and women in North America (and a handful in Britain) and had spent over $2.3 million doing so. Almost all of these veterans were Canadian, with their proportion rising the more recent the war. (See Table 1.) Still, many of those from the South African War and the First World War were British-born veterans of Canadian service or British veterans who emigrated to Canada following their respective wars. Others, Canadian and British born, had served in several conflicts.

Table 1 Wars in which veterans buried by the LPF served, to summer 1955

First World War	18,200
Second World War	1615
South African War	312
Northwest Rebellion	42
Fenian Raids (1866–1871)	18
Egyptian Campaign (1882)	6
Korean War	5
Indian Mutiny (1857)	1
Zulu Wars (1870s)	1
Total	20,200

Others served in the Crimean War, on the Northwest Frontier of India, and in many other imperial wars scattered across the globe. Some of the decorations held by these men included a Victoria Cross (V.C.), at least one Distinguished Service Order (D.S.O.), two Officers (O.B.E.) and four Members (M.B.E.) of the Order of the British Empire, 11 Military Crosses (M.C.), two Distinguished Flying Crosses (D.F.C.), one Distinguished Flying Medal (D.F.M.), 21 Distinguished Conduct Medals (D.C.M.), 78 Military Medals (M.M.), and five French *Croix de Guerre*. Many other holders of such awards, including Victoria Crosses, would follow in the decades ahead.

To understand better exactly *who* the LPF interred in these years, we can look at a single year's burial profile. The breakdown of the 892 burials across Canada for the year ending March 31, 1959, is as follows: 572 were veterans of the First World War, 299 of the Second World War, 12 served in South Africa, and nine in Korea. Two-thirds of the total were Protestant, most of the remainder being Catholic, although there were five Jehovah Witnesses, two Jews, and one Druid. Only 16 had been officers, including seven from Britain. As was the case every year, the overwhelming majority came from the army, there being but 38 naval and 28 air force veterans. Most cases were of Canadians who had seen service in Canadian forces, although about 10 per cent were Britons having served with imperial forces, including one former Royal Marine. Commonwealth veterans included 12 South Africans, and a handful of Allied veterans included Americans, Poles, a Belgian, and a Russian. This was a typical LPF year.

At the May 1964 annual meeting, A.G. Edward suggested that in future the LPF's annual report not mention the religious denomination of those buried. The Fund was set up on non-religious principles, and reporting such information was not relevant to its operations. The Dominion Council accepted these arguments, and the practice was discontinued.

In the early 1960s, the LPF experienced a sharp rise in the need for its services. In fiscal year 1960-61, there were 983 burials, including 350 in Ontario, which experienced the largest increases of any branch in these years. Alberta surpassed Québec for third place, behind Ontario and British Columbia in the number of burials. The LPF exceeded the 25,000-burial mark in 1961, which meant that it had interred an average of 480 veterans annually. Also, DVA calculated that approximately 12,000 Canadian veterans would die that fiscal year, and it expected the annual figure to be more than double that amount by the end of the century.

In fiscal 1964-65, the LPF buried 427 First World War veterans – a decrease of almost 15 per cent from the previous year; their ranks were beginning to thin out. At the same time, the Fund interred 514 veterans from the Second World War – an increase of nine per cent; the era of the LPF's burying that generation had begun in earnest. The veterans of South Africa had nearly disappeared. Twelve Korean War veterans were buried that year – double the number of the previous year. These men, too, were reaching middle age. A new single-year burial record of 1,100 veterans was set in 1965-66 – about 60 per cent of them from the Second World War. The next fiscal year saw yet a new record: 1,177. In 1969, the Fund's 60th anniversary, total burials had reached over 34,000, of which more than 33,000 were in Canada, 750 in the United States, about 100 in Britain, and one in Australia. In September 1968, DVA reported there were at least 961,000 veterans living in Canada, of whom 121,000 were from the First World War and the remainder from the Second World War and the Korean War. In the years ahead, tens of thousands would be buried by the Last Post Fund.

Throughout the postwar years, the Field of Honour in Pointe Claire was the Fund's 'jewel in the crown'. Although the Québec branch did not inter as many veterans there as some other branches did in military sections of civil cemeteries, the Field remained the Fund's showpiece and the focal point for its commemorative activities. To April 1949, 1,600 burials had taken place at the Field of Honour.

But the cemetery required constant upkeep to ensure its reputation as one of Canada's most beautiful final resting places and the Québec branch had to allocate scarce funding for this purpose. It needed to install or repair drains; purchase lawn mowers, tools, and a vehicle for the groundskeepers; pay on-site personnel; eventually enlarge the cemetery and improve its infrastructure; and maintain the heating, plumbing, electricity, masonry, and stonework of the Gate of Remembrance – all of this at considerable expense. In early 1946, S.J. Smith, the Québec branch's secretary-treasurer, estimated these combined costs to be approximately $4,500 per annum. Already, by 1941, the cement at the Gate of Remembrance (built in 1937) was leaking. By 1953, serious deterioration had set in to the stone work, and in the mid-1960s costly renovations had to be made to ensure the structure's survival. In the postwar period the Field of Honour grew and developed considerably. By 1961, a series of paths and roads crisscrossed its territory bearing the names of famous individuals or battles in Canadian military history. The LPF also named roads in honour of Arthur Hair and Norman Holland.

The Field of Honour was expensive to maintain. Unless the volume of burials increased, and brought down the costs of individual interments, the Field would continue to run a significant deficit. Smith calculated that a minimum of 107 indigent burials per annum would provide an equilibrium, whereas the current average was only about 80. Numbers grew in the 1950s, but burial costs rose too. That same year, Holland spent $187 of his own money on the Field. As a non-profit organization, the LPF did not expect the Field to generate income, but the Fund's administrative burden would be eased the more self-supportive it became.

Between 1957 and 1965, there were 1,330 burials at the Field (660 indigents and 670 reservation burials) and a deficit of over $39,000 accumulated (equivalent to about $30 per burial). This figure does not include building or equipment depreciation. As a result, the actual financial loss per burial (including pre-paid cases) was closer to $36. (It would have been twice that amount if all burials had been of indigent cases.) The main reason for this shortfall was that DVA allowed the LPF to charge it no more than $82.50 per indigent burial in the Field. This was a ridiculously small amount. The LPF requested an increase to $122.50, still well below market costs in either Montreal or Toronto, for example, and less than the $130 charged for reserved burials in the Field of Honour. These latter burials, too, needed to rise in price considerably nearer to market rates. In 1966, DVA authorized the increase to $122.50, which greatly helped the Québec branch to pay for maintaining the Field.

Over the years, the weather damaged the LPF's four cannons at the Field of Honour. Their wheels, ball ammunition, and equipment boxes, and part of their support bases, which were made of wood, had fallen into disrepair and become "an eyesore", in the words of S.J. Smith. In 1947, 1950, and 1953, and at irregular intervals thereafter, the Montreal-area Royal Canadian Electrical and Mechanical Engineers (RCEME) and the Royal Canadian Ordnance Corps (RCOC) offered their expertise in refurbishing the 1875-vintage, British-cast guns. The repair work was undertaken with pleasure by the craftsmen of the RCEME and symbolized the Fund's continuing close co-operation and good relations with local military authorities. On occasion, the carriages were removed to the RCEME's Base Workshop at Longue Pointe. The fact that Major-General J.P.E. Bernatchez, C.B.E, D.S.O., who was GOC of Québec Command in the 1950s, took a personal interest in the project, facilitated and expedited the work. Bernatchez went on to become a vice-president of the Fund in the late 1960s and its president in the mid-1970s.

In March 1965, the LPF held a joint meeting of the Dominion and Québec directors (many present represented both bodies). DVA had approached the Fund with a request to inter in the Field of Honour, at DVA's cost, the department's approximately 150 annual burial cases in the Montreal area. DVA's plots in Mount Royal and Côte-des-Neiges cemeteries were nearly full. Was there sufficient space in the Field for long-term LPF *and* DVA needs? Nearby residential and industrial growth had left little room for expansion. The Fund feared that accepting this proposal would halve the projected 30-years' worth of remaining space for LPF interments. Still, the Dominion Council agreed to inter DVA cases at the Field.

The Fund also began exploring the possibility of acquiring more land from adjacent cemeteries. To November 1965, there had been 3,917 burials in the Field of Honour, of which 2,680, or slightly more than two-thirds, were indigent cases. In September 1966, the LPF calculated that there remained 6,000 burial spaces (at two interments per space). An average year's 200 burials would usually be equally divided between indigent cases and veterans' reservations. Adding the DVA cases meant approximately 350 burials a year, or about 18 years' of burials given space remaining. The directors of the Québec branch did not expect burials to increase dramatically, since Canada's welfare legislation would prevent at least some indigence among poorer veterans and their families.

The Field of Honour continued to be the focal point for the Fund's annual May 24 Decoration Day ceremonies. These grew in size throughout the 1950s, and the media accorded them considerable attention. The LPF estimated that normally between 3,000 and 4,000 people attended. Much work was necessary to make these solemn occasions successful. They also cost money. Norman Holland had usually helped out with his incomparable generosity. He exploited his contacts throughout the community to arrange for some free services in connection with these events. In July 1947, Holland wrote S.J. Smith (whose relations with Holland were rather cool): "I have been going to a very great deal of expense each year in order to see that everyone who does anything for us is looked after, and you may, or may not, know that is the reason we get so many favours from all sources as regards our ceremonies." That year alone Holland "looked after" 43 people and sent 104 gifts at his own expense to members of the guard of honour, the man who fired the rocket at the harbour ceremony, officiating clergy, members of the press, policemen, and many others.

Since 1930, most governors general, as patron-in-chief, honorary president, or later honorary patron of the LPF, have been a guest speaker at the annual ceremonies at the Field. The speeches themselves and the prominence of the speakers indicated the importance of these annual ceremonies for Canadian veterans and for the families and friends of those who did not return. The list of those agreeing to speak at the LPF ceremonies over the years reads like a veritable who's who of Canadian military and vice-regal history. In the 25 years following the end of the Second World War a procession of governors general, Québec lieutenant-governors, ministers of national defence, ministers of veterans' affairs, admirals, generals, air marshals, and many others in prominent positions in the Montreal area, the province of Québec, and across Canada have spoken at the Field.

In 1949, Field Marshal Viscount Alexander of Tunis, Canada's governor general, delivered the oration. "This Field of Honour is a noble and fitting place for heroes and warriors and a worthy tribute to them from a grateful country", stated Lord Alexander. "It is fitting that the final resting place of those warriors whom we honour today should be here beside the great St. Lawrence…for it was down this stream that many of them journeyed on their way to the wars and years later were borne back again on its waters to their homeland." He paid homage to all with whom he served in both world wars and told the crowd, as the king's representative, that His Majesty would be pleased that he was being represented at the ceremony. His 12-minute speech, delivered in English and French before a large crowd of some 3,000 veterans, military personnel, and civilians, was broadcast live by CBC radio and rebroadcast coast to coast later that evening, when more people would be at home to tune in. Montreal radio stations also broadcast the ceremony. Most May 24 ceremonies between 1945 and 1960 were considered of sufficient national significance to be broadcast on the radio, either nationally or locally.

In May 1951, Lieutenant-General Guy G. Simonds, Chief of Staff, Canadian Army, and perhaps Canada's finest field commander of the Second World War, paid tribute to those who had served their country and had passed away in the preceding year. With the Korean War raging, Simonds also reminded listeners that freedom had its costs and that Canadians must stand ever vigilant against threats to democracy.

In 1967, the LPF arranged for an RCAF helicopter to drop

Governor General Viscount Alexander of Tunis giving speech at the Field of Honour, May 24, 1949.

15,000 poppies across the Field of Honour during the ceremonies. Similar features had formed part of the ceremonies 45 years earlier at Fletcher's Field on Mount Royal. The poppies were then gathered by school children and placed on the graves, already decorated with small Canadian flags. This was apparently the first time a drop of poppies was made during such an event in Canada, it was a common feature of ceremonies at military cemeteries in Belgium and Holland. The following year, the number of poppies dropped was doubled.

Operations Across Canada and Beyond

In the 1950s and 1960s, LPF branches solidified their organizations and honed their operations. Relations between the branches and Dominion headquarters were harmonious, thanks in no small way to the efforts of Kathleen Cobbett. In 1955, she visited branches in western Canada and in California, and she was warmly welcomed everywhere she went. On her return, she offered Dominion Council a glowing report of the LPF's operations across the country. Her trip cemented ties between HQ and the branches. On a trip to the Atlantic provinces in 1957, Cobbett was similarly received with open arms. She efficiently straightened out some administrative problems in Prince Edward Island and Newfoundland related to the cost of headstones and spent only 60 per cent of her travel allowance. She was a treasurer who guarded the LPF's funds very carefully. In 1959, she again visited the western branches on a shoestring budget and still did not use all her allotment.

The only serious problem occurred in British Columbia in the early 1950s. That branch's audited reports were always late and generally inaccurate. Montreal HQ and even DVA were growing extremely annoyed at this perennial problem, apparently the result of lax administrative and accounting procedures. Indeed, following the resignation of the long-serving secretary-treasurer, the BC branch discovered to its horror that its burial register had not been properly maintained since 1927 – a period of more than 25 years! The new officer, R.V. Waters, immediately turned around a nearly disastrous situation.

A dispute with the Southern Alberta branch in Calgary caused quite a stir at Dominion headquarters. In 1951, Reverend Canon W.H. Morgan, the branch president, refused a burial case but asked for a final ruling from headquarters which, perhaps unexpectedly, accepted the case. Morgan angrily denounced the decision and resigned, wondering what the use was of branches and branch presidents. This response angered Norman Holland, who termed Morgan a Calgary "czar", who had been branch president too long anyway. But Morgan's association with the LPF was far from over. In 1953, the branch lacked official representation on the Dominion Council, and the two Alberta branches agreed to rotate a member between them every three years to serve on the council. Southern Alberta's first delegate was none other than Morgan. Despite the underlying hostility between Morgan and Holland, the minutes show Morgan to have been rather discreet during meetings. Still, relations between him and Holland remained cool.

In 1957, Calgary's Field of Honour in Burnsland Cemetery more than doubled in size with the acquisition of 3,000 new plots. This was just in time since the original plot already contained the remains of 2,800 veterans and only 50 grave sites remained. In the 1970s, a new plot was opened in Rocky View Cemetery, in the east end of the city,

Norman Holland casting wreath from Sir Hugh Allan, *during LPF's river ceremony in Montreal harbour, May 24, 1952. At left, Ruby Hair, daughter of Arthur Hair, prepares to release symbolic dove of peace.*

available also to spouses of ex-service people buried by the LPF, under a "new concept", which was in fact as old as the Fund itself.

Manitoba's branch suffered a setback in 1950 when most of its records, including its original charter, were lost in the great Winnipeg flood. To October 31, 1958, 2,368 LPF burials had taken place in Manitoba, of which 1,418 were in Brookside Cemetery in Winnipeg. Brookside contained over 5,000 military burials, and so LPF cases accounted for more than a quarter of all veterans buried there.

The Ontario branch was by far the largest and busiest. As of 1960, it had organized a system of 55 local representatives throughout the province, and it added more in the course of the decade. The provincial government assisted the branch with a grant of $1,000 annually.

The LPF was least busy in eastern Canada. One representative sat on Dominion Council for all three Maritime provinces, each of which was served by a local representative. In the fiscal year 1960-61, there were only 30 burials in New Brunswick, 21 in Nova Scotia, and nine in Prince Edward Island, for an average of only about one a

photo Alex Bialosh

Brookside Cemetery, Winnipeg, 1999. Last Post Fund burial markers, flush with the ground, visible in right foreground.

week for the whole region. This volume did not justify the establishment of individual branches for these provinces, and not even a single branch for the Maritimes as a whole. Nevertheless, in New Brunswick, the soldiers' burial plot at Fernhill was becoming full. In 1959, a 600-plot military section was opened in Cedar Hill Cemetery, overlooking the Bay of Fundy near Saint John. In 1967, A.G. Edward visited the LPF's eastern operations and found everything in order.

Following the admission of Newfoundland into Confederation on March 31, 1949, a group of proposed trustees in St. John's applied to the Dominion Council to establish a branch of the Fund. The application was accepted on January 5, 1950, and the council sent $500 for an initial imprest fund. The first president of the branch was Major F.W. Marshall, M.B.E. In May 1950, Holland successfully requested the new province's lieutenant-governor to extend his patronage to the Fund, as all his counterparts in Canada had done. The new trustees were all members of the Great War Veterans' Association in Newfoundland and subsequently of its successor, the Canadian Legion. D.E. Macintyre, in welcoming the Newfoundlanders, also reminded them that "the LPF is a separate and independent Organization and has no affiliation with the Canadian Legion or any other Veterans' Associations, although we work in close harmony with all Veterans' Associations." He mentioned this because of the common perception in eastern Canada that the Canadian Legion played a role in determining the affairs of the LPF.

The Dominion Council was expanded from 15 to 17 members: seven from Québec, one each from the remaining nine provinces, and one representative from DVA. The Newfoundland branch eventually appointed Marshall to the council in 1953.

At about the same time, the LPF expanded its operations in California. In 1948, the Canadian Legion of Northern California initiated a fund-raising campaign for the burial of indigent Commonwealth veterans. The region was quite a distance from Los Angeles, where an LPF branch operated out of the local Canadian Legion branch, and so the Northern California Legion purchased a plot of land at Greenlawn Memorial Park in Colma. At the end of that year, this Legion branch applied for admission to the LPF. The Dominion Council issued the sub-charter effective January 1, 1949, and immediately dispatched $500 for an imprest account.

Without delay, the new branch removed the bodies of 33 Canadian veterans from local pauper burial grounds and placed them in LPF graves in Greenlawn. Each grave was duly marked with a bronze plaque like those formerly used by the LPF in Canada. Two flagpoles were raised in 1949, and in 1950 a memorial in the cemetery was dedicated in the presence of D.E. Macintyre. The branch offered grave sites for pre-purchase at reduced costs to any former serving member of Commonwealth forces, whether indigent or not. By 1972, there were some 200 Canadian veterans buried in the branch's plot. Most of the work of this branch was carried out through the generosity of the LPF's supporters in California, many of whom were members of the Canadian Legion. In the 1970s, the branch's president was one Douglas G. Hair, son of Arthur.

"To you from failing hands…"

In the twenty years following the death of Arthur Hair in 1947, most of the Last Post Fund's longest-serving members across Canada retired or passed away. Some among them had achieved national stature, and their association with the LPF was but one of their many accomplishments. With them went the personal connections to the Fund's formative years. The LPF's sense of its own history began to fade, even though the organization renewed itself with people of high calibre who shared the same sense of purpose.

On July 6, 1950, Dr. W.H. Atherton, M.B.E., K.S.G., Ph.D., died at the age of 82. A member of the LPF since 1910, he had served as its first national president in the early 1920s. For over 40 years, Atherton, a scholar and historian, contributed to community, reform, and charitable causes in the Montreal area. The next month, on August 30, 1950, Mrs. A.H.D. Hair (née Janet McIntyre), 82, was buried with her husband in the Field of Honour. Lucien C. Vallée, the last member still alive from the inaugural meeting in April 1909, but who had not been active with the Fund for a number of years, died several years later. Major Louis Gosselin, an LPF honorary legal counsel since the First World War, passed away June 18, 1954.

After a brief illness Norman Holland died at the age of 75 on February 4, 1956, less than one year after he resigned as president of the Fund. His funeral was attended by 15 top-ranking members of the LPF, and every branch sent a floral tribute. Paul Earl stated at the May 1956 annual meeting that "the unselfish devotion to the Fund of this great man will never be forgotten". With typical generosity, Holland left a $5000 bequest to the Québec branch for the Field of Honour Endowment Fund.

Lieutenant-Colonel G.S. Macfarlane, for many years DVA's representative on Dominion Council, died July 25, 1957. Kathleen Cobbett remarked that his expertise and presence on the council had yielded "untold benefit" to the Fund. After Macfarlane left, most DVA representatives to the council changed over rapidly, often year to year, and much of the sense of continuity, personal collaboration, and commitment seemed lost. In 1958, A.J. Dixon retired from DVA. Working with the Department of Pensions and National Health and later with DVA, he had been involved with the LPF for 30 years. He was a key behind-the-scenes player in helping the LPF obtain greater burial and administrative funding from Ottawa.

Many stalwarts in the branches also passed away at this time. In 1957, death took Howard Stutchbury, an original member of the LPF's Alberta organization. He devoted his life and career to soldiers' civil re-establishment and to the ideals of the LPF. In the year before the 1960 annual meeting, Newfoundland's Major F.W. Marshall passed away. On July 30, 1960, Lieutenant-Colonel H. St. J. Montizambert, long the president and inspiration of the BC branch, died. The Saskatchewan branch lost much of its personal connection with the past in this period. In 1959, W.D. Dewar retired as secretary-treasurer, and he died the next year; he had served the LPF for 25 years. On April 26, 1961, James S. Woods, long-serving Dominion Council representative from that province, also died.

The year 1963 struck several hard blows to Dominion Headquarters. On May 16, Judge Gerald Almond died. He had served the Fund since 1938 as a legal counsel. His demise ended more than 50 years' affiliation between the LPF and the Almond family. Brigadier-General Walter Leggat, D.S.O., Q.C., honorary legal counsel for the Québec branch, joined Lieutenant-Commander E. James Lattimer, as worthy successors to Almond. Less than two weeks after Almond's death, Commodore Paul Earl died. His tenure with the Fund was not as long as that of some of his colleagues, but it was one filled with hard work and devotion. He succeeded Holland as president – a tough act to follow – and served two years in that position, ensuring a smooth succession. He was a minister in the Québec cabinet at the time of his death. Finally, Stuart Rolland, president of the LPF from 1957 to 1963, died in October 1963.

More changes came in 1964. That year both John H. Molson and Fred Thom resigned from the LPF. Molson had more than 30 years' service with the Fund, while Thom had joined in February 1910, giving him nearly 55 years of service as a member, director, and head of various committees, including the Grounds Committee. His length of service remains an unofficial "record" with the LPF. Thom died in February 1966. Also in 1964, 92-year-old Major-General John H. Gunn, who had been with the LPF in Ontario since 1935, and had been the first vice-president of the Fund for many years, lay immobilized in a Toronto hospital. It was obvious that he would never again take up any LPF duties. With the other vice-president, Major R.H. Tupper, located in Vancouver, it was imperative to find a replacement for Gunn closer to Montreal. In early 1965, the Québec branch's Major-General J.P.E. Bernatchez agreed to serve as first vice-president, replacing Gunn, who was named an honorary vice-president. Bernatchez was a Second World War brigade commander who had served in the Italian campaign. Gunn passed away in May 1966.

Air Vice-Marshal Clifford M. McEwen died August 6, 1967. He was 69. Along with Arthur Currie, McEwen was one of the most famous Canadian military figures to serve the Fund. He had been a fighter 'ace' of the First World War, scoring 24 kills on the Italian front with the Royal Flying Corps. During the Second World War, he commanded the RCAF's No. 6 Bomber Group. From 1959 to 1961, he was a director of Trans-Canada Airlines (now Air Canada). Although he died in Toronto, his remains were transported to Montreal, and he was buried in the Directors' Circle at the Field of Honour. In the same year, long-time director, Lieutenant Colonel Rolland Bibeau, formerly of the *Régiment de Maisonneuve*, was also interred in the Directors' Circle.

Other changes affected the LPF in these postwar decades. In 1954, the LPF moved to new offices in the Post Office Building, a federal government facility, at 1254 Bishop. This satisfactory move was arranged by Lord Shaughnessy, a prominent member of the Québec branch and later its president. (Shaughnessy, Canadian born and raised, was a British peer, the 3rd Baron Shaughnessy of Montreal and Ashford, County Limerick. His grandfather had been the third president of the Canadian Pacific Railway.) In 1963, Ottawa decided that the Fund, not being a department of the government, should start paying rent of $100 a month. The order-in-council governing the LPF's administrative budget was promptly amended to increase the amount from $15,000 to $16,500 per year, so that the LPF in effect gained $300 a year by being a tenant of the federal government.

In May 1964, Kathleen Garrett (née Cobbett) and C.M. McEwen were awarded honorary life memberships. Arthur Hair's two daughters, Jessie and Ruby, received the same honours at this time as did subsequently John Molson and Fred Thom. All were given framed certificates to this effect.

By the late 1960s, there were many new faces at the LPF and a fairly high turn-over among the directors. More and more French Canadians were attracted to executive positions in the Québec branch and also as directors of the national organization. Accordingly, in 1969, after 60 years of existence in Montreal, the Fund officially began the search for a French translation of "Last Post Fund". This quest was destined to remain curiously unsuccessful for the better part of a decade.

A weekend of ceremonies marked the LPF's 60th (Diamond Jubilee) anniversary in 1969. On May 23, Miss Ruby Hair released a symbolic dove at the river ceremony. The next day a Round Table Conference of LPF delegates convened at the Ritz-Carlton Hotel to discuss administrative procedures and accounting practices. There followed an unusually well-attended annual meeting with strong delegations present from branches across Canada, and four officials from DVA. That evening, "as an expression of the Government's appreciation of the dedicated efforts of all who have helped achieve the Fund's objectives", J.-E. Dubé, minister of veterans affairs hosted a dinner for the officers and supporters of the LPF at the Windsor Hotel. Ruby Hair was at the head table. On May 25, Governor General Roland Michener was the invited speaker at the Field of Honour ceremonies. The attendance of delegates from across Canada gave the event a strongly national flavour. Also present were a 100-person honour guard from the *5e Groupement de combat*, Black Watch pipers, and the Royal Canadian Artillery band. Michener held a reception for the LPF at the Ritz-Carlton Hotel that evening.

The LPF used the anniversary year to publicize its activities. Commemorative brochures outlined the benefits provided by the LPF and briefly explained its history. The Ontario branch, too, made special efforts during a five-week publicity campaign organized by Stan G. Olsen, its excellent secretary-treasurer, who prepared an article that described the Fund and distributed it widely to Ontario's press and media, churches, Royal Canadian Legion branches, police departments, social service organizations, hospitals, nursing homes, and funeral homes. He asked Ontario's local representatives to find some means of publicizing the Fund in their communities. The campaign ended very deliberately on November 11 – a date when so many people think of war and of veterans. The Ontario branch found that, despite a well-organized network of 65 local representatives throughout the province, "a lot of people have never heard of us", as Olsen phrased it. Accordingly, "quite a few widows and other indigent next-of-kin saddle themselves unnecessarily with expensive funerals, and go into debt to pay for them, instead of applying to the Last Post Fund." This must have been a sentiment shared by all branches of the LPF.

In 1969, in one of the Fund's final acts of the decade, and in accordance with federal government practice, the LPF dropped the word "Dominion" from the title of its executive body, henceforth to be known simply as the "National Council". The use of the word "Dominion" was being phased out by the federal government, corporate entities, business enterprises, the press, and even by the general public. (The Royal Canadian Legion, however, continued to term its headquarters the "Dominion Command".) The 1970 LPF annual meeting formalized this decision.

The next three decades would produce the greatest workloads ever for the Last Post Fund and also the greatest changes.

7

TOWARDS THE TWENTY-FIRST CENTURY, 1970–1999

I have completed a memorial more lasting than brass.

HORACE

The Last Post Fund has changed enormously in the last 30 years, especially during the last decade. It will be a restructured and reorganized Fund that enters the twenty-first century, one which has taken on a vastly increased number of cases and has become the sole agency for burial of veterans in Canada. And yet throughout its 90-year existence the LPF's guiding principle has continued unchanged: it has never been a charity and has always provided a service that the veterans themselves earned.

Given altered national and demographic circumstances, not to mention shifting government priorities and considerable self-examination, the Fund's organization and operations have evolved considerably from those established in 1909. The LPF's operating methods, its mandate and responsibilities, and even its independence of action have changed. The Fund's rather unique position for decades as a corporation undertaking benevolent work with government subsidy (and some government regulation) gave way in the 1990s to an LPF more or less merged, as a visibly separate entity, with Veterans Affairs Canada (VAC). (This new "applied title" for the Department of Veterans Affairs came into use in the 1980s as a result of Ottawa's Federal Identity Program, which made mandatory the use of the word "Canada" to describe government departments. Federal statutes continue to use "Department of Veterans Affairs".)

The face of Canada's veteran community was also changing. Despite contributing some combat forces to the Gulf War in 1991 and to NATO operations against Serbia in 1999, Canada has not been involved in sustained military operations since the Korean War. As the twentieth century gives way to the twenty-first, Canada's veteran population is thinning out rapidly. Roughly 450,000 veterans will enter the new millennium, and their mortality rate will increase exponentially. The need for the services of the Fund will probably rise as dramatically. Then, by the end of the first decade of the new century, the need will decline. The LPF will face new choices and new challenges.

Old Policy, Same Practice

Since its inception, the LPF has carried out its principal function of burying Canadian veterans in a dignified manner, especially those fallen on hard times. In at least one respect, the last three decades of the twentieth century were no different than the previous six for the LPF: money was scarce and expenses were high.

In 1972, the LPF complained to DVA that Ottawa's maximum approved burial rate of $315 for indigent veterans was terribly inadequate. After all, legislation allowed $360 for welfare-funded burials, and, not surprisingly, funeral home directors across Canada preferred to treat deceased indigent veterans as welfare cases rather than as LPF burials. This long-lasting inconsistency was embarrassing to the Fund and shameful to the veterans. Finally, in response to several years of rampant inflation in Canada, in November 1975 DVA raised allowable LPF funeral expenses to $500 – although Ottawa also increased maximum costs of welfare burials to $650! Soon the increments occurred more quickly and in greater amounts. In January 1983, permissible funeral expenses rose to $1,000 and they reached $2,000 by 1988. Notwithstanding this increase, at the 74th annual meeting in May 1983, a frustrated James Lattimer, then national president of the Fund, noted that "the funeral directors never seem to be satisfied." It was a sentiment shared by all his predecessors. In the 1920s, Sir Arthur Currie had complained about the rapacious and even unpatriotic ways of some Canadian undertakers. Nevertheless, the issue was not about funeral directors' sense of patriotism. Though perhaps not always as flexible as the LPF would have liked, they were business people and ensuring the success of their businesses constituted their prime motivation. Some, in fact, undertook LPF burials at a loss. The root of the problem lay elsewhere.

In the 1980s, the LPF improved its burial casket standards, and DVA assured the Fund that its funerals would henceforth receive the same level of service as those granted deceased members of the RCMP or the armed forces. The LPF had lobbied very hard for this measure of equality, which seemed an inordinately long time in coming. In 1989, the allowable estate exemption climbed to $19,780 and was linked to rises in the cost-of-living index.

In early 1975, total LPF burials since 1909 broke the 40,000 barrier. In the next two decades, the LPF recorded a spectacular increase in its caseload, with total burials reaching 60,000 in 1990 and over 80,000 by 1994. The figures could easily have been higher but for the death benefit associated with the Canada Pension Plan, which helped many otherwise impoverished veterans and their families obtain dignified burial services without recourse to the LPF. After 85 years of public service, the LPF had buried over 78,000 veterans in Canada, 1,400 in the United States, nearly 300 in Britain, and a handful in other countries including Australia, Greece, and Spain. Over 260 of these veterans were women.

Firing party from Montreal's Naval Reserve unit, HMCS Donnacona, at river ceremony, June 1999.

Although burials declined somewhat in the period 1978-1982, new marks were set routinely during the 1980s and 1990s regarding the number of cases per annum, percentage increases from year to year, and the amount spent by the LPF in carrying out its appointed tasks. The huge increases were the result in large part of advancing veteran mortality rates. By 1991, the average Canadian male veteran was 73 years old. Moreover, DVA transferred a growing proportion of its cases to the Fund. This included the burials of most veterans dying while on strength of DVA hospitals and medical facilities or in receipt of a disability pension. The LPF began to assume a greater role in total veterans' burials in Canada. In 1991-92, for example, it carried out 5,000 of 8,000 VAC funerals. Another contributing factor was the establishment of an LPF branch in the Maritimes, which resulted in a greatly increased caseload there. The Fund's spending on funerals and burial services topped $1 million a year for the first time in the fiscal year 1978-1979. Funeral costs spiralled upward in the 1980s, and LPF annual burial expenditures rose from $2.5 million in 1987 to over $20 million in 1993.

This rapid growth led more and more Canadian families into contact with the Fund. The LPF had become important in the lives of tens of thousands of bereaved Canadians. An article appearing in the Hamilton *Spectator* in July 1991 showed just how much the Last Post Fund meant to those whom it assisted. In March 1991, Ross Thompson, a former member of the Royal Hamilton Light Infantry during the Second World War, passed away without any insurance. In order to care for him during his illness, his wife, Ava, had given up her job. When he died, she was obliged to cope not only with the pain of her bereavement but also with the difficult financial truth that she was unable to pay for his burial. VAC put her into contact with the LPF. "I think they're wonderful", she is quoted as saying. "I don't know what I would have done without them". Another Hamilton widow, Mary Wood, noted that the LPF "helped me out tremendously because I was on my own and trying to keep my home". Mrs. Wood went on: "Not very many widows know about [the LPF], especially the ones that really need it."

The Fund's determination to mark the grave sites of Canada's veterans, wherever these might be found, has taken its familiar grave marker to some exotic locations. In the early 1980s, the LPF marked one Canadian naval veteran's grave in Guyana apparently by "shipping a marker by dugout canoe deep into the Amazon", according to Nick Auf der Maur, then a columnist with the Montreal *Gazette*. In 1984, the LPF erected a marker in Zimbabwe. The LPF's reach had become world-wide. In 1996, the LPF added in its letters patent the responsibility to mark any veterans' graves, or those of other service-eligible persons, that had gone unmarked in the previous five years. The LPF had been doing this from its earliest days, as finances permitted. Ottawa provided it with $50,000 per annum for this purpose. By 1998, over 300 hitherto unmarked graves across Canada had been marked, including one in Thunder Bay which had been without a proper marker since the 1940s.

Sometimes LPF directors went to extraordinary lengths to arrange for the dignified interment of a veteran. In 1994, the Manitoba branch had arranged to cover the costs of a veteran's burial, but, to the Fund's chagrin, the designated funeral home handled the burial not as an LPF case, but as a welfare case, which meant a pauper's grave without a marker. The Manitoba branch refused to accept this, and circumstances dictated immediate action. The branch had the man's remains exhumed and laid to rest in the veterans' section of Brookside Cemetery. An immense amount of legal wrangling and administrative difficulty resulted, but a principled adherence to the very cause for which the LPF was founded inspired the Manitoba branch directors. Most of them were present at the final burial service, as were representatives of the Royal Canadian Legion. The deceased veteran's son, at the time serving a term in a federal penitentiary, attended the ceremony – escorted by a prison guard!

The Field of Honour in Pointe Claire was the scene of much activity during this period. By the early 1970s, more than 250 burials took place there annually. As veterans' mortality accelerated, and demands for the LPF's services grew, space limitations at the Field became a concern for the Québec branch. In early 1978, the LPF estimated that only 2,573 graves remained in the Field which, with two burials per grave, would allow for a maximum of 5,146 burials. At such a rate, the Field would be full in about 12 years. A solution to this impending problem had to be found.

Fortunately, cremation became a growing funerary practice in the postwar period. It was cheaper and required less burial space; in many cases, the ashes of the deceased were not actually buried, but either retained or scattered by surviving family members. In 1977, to save space and to satisfy the wishes of many of those seeking the services of the Fund, the Québec branch set aside a small section of the Field for cremation burials. This provided for five times as many burial sites as would have been possible with conventional interments in an equivalent area and extended the life of the Field by over four years. Cremations became a large part of the answer to the LPF's space problem. The Fund modified its regulations on expenses to make allowances for a cremation service, a cremation urn, and the rental of a casket for public viewing.

Financing for the Field came mostly from donations and from income derived from pre-sales of grave sites, which grew enormously in number. Nevertheless, the Field often paid for itself in the early 1970s, even registering a surplus of $18,000 in 1974. But, before the decade was out, this situation was completely reversed. By 1978, the Field was absorbing an annual administrative budget of $20,000 and was running an annual deficit of $4,000 which, under inflationary circumstances, the branch directors felt was an excellent result. Expenditures for salaries and burials rose sharply during the 1980s; the Field needed more money.

Major benefactors came to the aid of the LPF. In 1973, Bruce Brown, a long-time director of the Fund passed away. He bequeathed $25,000 to the LPF for improvements to the Field of Honour. Brown wanted his money used to build a caretaker's residence and to incorporate a memorial chapel in the Gate of Remembrance. Thanks to his generosity, in 1975 the LPF erected a modest house for the superintendent and remodelled the Gate of Remembrance to include an office and a chapel which was dedicated in June 1975. In 1990 and 1991, the estates of Henry E. McKeen and his wife, Marguerite, made donations of $100,000 and $80,000, respectively, to the Fund. Henry McKeen was a veteran of the First World War; he died in 1977, and his wife, in 1989. The money came as a welcome surprise to the directors of the LPF, none of whom had known of the McKeen family. Thanks to this thoughtful donation, the Fund was able to make inquiries about the purchase of additional land to enlarge the Field – an urgent matter.

In 1994, following complex and lengthy negotiations, the LPF purchased two and one-half acres of undeveloped land from the Eternal Gardens, a cemetery adjoining the Field. This brought the Field's total area to 14.5 acres. The Québec branch christened this 100,000-square-foot acquisition the 'Peace Section'. Costs amounted to $100,000, not including landscaping and road development. The purchase of this land caused a minor protest from nearby homeowners who felt that the transaction had violated a provincial law limiting burials to within 40 metres of residences. However, the land had been zoned for burial purposes in 1955, long before the residential zones came into being. The provincial authorities responsible for the environment dismissed the citizens' complaints. The addition of this land came just in time: after more than 15,000 burials at the Field since its opening in 1930, there were virtually no casket spaces left, although several years' worth of cremation burial plots remained.

The land was expensive enough on its own, but the Québec branch feared that the cost of clearing and developing it would be prohibitive. In 1993, Colonel Douglas Briscoe, base commander in Montreal, and a director of the LPF's Québec branch, proposed that the clearing and levelling of the land might be an ideal militia training exercise. Francis Lamarre, the Field's superintendent and a chief warrant officer in 3 Field Engineer Regiment, a militia unit in Montreal, expressed confidence that his unit could accomplish the task and, what is more, benefit professionally from the experience. Members of the regiment took up the task in the autumn of 1994, under the command of Lieutenant-Colonel Jean-Luc Fournier. The military engineers acted on the professional advice of landscapers, designers, and architects, who worked on a voluntary basis, and of experts employed by the municipalities of Beaconsfield and Pointe Claire. Lamarre, who obviously knew the site intimately, co-ordinated and managed the enormous project, which involved the use of heavy equipment brought from Canadian Forces Base Valcartier. The job was completed in May 1995 and the results were excellent. As so often in the history of the LPF, close co-operation between the Canadian Forces and the Fund had overcome what might have been a thorny problem.

Maintenance and renovations at the Field had always constituted a major expense. At roughly ten-year intervals beginning in the mid-1970s, the Québec branch made substantial improvements to the site. In 1985, the LPF announced major plans to renovate the Field and purchase new and sorely needed equipment. The naturally shifting ground had begun to play havoc with the alignment of the tomb-stones. A federal grant of $94,000 allowed the Fund to employ 14 people for three months to level the worst-affected areas. Although only about half the Field was attended to, this was an impressive start. In 1994, the Québec branch's hard-working Cemetery Development Committee, overseen by Colonel Pierre Richard, the branch's vice-president and honorary treasurer, organized capital projects and notable improvements to the Field. By 1999, total interments at the Last Post Fund's Field of Honour exceeded 17,000.

Since LPF branches increasingly viewed the Field of Honour as representing the Fund on a national scale, not merely as the purview of the Québec branch, others in the LPF were anxious to help with its development. In 1990, the BC branch gave the Québec branch $1,000 towards the upkeep of the Field. The Ontario branch followed with a generous cash infusion of $10,000. In 1992, the British Columbia branch provided a further $2,000, and Southern Alberta chipped in with $1,000. In 1997, the Saskatchewan branch made two $1,000 donations and the by-then amalgamated Alberta branch gave another $5000. This was an outstanding show of internal support for Canada's only dedicated military cemetery.

Despite increased demands for burial space in the Field and major improvements to the site, by the early 1970s public interest in the cemetery was declining. The media no longer considered the annual commemorative ceremonies particularly newsworthy. The public profile of the Fund itself began to wane, even as its role in Canadian veteran burials was expanding. The work more than ever went on in quiet anonymity. Nevertheless, in June 1986 about 500 people attended the commemorative ceremony at the Field. As always a distinguished speaker was present – Major-General J.A.G. de Chastelain, deputy commander, Mobile Command. Twenty-three Legion branches were represented, while pipers from the Black Watch and an honour guard from Canadian Forces Base Montreal added solemnity to the proceedings.

Some well-known Canadians were interred in the Field during the 1980s, among them Major-General J.P.E. Bernatchez, a former president of the Fund, who was buried next to the Cross of Sacrifice in 1983; Clarence Campbell, former long-time president of the

National Hockey League, interred in 1984; and Thomas Harold Beament, a distinguished Canadian war artist, who died in 1984.

Ottawa considered the LPF's cemetery a most appropriate location to honour all of Canada's war dead. In May 1987, DVA erected at de Salaberry Circle in the Field a granite monument with a bronze plaque commemorating those Canadians who served and died in Canada's major wars this century: the two world wars, and the Korean War.

On September 11, 1997, the Last Post Fund officially inaugurated the new section of the Field of Honour purchased in 1994. It dedicated a monument in the circular Peace Garden, which Minister of Veterans Affairs Fred Mifflin unveiled. Distinguished guests included Pierre Richard, by then president of the Québec branch, and Harvey Bishop, national president of the Fund. The Peace Monument was erected through the financial assistance of VAC, the Royal Canadian Legion's Québec Command, the Montreal Division of the Canadian Corps of Commissionaires, and the ABN-AMRO Bank of Canada. The involvement of this last-named group followed a 1995 conversa-

Peace Monument in new section of the Field of Honour, unveiled September 1997. From left: Fred Mifflin, minister of veterans affairs; Jean Bernard, designer of monument; Brigadier-General J. Richard Genin, vice-president of LPF's Québec branch; and Colonel Pierre Richard, president of Québec branch.

Department of National Defence

tion in the Dutch town of Apeldoorn between Lieutenant-General
Gilles Turcot, a former president of the LPF, and the president of
ABN-AMRO. Turcot, who commanded the *Royal 22e Régiment* during the campaign, was attending the 50th anniversary ceremonies held
to mark the liberation of the Netherlands. Upon learning from Turcot
of the LPF's plans to erect a Peace Monument, and as a symbol of his
gratitude for Canada's role in liberating his country, the bank president arranged for ABN-AMRO to financially assist the project. The
monument is a simple block of granite with the words "Paix – Peace"

*Aerial view of the Field of Honour, 1997. D'Urban Monument in
foreground, de Salaberry Circle at top.*

inscribed on it. Perched atop the memorial is a fibre-glass dove with a laurel leaf in its beak, also meant to symbolize peace. The monument was designed by Jean Bernard, an accomplished artist and a Second World War veteran of the RCAF. Fittingly, the path leading to the monument became McKeen Roadway, after the benefactors who made purchase of the land possible.

Only two weeks later, the LPF rededicated the old St-Helen's Island Cemetery which it had restored in keeping with its tradition of caring for military burial grounds. The virtually forgotten cemetery, which closed in 1869, contained the remains of about 100 soldiers of Montreal's British garrison and members of their families. The LPF had interested itself in this historic site since the 1920s, but it had fallen on hard times. In the mid-1990s, Brigadier-General J. Richard Genin, the Québec branch's vice-president, implemented a project to restore the site. The rededication ceremony took place under the auspices of the Fund, on September 30, 1997, with the

Rededication of St. Helen's Island Memorial and Cemetery, September 30, 1997. Left: Brigadier-General J. Richard Genin; right: Robert Côté, member of Montreal municipal council, representing the mayor.

financial support of the City of Montreal and the co-operation and technical assistance of the David M. Stewart Museum. The Royal Canadian Legion laid a wreath during the ceremony as did Pierre Richard. Representatives of the LPF unveiled an historical marker and the restored memorial plaques listing those interred there. The remaining headstones had been repaired, and the site was more presentable than it had been for decades.

During the Decoration Day ceremony at the Field of Honour in June 1998, a spectacular stained glass memorial window was unveiled in the Gate of Remembrance. This moving artwork, the creation of Montreal artist Nicole Gascon, depicts a Canadian soldier of the First World War with his head reverently bowed before the grave site of a fallen comrade. The window was a generous donation to the Fund by the Dominion Command of the Royal Canadian Legion, and symbolizes the cementing of their relationship in the 1990s. In December 1999, the LPF presented Veterans Affairs Canada with a framed copy of the window for display at its headquarters in Charlottetown.

Administration: the 1970s and 1980s

In 1971, the Last Post Fund's national headquarters and Québec branch were amalgamated and moved into a federal government building located at 685 Cathcart in downtown Montreal. This convenient and comfortable new location has proved the most lasting home in the Fund's history, and it is from here that the organization's headquarters ushered in the new millennium.

During the last decades of the twentieth century, the LPF underwent frequent changes in leadership. The president of the LPF, Senator Romuald Bourque, died August 14, 1974, at the age of 84. He had led the Fund for 12 years. This would be the last time a president served so long in office. Bourque's death signalled the start of a regular rotation of LPF national presidents. For the next 25 years, the leader changed on average every two years. Major-General J.P.E. Bernatchez replaced Bourque; Judge J. Redmond Roche became first vice-president, and Canon A.W. Wilcox second vice-president. Bernatchez was another high-profile president for the Fund. He had commanded the *Royal 22e Régiment* in action in Sicily and Italy before being promoted brigadier-general in 1944. He had continued to serve with distinction in the postwar army.

In the 1970s, the directors of the LPF finally settled one nagging and even embarrassing issue: the official translation of "Last Post Fund". The growing number of prominent French-speaking directors from Québec made the LPF's unilingual appearance incongruous. Yet, for reasons difficult to explain, finding a suitable French translation seemed difficult. The Fund struggled with the question throughout 1970 and 1971. Despite having studied the matter, both Bernatchez and Roche failed to suggest appropriate translations. Shockingly, by 1975, no progress had been made. In despair, Roche simply claimed that the phrase "Last Post Fund" defied translation. Some of the better, though by no means adequate, translations that he and others brought forward included: "*Le Dernier Appel*" and "*Sonnerie aux morts*". Very sensibly, a decision was deferred, and a committee was struck to investigate this resistant conundrum.

Finally, in 1975 Governor General Jules Léger requested that the LPF select a French translation as soon as possible. Accordingly, the National Council advanced and seemingly accepted the phrase "*Fonds du Souvenir*". The matter appeared settled. But three years later, in an astonishing twist, the council took up the issue yet again. Gordon Lawrence, DVA's representative formally requested that the LPF, a federally financed institution, select a French translation. The lip-service of 1975 had never led to the official use of "*Fonds du Souvenir*". Once again, three selections were offered: "*Le Fonds Arthur Hair*", "*Le Fonds de Secours du Souvenir*", and "*Le Fonds du Souvenir*". The choice was obvious, and "*Le Fonds du Souvenir*" was officially adopted and ratified at the annual meeting on May 25, 1978. This process had taken more than a decade, and the National Council as a whole appears not to have taken the issue very seriously.

Bernatchez's tenure as leader was brief; he resigned in October 1975 for "personal reasons". There was probably more to it than that. Bernatchez was a dynamic, but impatient man, and a careful reading of relevant correspondence and minutes reveals a strained working relationship between him and the secretary-treasurer, A.G. Edward. In fact, Bernatchez was dissatisfied with Edward's work and hoped to induce him to retire. The two men also disagreed on major issues. For example, Bernatchez continuously sought to heighten the LPF's presence in the Maritimes, where he hoped to establish a branch. Edward resisted this course of action. In any event, Bernatchez had had enough of the presidency and, while remaining an influential director on the National Council, yielded the leadership to Reverend Canon Arthur W. Wilcox, the second vice-president from Calgary.

Wilcox was president of the Southern Alberta branch from 1965 to 1972 and represented Alberta on the LPF's council from 1965 to 1988. The Winnipeg-born Wilcox, the Fund's first non-Québec-based president, was a Second World War veteran of the RCAF and had been ordained a minister in 1947. Wilcox was the first clergyman since John Almond to head the Fund.

Being in Calgary presented Wilcox with some serious disadvantages as president. He admitted to feeling "out of touch" and "far removed from the HQ scene". Still, he expressed confidence that affairs were being expertly handled by Roche, other officers, and the small staff in Montreal. Roche was actually administering the LPF, with Wilcox exercising only limited control – a testament to Roche's outstanding abilities, which Wilcox acknowledged. At the LPF's 68th annual meeting in May 1977, Wilcox made known his preference that "future presidents should be chosen on a national basis". Yet, only a year later, when he resigned the presidency, he emphasized that the leader should be "nearer to the action".

At a directors' meeting held at the United Services Club in Montreal on May 25, 1977, Wilcox stated: "I speak from experience when I say that the work you are doing on behalf of deceased veterans and their families is valued above measure. When a father is buried with solemnity and dignity a family...is fortified by the precious memories they have of their loved one. One has but to...conduct the burial service for one of these veterans, as I have done, to realize just how worthwhile our work is." Others obviously agreed. At the 69th annual meeting in 1978, Wilcox announced that seven members of the Fund had been awarded the Queen's Jubilee Medal for meritorious national service: Lieutenant-Colonel J.P. Duhaime, A.G. Edward, Lieutenant-Commander E.J. Lattimer, Gustave LeDroit, Brigadier-General W.C. Leggat, Frank Starr, and Wilcox himself.

In 1978, Brigadier-General James A. de Lalanne replaced Wilcox as president. A chartered accountant and veteran of both world wars, he had long been heavily involved in an executive capacity with both the LPF and the Legion. In 1972, he was named national treasurer of the Legion, and the following year became vice-president of the Québec branch of the LPF, and president in 1976.

Born in Montreal in 1897, de Lalanne had served with the Princess Patricia's Canadian Light Infantry during the First World War, rising from private to captain. He was wounded three times and won the Military Cross and Bar. The grateful village of Vimy, France, named a street after him, for it was he who led the Canadian patrol that liberated it in 1917. He enlisted during the Second World War as a major and held staff positions in Canada until 1943, when he was promoted to brigadier-general. He was awarded a CBE for his service. De Lalanne devoted his life to community affairs. He was a director or member of the board of numerous corporations, professional associations, charitable and benevolent organizations, and educational institutions. He somehow found time to serve as mayor of Westmount in 1955-56.

In the mid-1970s, Bernatchez asked de Lalanne to conduct an audit of the LPF's office procedures, its accounting practices, and the channels of communications between headquarters and the branches and also between the LPF and DVA. Foreshadowing later reports, de Lalanne found no clear division of responsibility among LPF staff

Reverend Canon Arthur W. Wilcox, president of the Last Post Fund, 1975-78.

Brigadier-General J.A. de Lalanne, president of the Last Post Fund, 1978-80.

members, especially for those individuals representing both HQ and the Québec branch. He found the accounting system a shambles, the legacy of years of confusion and inefficiency, and hoped to improve internal reporting procedures and streamline operations. Moreover, he was "not at all happy" with past financial statements about operations of the Field of Honour. In 1978, Edward retired as secretary-treasurer. De Lalanne, who changed the name of the National Council to the Governing Council, had begun a process of critical self-review at the Fund that would continue for 20 years.

In 1980, just prior to giving up the presidency, de Lalanne, in a confidential report, noted a serious lack of communication between headquarters and branches. He believed that HQ informed branches infrequently and unevenly of evolving policies and practices. Despite his insistence as president on dispatching many informative circular letters and memoranda to branches, uniform procedures were difficult to establish across the country, especially for cases seconded to the LPF by DVA. Branch representatives had little effective input into national policies, he noted, and the annual meetings had degenerated into social events. He wondered if delegates' travel costs were even justified. When de Lalanne died in August 1988, at the age of 91, an editorial in the Westmount *Examiner* noted that, despite his fervent interest and abiding commitment to many organizations, the Last Post Fund was "dearest to his heart".

In 1980, Colonel J. Redmond Roche, a court of sessions judge, became president. Like de Lalanne, he had long been affiliated with both the Legion and the LPF. He had served during the Second World War and was elected president of the Legion's Québec Command in 1963. He was elected a vice-president of the Legion's Dominion Command in 1964 and was president in 1970-71, by which time he was also a director of the LPF. His management style was conciliatory, and he presided over the Fund on the cusp of its entry into a more modern operating environment.

One long-standing tradition and several old friends died during Roche's administration. In 1981, the LPF held its final annual meeting at the Ritz-Carlton Hotel, ending a decades-long relationship. Beginning on a permanent basis in 1982 the United Services Club made available its pleasant facilities in Montreal for LPF meetings. In June 1973, the aging General E. de B. Panet resigned after 36 years

Colonel the Honourable Judge J. Redmond Roche,
president of the Last Post Fund, 1980-82.

with the Fund; the National Council named him an honorary vice-president. Long-time director and trustee Major-General C.B. Price died in February 1975. Both honorary vice-presidents, John H. Molson and E. de B. Panet, died in 1977-78. Arthur Hair's son Douglas, who had been very active in the Northern California branch, died in San Francisco on November 20, 1979. His remains were flown to Montreal and he was interred in the Field of Honour. His sister Ruby died in 1987. From this point on, the family's only connection with the Fund was Arthur Hair's grandson, Arthur "Chip" Hair, a resident of Ottawa, who, as this book went to press, still occasionally attends LPF annual meetings.

In 1982, Lieutenant-Commander E.J. Lattimer became president. A lawyer, he had been affiliated with the LPF's Québec branch and national office since 1961 and had proven himself a tireless administrator and legal advisor. The LPF benefitted from his enormous experience and his valuable legal counsel into the new millennium.

In 1984, the LPF discarded use of the word "indigent" to describe most cases in favour of "regular" – less damning, it seemed, of the deceased's social situation. It would take several more years before "indigent" was excised from the constitution and by-laws of the Fund. By 1989, official LPF forms using such words as "charity" and "pauperism" were also amended. The LPF of the 1980s found these terms unnecessarily patronizing.

Lieutenant-General Gilles Turcot succeeded Lattimer as president in 1984. Turcot had served in the *Royal 22e Régiment* during the Second World War and was the highest-ranking former officer to head the LPF since Sir Arthur Currie. The new president was extremely conscious of the need to modernize the Fund: he set up a Maritime branch and laid the groundwork for the acquisition of computer technology at the Fund's office. In 1988, Major John O. McArthur replaced Turcot and Colonel Richard J. Connor succeeded him in 1989. Both McArthur and Connor were Second World War veterans and helped propel the Last Post Fund towards the new, important phase in its history for which Turcot had prepared the ground.

Lieutenant-Commander E. James Lattimer, vice-president of the LPF's Québec branch and the Fund's senior naval representative, with Jessie Hair, daughter of Arthur Hair, at 1967 river ceremony. Lattimer served as president of the Last Post Fund, 1982-84. La Presse, *May 27, 1967.*

Lieutenant-General Gilles A. Turcot, president of the Last Post Fund, 1984-88. Photo taken at 1985 river ceremony; Ruby Hair at left.

"Hectic Years" and "Drastic Changes"

Perhaps it was inevitable that Ottawa would seek greater control over the affairs and policies of the LPF. After all, although it had in large measure been supporting the LPF for over 60 years, there had always been a comfortable distance between the two parties, at least at an official, policy-making level. The relationship was mutually convenient, and the Fund's ultimate independence was never seriously called into question. Things began to change – though not necessarily for the worse – in the late 1970s, accelerating in the 1980s.

In 1977, the Department of Veterans Affairs changed the existing practice for paying LPF burial accounts. It discontinued funeral imprest accounts and instituted a more decentralized system of financing. Starting July 1, 1977, all charges for burial, cemetery services, and grave markers were paid by DVA's local district director of veterans services, on the request of the secretary-treasurer of the LPF branch who forwarded the appropriate invoices. Both DVA and the LPF agreed that the old system had become "unwieldy" and welcomed the change. The Fund's California branches were to use DVA's offices in Vancouver to process payments. The LPF also hoped that this new procedure would accelerate payments to funeral directors across Canada; it certainly implied greater direct control by the Department over LPF spending practices.

In 1988, Veterans Affairs Canada was anxious to formalize its relationship with the LPF in a Memorandum of Understanding (MOU). Ultimately, as Canada's veterans aged, VAC foresaw the day when the LPF would be the premier and even sole organization responsible for their burial. But VAC also sought to codify regulations for burying veterans in such a manner that the LPF would execute pre-ordained government policy. Since both groups agreed on principles, this approach made sense. In effect, the LPF expanded its operations and grew in stature but in exchange was held to greater accountability by VAC. While the Fund remained a separate entity, with its own board of directors, its formal ties with Ottawa became much closer.

In 1987, Treasury Board asked VAC to be more precise with its budget estimates concerning LPF costs. Accordingly, VAC obliged the Fund to submit a business plan for approval and funding. It scrutinized particularly the LPF's cash flow derived from reclaims, which were public monies. All branches had to submit standardized annual operating budgets to National HQ beginning in 1988-89. Headquarters consolidated these and sent them on to VAC. Moreover, the LPF instituted job classifications for its employees to ensure appropriate and consistent remuneration throughout the Fund. Ottawa was paying the bills and wanted the LPF to fall into line with federal government practices and procedures. The old ways of the LPF were gone for good; so, too, as far as some of its members were concerned, was its traditionally powerful sense of institutional independence.

The 1988 Memorandum of Understanding was the basis of a new administrative arrangement. VAC would henceforth pay for the Fund's administrative expenses after approving its annual budget. Employee salaries became subject to VAC approval. The closer monitoring seemed to work: branch spending went down, while reclaims went up. VAC underwrote the annual Field of Honour and river ceremonies, formerly a drain on tight LPF finances. Perhaps unnecessarily, given the LPF's record of leniency and compassion over eight decades, VAC wanted the Fund to adopt a "broad interpretation" towards burial cases brought to its attention, bearing in mind the need for "courtesy, speed, and generosity" in providing a uniform level of treatment. In these respects, the LPF had little to learn from anyone.

The signing of the MOU in 1988 was a milestone for the LPF. The Fund altered some of its administrative practices to conform with those in place for the federal public service. It was time to move forward for the benefit of Canada's veterans. The closely intertwined relationship between the LPF and the federal government ultimately translated into an enhanced national burial program that was more uniform and better administered. G.A. Turcot, E.J. Lattimer, Colonel Jean-Marc Fournier (secretary-treasurer), Ross O'Farrell (director), and others had worked extremely hard to bring this matter to fruition. The president, J.O. McArthur, called 1988 "a good year" for the LPF, one of "progress and consolidation". He was right: by 1989 the Fund had entered the modern world, with computers, fax machines, and other technological improvements.

Some changes were taking place in branch operations as well. In April 1981, the Saskatchewan branch moved its headquarters from Saskatoon to Regina, a location that the local LPF considered more practical. The LPF's position in the province had taken time to con-solidate in the 1920s and 1930s, mainly because of the opposition and even hostility of local Legion officials. In 1986, in contrast, the branch changed its directors by simply appointing the executive of the Legion's Saskatchewan Command as its new executive! After more than half a century of sometimes thorny relations, the Legion had swallowed the Saskatchewan LPF, at least in the sense that the same individuals controlled both operations in the province. Roche and de Lalanne had helped bring the two organizations into harmony. No immediate alarm bells rang out at LPF headquarters when the Saskatchewan branch initiated this changeover. It was a welcome change and all concerned understood that both the LPF and the Legion assisted Canada's veterans.

Despite the Legion's helping hand, the LPF branch in Saskatchewan was on the wane. When its hard-working secretary-treas-urer, F.W. Eason (who operated the branch from his Regina home), passed away in 1988, the national headquarters transferred Saskatchewan's caseload to the Northern and Southern Alberta branches and moved the files to the offices of the Legion's Provincial Command. The Saskatchewan branch was stood down. It was reacti-vated in Saskatoon in January 1991, without its previously obvious link to the Legion, and located with the local VAC offices. As the new branch directors themselves admitted, there were some initial "growing pains"; soon thereafter, the rejuvenated branch boasted excellent results.

The Alberta branches, too, experienced organizational change. Because of advancements in communications, and a desire to avoid duplication, the province's two branches merged in 1995. Edmonton became branch headquarters, and Calgary a branch office. The Calgary office closed on March 31, 1997, although Southern Alberta continued to enjoy adequate representation on the provincial board of directors.

A less happy situation in British Columbia had nothing to do with restructuring. Unfortunately, the first and only recorded "dishonest application" of LPF funds took place there in 1992. The BC branch secretary-treasurer, Major C.A. Buchanan, was removed from office and charged with defrauding the LPF of over $62,000. He was convicted in 1993 and ordered by the court to pay back $40,000. The scandal induced the branch's president, Commander Johnston, to resign. Despite this crisis, and the branch's less-than-stellar choices of secretary-treasurers over the years, the branch recovered nicely and put the matter behind it.

In 1994, the Manitoba branch completed a five-year project to restore the military section of Brookside Cemetery, renamed the "Field of Honour". It repaired or replaced existing markers and overhauled and re-landscaped the entire section. It did so with the cooperation of the City of Winnipeg, the Commonwealth War Graves Commission, the Royal Canadian Legion, and Veterans Affairs Canada.

By far the biggest change took place in the Maritimes, where a new branch was organized. In 1975, LPF president Bernatchez had complained of serious organizational problems in the region, which had two directors on the National Council, three local representatives, one in each province, and no actual branches. The local representatives gathered applications and dispatched them to Montreal for processing but received virtually no remuneration for their efforts. Few LPF burials took place in the Maritimes. Bernatchez requested DVA funding to improve the situation and increase liaison visits to branches across Canada to enhance the Fund's "national character". Branch financing came out of provincial and municipal grants, private donations, and reclaims, but the Maritimes, lacking a branch had no such support. Wilcox, Bernatchez's successor, considered that "the thinking concerning the LPF is back about 50 years" in the Maritimes. The Fund was simply unknown to most veterans there, and so Wilcox enlisted the co-operation of the Legion in publicizing the Fund.

Finally, in January 1985 Gilles Turcot, president, visited the Maritimes to establish a branch. He met with the LPF's local representatives and military officials in all three provinces, and in April 1985, a branch was inaugurated, with headquarters in Halifax. Vice-Admiral H.A. Porter became its president and representative on the Governing Council. Legion officers from each province's Command were appointed to the large board of directors. Turcot announced at the Fund's May 1985 annual meeting that creation of this branch was "without a doubt the highlight of my first year as President". Bernatchez, who died in 1983, had long desired a branch there and Turcot expressed sadness that he did not live to see it realized. National HQ funded operations until enough reclaim money became available.

As soon as the branch was established, LPF business in eastern Canada rose dramatically, by some 30 per cent in the first year of operation. Nevertheless, local directors of the Fund still ruefully considered it the "best kept secret in Canada". Awareness programs were launched immediately with the close co-operation of the Legion. LPF officers visited Legion branches and spoke to well-attended gatherings to make the veteran community more fully aware of the Fund's services and eligibility criteria. Cases jumped from 59 in 1985–86, costing about $63,000, to 1,032 in 1989–90 costing over $2 million – a remarkable turn-around that only became more dramatic in the next several years. Turcot gave Bill Byatt, the branch's secretary-treasurer, credit for "changing the image" of the Fund in the Maritimes. Turcot himself could share the credit.

By 1989–90, it was obvious that volume in New Brunswick warranted creation of a separate branch there, as did the increasing number of inquiries from the province's French-speaking veterans and their families, who would be better served locally than from Halifax. In January 1991, the Governing Council split the Maritime branch. A bilingually-staffed New Brunswick branch opened in Saint John, with responsibility for Prince Edward Island as well. All of the new officers were also Legion members, including many former executives. Long neglected, the Maritimes proved to be a phenomenal growth area for LPF services. Better marketing helped enormously, but as well the LPF conducted almost all VAC burials in this region, as it did in much of western Canada. For similar reasons, Newfoundland's LPF cases rose dramatically in the early 1990s. In addition, the arrival of Hugh Peden as secretary-treasurer there in 1989 had much to do with reviving the fortunes of this nearly moribund branch.

The Fund was still "best known" in Québec, according to a March 1991 article in *Legion* magazine. At this time, burials remained fairly stable at about 400 per annum. Many veterans in Québec considered it a privilege to be buried by the LPF in the Field of Honour. Montreal-area burials increased rapidly in the early 1990s, as the hundreds of aging veterans who had pre-paid a plot at the Field passed away in steadily growing numbers.

In the late 1980s and early 1990s, the Fund made a strong nationwide effort to publicize its activities through seminars and information sessions at Legion branches or with groups of funeral directors. Many branches developed communications and advertising strategies, including the use of 15-minute videos.

In 1988, in the course of overhauling the constitution, by-laws, and written procedures of the Fund, the Governing Council altered its own composition starting in 1989-90. The preponderance of Québec members on the council – in recognition of the fact that they often had national and branch duties as well as responsibility for the Field of Honour – had rankled the Ontario branch, among others, for years. Henceforth, Québec would have four members (down from seven), and the Alberta, Maritimes, and Ontario branches two each. This change seemed to satisfy the non-Québec members – at least for the moment.

Following decades of discussion in LPF and VAC circles regarding the eligibility of merchant navy veterans for LPF services, the matter was finally settled in 1993. Pursuant to an amendment to its letters patent in October of that year, the LPF began accepting applications for funeral and burial benefits on behalf of merchant navy veterans who had died on or after July 1, 1992. The guidelines employed were based on the applicable conditions set out in the Merchant Navy Veteran and Civilian War-related Benefits Act. To qualify, at least one of the following conditions had to be met: a) a person with service aboard a Canadian ship while on a high-seas voyage in either the First or Second World Wars; b) a Canadian national with service aboard an Allied ship on a high-seas voyage in either the First or Second World Wars; c) a Canadian national who was awarded the 1939-1945 Star in respect of Merchant Navy service; or d) a person with service on a Canadian ship in "dangerous waters" (any one of five defined "risk zones" surrounding the Korean Peninsula) while on a high-seas voyage during the Korean War. Eligible merchant seamen were finally accepted by the LPF and Ottawa as if they had been uniformed service personnel.

In the early 1990s, there was some question as to whether or not the approximately 3,000 Canadians who saw service in the Gulf War in 1991 held the status of veterans. In 1993, VAC announced that military service in "special duty areas", including the Persian Gulf, Bosnia, and Croatia, qualified participants to a range of benefits, including death benefits, if death was the result of war-related activities. However, the ruling was clear: these individuals were not veterans as such and were therefore ineligible for LPF services. This decision applied to Canadian military personnel on United Nations or other peacekeeping missions and also later to aviators who flew combat missions over Serbia and Kosovo in the spring of 1999. However, in June 1999 the Governing Council authorized that any veteran of these operations wishing to do so could be buried in the Field of Honour.

In 1993, another federal policy restricted 'after the fact' burials. The LPF would have only one year after burial to accept financial responsibility for eligible cases after interment had already taken place without its involvement. This was intended to remedy the LPF's confusing policy in this area; it also led to a significant decrease in the number of such cases.

Colonel Richard Connor retired from the LPF presidency in 1992 after what he described as three "hectic years which have seen many drastic changes". No one could argue with Connor's assessment, although this period was merely a forerunner of greater changes to come. Mark Devlin replaced him as president. The two vice-presidents were Capt (N) P.G.A. Langlais and Brigadier-General Douglas Anderson.

Under the Microscope

In 1993, Veterans Affairs Canada subjected the Fund to rigorous scrutiny and the LPF itself even commissioned an independent review of its administrative structure. Ottawa planned major changes to its veteran burial policies and, to remain relevant to those plans, the LPF had little choice but to tighten up its procedures. That year, VAC sponsored two separate, in-depth studies of the Fund's organization and activities. These reports engendered far-reaching consequences for the management of the Fund and introduced changes that prepared the LPF for the twenty-first century.

In 1992, VAC had conducted an extensive review of its funeral and burial programs with the goal of streamlining and consolidating its services. This exercise included an audit of the LPF's administrative practices, particularly its operations and organizational framework. The objective of the audit was to recommend ways and means to improve the Fund's services and strengthen its overall administration so that it could eventually handle VAC's large burial caseload in addition to its own. Ronald Wybou of VAC conducted the audit between November 1992 and January 1993. His exhaustive program review (the Wybou Report), issued in March 1993, made 56 recommendations.

Wybou judged that, since the LPF had from the mid-1980s successfully taken over a growing percentage of VAC cases (mainly because of budget constraints within VAC), the Fund would be well-suited to take over all of VAC's funeral and burial services in the near future. However, an administrative overhaul and a carefully managed phasing-in of the increased workload would have to precede official transfer of authority. As well, Wybou showed that staffing arrangements and program practices needed to be improved and made consistent throughout the LPF's branches. The respective jurisdictions and activities of both the national headquarters and the branches required greater definition. Moreover, the report recommended reconciliation of certain nation-wide deficiencies and inconsistencies in budgeting and financial reporting and improvements in channels of communications and working arrangements within the LPF and between the Fund and VAC. James de Lalanne had identified these problems nearly 20 years earlier.

The VAC auditor condemned the increasingly unworkable dual

nature of the national office and the Québec branch: "The LPF Headquarters is in fact the Québec Branch Office with several of the staff also having responsibility for national operations." Such onerous "double duty tasking", Wybou believed, was inefficient and inimical to the best interests of the Fund. He also hinted that this practice was unfair to the overburdened personnel involved. Even while noting that an independent consultant hired by the LPF (H.J. Carter) was addressing the very question, Wybou stated categorically: "There is a definite need to establish an organizationally and physically independent Head Office unit with a National Secretary-Treasurer separate from the Québec Branch in order to provide for adequate management of LPF activity. Such a position, together with additional support, will be imperative should the LPF's role be expanded." Clearly, a division of functions was a *sine qua non* for VAC's allowing the LPF to assume its funeral and burial responsibilities. Since the Fund was willing, perhaps eager, to expand its operations, a major restructuring was essential.

He thought the head office's monitoring of branch activities and procedures woefully inadequate, particularly in case eligibility and collection of reclaims. He suggested a form of internal audit based on 'spot checking', or sampling. He expected that this would oblige branches to adopt standard information-gathering techniques and institute more rigorous reporting procedures. Wybou believed that procedures for estate valuation and reclaims were unsatisfactory. He doubted that the Application for Funeral and Burial Services (Form B) provided sufficient information on which to base acceptance of a case. Often, applicants left the section related to asset holdings blank or completed it only very sketchily. Rarely did the branches seek or obtain independent proof regarding assets claimed as jointly held by the deceased and the surviving spouse; applicants submitted few probate documents or other material pertaining to the value of the estate. According to the auditor, the LPF needed to investigate claims more thoroughly.

Wybou's views on this score did not meet with the approval of some LPF directors across the country, who believed that the Fund's work was about interring veterans and honouring their services, not mounting a financial inquisition of the surviving spouse and family. Indeed, the Fund had traditionally existed to provide a necessary and patriotic service in a compassionate manner not, they felt, to 'nickel-and-dime' bereaved families. Still, Wybou had a point and a workable compromise had to be found before VAC would formally turn over to the LPF its responsibilities for burying veterans.

Estate valuation was essential in determining a claimant's eligibility. It also heavily influenced reclaims policy. But, the auditor noted, there was no consistency in reclaims procedures from branch to branch. Some branches sent letters seeking additional funds from the survivors if the deceased's Canada Pension Plan death benefit increased their estate beyond the LPF's basic exemption. A majority of branches pursued reclaims only when the veteran had no surviving spouse, reasoning that a surviving spouse might be in serious need, notwithstanding LPF regulations. In fact, in 1992 the BC branch specifically instructed its branch secretary-treasurer *not* to seek reclaims if a dependant survived. While morally defensible, this position was contrary to the LPF's own regulations. While Wybou acknowledged that the LPF should not harass families, it had to increase the volume and amounts of reclaims by designing more exacting application forms and implementing more stringent recovery of reclaims.

The LPF also required additional staff at the national office and in Ontario and British Columbia. A redefined relationship between VAC and the Fund would include enhanced 'contractual' obligations between them and the establishment of a reasonable system for VAC to monitor LPF operations and expenditures. Wybou was explicit in noting that it was VAC's responsibility to prepare a smooth transfer of authority.

Wybou's report was honest and judicious. Not many of his recommendations came as a great shock to the LPF. As he suggested, the LPF "realized" some of its own shortcomings and had been "actively pursuing improvements". But the Fund was perennially strapped for cash and under-funded. It could not do everything demanded or desired of it on a shoestring budget. Although VAC spent over $107,000 per year in administering the LPF, the directors felt this "a small amount for a program of this magnitude". Criticism was easy; Ottawa would have to help pay for the solution. "Before any additional workload is transferred to the LPF", Wybou concluded, "it is our opinion that steps be taken by VAC to ensure that the operations of the LPF are meeting the spirit and intent of the legislation pertaining to the funeral and burial program." The next several years would see the LPF and VAC implement procedures to remedy Wybou's concerns.

Wybou had noted the pressing need for a *national* secretary-treasurer and for a clear definition of the roles, authority, and responsibilities of the national and branch offices. Many LPF administrators across the country had already arrived at the same conclusions. It was up to H.J. Carter, a management consultant hired to report independently, to suggest the necessary improvements. Carter's main term of reference was simple: to "examine the feasibility of establishing a separate National Office" for the LPF. Currently the national secretary-treasurer also acted as secretary-treasurer for the Québec branch. Was this arrangement appropriate? Was it efficient? Was the dual role simply too much for one person to handle? These were the questions to which Carter sought answers.

Carter launched his investigation in early 1993 and submitted a modified final report on April 30 of that year. VAC supported and funded the study. Carter interviewed the LPF national executive, branch staff, and representatives of VAC and reviewed all pertinent LPF and VAC documentation to determine the exact nature of the administrative relationship between the branches and the national office. He also closely studied the entire operations of the Fund, paying particular attention to administration and head office costs, caseloads, and reclaims. At the time of his study, the Fund's national office and the Québec branch were located in the same office in Montreal, sharing an address, telephone numbers, and fax facilities. The national secretary-treasurer and the Québec secretary-treasurer were one and the same person, who further had to manage the Field of Honour. Worse, the incumbent's two superiors, the national president and the president of the Québec branch, at times made "competing demands", which resulted in "confused priorities". Other LPF officials were similarly double-tasked: a financial officer handled accounting at both the national and branch levels, and a staff of counsellors handled both national and branch issues.

Should a national office be established physically removed from the Québec branch and staffed by completely different people? Carter's answer was resoundingly in the affirmative. He believed that the national structure of the LPF was inconsistent with its constitutionally prescribed functions. In fact, he concluded, perhaps with some exaggeration, "there is no distinct national structure" and the "powers and authority of the national office are not understood nor exercised effectively". It was time to remedy this deficiency and establish a "distinct national office with adequate responsibility and authority to effectively manage the national operations of the Fund".

Many LPF officers across Canada felt that the Fund was "dominated by Québec branch". They were annoyed because the Québec branch held four seats on the Governing Council and the national president normally came from Québec. Non-Québec members strongly identified the Field of Honour, a national responsibility, as a purely Québec branch affair; to a large extent it was. This perception was slow to change. What *was* the national office? The too-close affiliation between the Québec branch and HQ lessened the national office's credibility among branch officials. How else explain the BC branch's willingness to act independently regarding reclaims?

Some branch officials believed that the national office lacked direction, which harmed LPF operations across Canada. Their queries to Montreal regularly went unanswered, they claimed, and so they directly contacted DVA officials in Ottawa for information. This created the impression within and outside the LPF that internal communications were poor. They were. While these problems had existed in one form or another since the 1920s, without necessarily hampering the LPF's delivery of services, this was hardly the image that the Fund wanted conveyed to Ottawa. The fact that the Governing Council met only once a year, and initiated little policy discussion or strategic planning when it did meet, only worsened matters.

Carter proposed a strong central authority to impose standardized operating procedures and a consistent nation-wide application of LPF regulations. The national office also had to develop and maintain a strict financial and administrative grip on policy implementation. The first step was to arrange for a physical separation of the national office from the Québec branch and to appoint a separate national "Executive Director" – a form of executive secretary-treasurer. The LPF was in transition.

The Governing Council accepted the Carter Report, in principle, in June 1993. Branches were given 90 days in which to offer their points of view. An LPF Study Group carefully reviewed Carter's recommendations, achieved a consensus, and suggested minor modifications. It insisted on clarification of the proposed relationship between the executive director, the branch presidents, and the branch secretary-treasurers. In essence, however, the study group considered the Carter Report a step in the right direction.

The Québec branch, too, strongly endorsed Carter's proposal of strengthening the national structure, even if that lessened its own influence. Although the Carter Report had recommended equal representation from every branch on the Governing Council, the LPF Study Group felt it advisable and justifiable to allow a second representative from Québec to represent the Field of Honour, which it called the LPF's "National Field of Honour", to indicate the Field's status as the cemetery of the entire LPF, and not specifically of the Québec branch. The proposal to allow Québec a second member, which did not originate in Québec, met with consent. It was a united LPF which looked to the future.

The Governing Council was re-organized and consisted of a president, and one representative from each branch (nine), the Field of Honour, and VAC. No president, vice-president, or treasurer was to serve more than two consecutive years at a time. The executive director would report to the Governing Council through the national president and be responsible for day-to-day operations, including supervision of branch secretary-treasurers' financial reporting. As before, all terms of reference for branch boards stemmed from the authority of the Governing Council.

In July 1993, the LPF hired Desmond Rive as a consultant to organize the implementation of the Wybou Report. Rive had been an assistant deputy minister with VAC and was well acquainted with the Fund. By January 1994, he began a two-year assignment as special advisor to the president on restructuring. Rive was in large part responsible for an effective transition and became acting executive director of the LPF.

On April 8-9, 1994, the Governing Council held a milestone meeting. The president of the Fund, Mark Devlin, who had worked very hard to restructure the LPF, had recently suffered a serious accident and was unable to attend. In his absence, Captain (N) P.G.A. Langlais, second vice-president, was in the chair. (Brigadier-General

Douglas Anderson, first vice-president, battling cancer, was present but felt too ill to lead the proceedings.) Some senior VAC officials were on hand – David Nicholson, acting deputy minister, and Serge Rainville, assistant deputy minister for veterans services.

The VAC officials assured the meeting of their department's support for the restructuring based on the Wybou Report and the Study Group modifications to the Carter Report. Ottawa would fund the establishment of a national office. Further, the department would soon streamline its operations, perhaps even merging VAC and LPF burial programs. All agreed that the modified Carter recommendations would be attended to first. Once the national office was operational, the detailed findings of the Wybou Report could be addressed. The meeting launched the start of a new Last Post Fund.

E.J. Lattimer, long-time honorary legal advisor to the LPF, was instrumental in amending the by-laws to reflect the changes. Following this demanding assignment, in June 1994, he announced that he was retiring as honorary legal advisor after many years of service in that capacity. In 1993, Mark Devlin had praised Lattimer's "outstanding" assistance to the LPF. The LPF had kept him exceedingly busy, and Devlin called him a "tower of strength in this organization

Captain (N) Peter Langlais,
president of the Last Post Fund,
1995-96.

for many years". Lattimer stayed on as a valued director of the Québec branch until his death in 2000.

In 1995, Rive set up a national office physically separated from the Québec branch in the Cathcart Street building. In September 1994, the Québec branch had appointed a secretary-treasurer, Colonel René Pothier, who would also manage the Field of Honour on behalf of the national office. In April 1996, the LPF hired Colonel Alex Bialosh as the first permanent executive director of the national office, a position that he held at the time of writing. Bialosh, an experienced administrator, guided the Fund through the final stages of implementing the recommendations of the Wybou and Carter reports.

The national office immediately appointed an officer with responsibilities for financial management and control and soon the staff increased from three to eight full-time personnel. In September 1997, the national office moved to a different floor of the Cathcart Street building, further cementing its distinctiveness from the Québec branch.

The Challenges of the Future

By the mid-1990s, the federal government was struggling to contain its run-away budget deficit. It had already made significant progress, but mainly by curtailing the public-sector workforce and cutting government programs. Veterans Affairs Canada would not be spared; it, too, had to reduce costs. A major VAC program review, whose findings were announced in the federal budget of February 1995, had a powerful and long-term impact on the Last Post Fund and on Canada's veterans. Few of the changes seemed positive from the perspective of the LPF. Worse, under the veil of budget secrecy, the LPF was not consulted about these modifications, which came as a profound shock to the organization.

Ottawa insisted that: "The increasing costs of veterans' programs, combined with the large public debt, have forced the Government to implement several cost containment measures within the funeral and burial programs. To ensure the future longevity of the program for needy veterans and their families, changes were required to guarantee that benefits are being directed to those that are truly without the necessary resources." In one fell swoop, it slashed in half the estate exemption from $24,030 to $12,015 – the 1981 rate. The new amount, far below the federal government's 'poverty line', was not difficult to attain, even among the poor, with the result that many veterans' families truly in need of LPF services were no longer eligible to receive them. Similarly, VAC reduced the LPF's dependent child maximum estate exemption of $2,100 to $700, in line with existing VAC Veterans Burial Regulations (VBR). Moreover, the Canada Pension Plan's death benefit, previously exempt, thereafter became for both the department and the LPF an asset of the estate. Spousal assets also affected the assessed value of an estate. Under these conditions, it would be much more difficult for veterans to qualify. Other changes ensured that the LPF would arrange for the lowest available "earth burial" costs and minimize allowable transportation charges. In addition, "resistance fighters" – veterans of the struggle against the Nazis in occupied countries during the Second World War – were no longer eligible. On a positive note, any "reasonable debt" of an eligible veteran was held to be a debt against the estate, and hence reduced its value. These changes came into effect October 1, 1995.

VAC claimed that its cost-cutting measures would allow it "to slow down its expenditures towards the ever-escalating costs of burial" yet "still allow the Department to ensure that veterans receive a dignified funeral and burial". Nevertheless, despite VAC's stated intention of returning the LPF's program to "its original mandate of assisting the truly financially needy veteran", the pendulum had probably swung a little too far to one side. Who could say how many "truly needy" veterans would henceforth be denied the fitting burial they deserved? Moreover, VAC estimated that reduced veteran eligibility would yield savings of $5.7 million annually. In fact, $11 million was saved in the first year .

It all seemed a bit heavy-handed. Serge Rainville, from VAC, admitted that the budget cuts by way of reduced veterans' eligibility had "strained" LPF-VAC relations, although few VAC officials were aware beforehand of the details contained in the February 1995 budget. David Nicholson, the deputy minister, was blunt when he spoke to the LPF's Governing Council on June 1, 1995: "Let there be no misunderstanding, the funding of services which are delivered by VAC or the LPF [is] financed by the government [which] controls the agenda." Thus was policy born, and thus was it implemented. Peter Langlais, the LPF president, who acknowledged realistically that the

LPF was entering the "sunset of its mandate", was left with little choice but to make the best of a tough situation. In the first year following the policy changes, the LPF experienced a 47 per cent drop in the number of cases it handled and a 58 per cent reduction in the amount of its payments. Ottawa's "cost containment" efforts had been successful.

One change in LPF policy proved a significant break with tradition. All LPF burials followed a standard funeral and interment practice, with common grave markers. After October 1, the Fund offered a choice: next-of-kin could either accept the standard LPF funeral package or make arrangements themselves, with the Fund contributing to the expenses up to its ceiling of $2993 for the services of a single funeral director.

Not all the news in these years was bad – far from it. An LPF/VAC pilot program in Saskatchewan from September 1996 to February 1997 saw that branch assume full responsibility for all LPF and VAC burials in its jurisdiction. It was a major test; failure might destroy the Fund's chances of becoming the sole veterans' burial organization in Canada. Although the initiative was sanctioned by VAC, some of its officials were at first sceptical that, nationally, the LPF could handle the department's caseload in addition to its own. However, Dennis Wallace, VAC's assistant deputy minister for veterans' services, was a key supporter. Some VAC personnel outside Saskatchewan opposed the pilot project, which created tensions with the LPF during its implementation. Still, as the Saskatchewan branch subsequently declared, "with careful planning, meticulous briefings and close liaison with Veterans Affairs officers in Saskatoon and Regina, the pilot project was an unqualified success." As Lieutenant-Colonel Harvey Bishop, who succeeded Langlais as national president in 1996, stated in May 1997, the LPF was on the upswing: it had "increased the tempo of its activities and...gained momentum". (As a Newfoundlander, Bishop was only the second non-Québec head of the LPF.) Despite the Fund having had its recent differences with VAC, it was on the verge of accepting burial responsibilities "unthinkable" only a few years earlier. Ottawa agreed that the LPF was in the best position to assume this task nation-wide, and, on April 1, 1998, the Fund assumed the responsibility for VAC's funeral and burial program across Canada. This included VAC's "means tested" cases, as defined under Ottawa's Veterans Burial Regulations, which awarded burial subsidies on behalf of veterans who, at the time of death, were in receipt of either income support, disability pension benefits, or health care benefits from VAC and whose funeral expenses could not be met without government assistance. "Matter-of-right" benefits available under the Veterans Burial Regulations were granted on behalf of veterans who died as a result of pensioned conditions, from military service, or while on strength of VAC medical facilities.

According to the LPF's Program Implementation Report, issued in June 1998, "the consolidation of administrative responsibility for all veteran-oriented funeral, burial and grave marker programs under the auspices of the Last Post Fund *will not result in changes* to either the scope of the benefits or the eligibility criteria for such benefits." VAC anticipated that since the LPF was the single point of contact for veterans and their families, this would result in "uniform application of policies and procedures, improved program effectiveness, and a rationalization of resources and costs". The Royal Canadian Legion, with which the LPF enjoyed a close and co-operative relationship, applauded the move as a sensible standardization of services co-ordinated by an experienced organization with a proven system. As Alex Bialosh, executive director of the LPF, reminded Legion service officers in October 1998 at a conference in Charlottetown, henceforward the bereaved families of veterans had only one thing to do to arrange a dignified funeral for their loved one: call their local LPF branch. And so VAC's plan had finally come to pass, a mere two years following the restructuring of the Fund.

The operational changes for the LPF's national office were significant. In addition to an increase in volume, the impact of assuming VAC's caseload affected budget planning and accounting, necessitated the careful amalgamation of program policies and increased staff training, and required an overall increase in managerial and administrative tasks. But the LPF at least had a head start: for a decade, VAC had been gradually transferring authority to the Fund for means-tested funeral and burial benefits. At the time of the implementation of the new policy, the LPF was already handling two-thirds of these VAC cases. Ottawa had invested the new, improved Fund with an immense responsibility, for which the LPF was nine decades in preparation.

LPF standard operating procedures held for VAC cases as well.

The LPF application process included initial contact by the client, completion of application forms, verification of service, establishment of financial eligibility, and arrangement for payment of approved benefits to applicants. The allowable LPF grant for funeral and burial services covered the cost of a casket, preparation of the body for burial, use of a hearse and one other vehicle, local transportation, graveside service, cost of the grave, opening and closing of the grave, and perpetual care.

Effective April 1, 1998, VAC transferred responsibility to the LPF for the issuing of all cheques in connection to its operations, replacing the practice whereby VAC issued government cheques to veterans' next-of-kin, funeral directors, and marker suppliers. This gesture was a measure of real progress and symbolized both growth in the Fund's capacities and the trust placed in its management system by government officials. Not unforeseen was the fact that VAC would effect savings this way, since the LPF could undertake the delivery of this service with fewer resources. As Harvey Bishop noted, the LPF cheques, with the Fund's watermarked logo prominently displayed, served "as an important advertising and communications tool in promoting our purpose among veterans." Bialosh reported in 1998 that the LPF's turn-around time for payments was, in fact, an improvement over VAC's previous practices. The Fund issued 150 cheques a week and was obviously earning its keep: at the June 1998 Governing Council meeting, Dennis Wallace, VAC's assistant deputy minister for veterans services, announced that his department was "thrilled at the progress and achievement" of the Fund in the previous year. VAC provided extra funding to the LPF to compensate it for the increased workload. Federal government auditors continued to scrutinize all LPF expenditures annually.

Confirming a sentiment that Nicholson had expressed three years earlier, Al Puxley, director of operations in VAC's commemorative division, reminded those in attendance at the October 1998 conference in Charlottetown that VAC retained control of burial policy and funding for the LPF; the Fund would execute this policy on its behalf. Indeed, that was the new reality for the LPF – enhanced responsibility, but less freedom of action.

The Last Post Fund has taken on an important challenge for the future. It has become the sole institutional authority for burying vet-

Attendees at the meeting of the Governing Council of the Last Post Fund,
June 1999. From left to right, first row: Lieutenant-Colonel Harvey Bishop,
past president; Colonel Ghislain Bellavance, first vice-president; Brigadier-
General Jacques Morneault, president; Levite Paradis, second vice-president;
Brigadier-General Richard Genin, honorary treasurer;
second row: Lieutenant-Colonel Vicky Percival, honorary legal advisor; Larry
Harrison, British Columbia director;
third row: Gene Bince, Alberta director; Simon Coakley, assistant deputy
minister, Veterans Affairs Canada; Arthur Christensen, Manitoba director;
Lieutenant-Commander William Byatt, Nova Scotia director;
fourth row: Stewart Kelly, British Columbia branch president; Colonel
Alexander Bialosh, executive director; Commander Michael Green, Ontario
director; and Lieutenant (N) Donald Newell, Newfoundland director.

erans in Canada. It is a curious reversal of roles. Virtually since the
time he founded the "Last Post" Imperial Naval and Military
Contingency Fund in 1909, Arthur Hair argued that it was the role
of government to fund the burials of veterans to whom the state
owed such a debt of gratitude. He would have been only too willing
to fold his operation into a generous government-sponsored burial
policy. But through two world wars and their aftermaths, Hair and his

successors kept their Fund alive in the face of government parsimony and exclusionary regulations. Within the confines imposed by Ottawa's willingness to pay, the LPF achieved its aim of serving needy veterans whose patriotism it sought to recognize with dignity at the moment of death. It is something of an ironic twist of fate, then, that 90 years after the founding of the Last Post Fund, it is the Fund that has emerged as the survivor, and it is the government that has folded its operations into those of the Fund. True, the Last Post Fund is an executor of government policy, but the policies are those which the Fund itself helped forge in the days when it stood alone on behalf of those Canadian service men and women who could no longer help themselves. Arthur Hair would have approved.

EPILOGUE

At the dawn of a new century, it is an inescapable truth that Canada's veteran population is diminishing rapidly. This will have an enormous impact on the Last Post Fund's operations. In 1998, the Fund received 8,000 burial requests from veterans' families, of which roughly 3,000 were approved and 5,000 denied, mainly because the estate of the deceased exceeded the maximum allowable exemption. According to a Veterans Affairs Canada study of mortality rates, the trend will be for an increase in LPF interments until the end of 2002. Beginning in 2003, the LPF can expect a progressive decline in burial requests until about 2005, at which time the decline will sharpen precipitously. By 2010, remaining Second World War veterans will average almost 90 years of age, and the LPF will inter relatively few, even taking into account its responsibilities for all veterans' burials in Canada. In the meantime, the LPF continues to handle thousands of cases annually and in 1999 operated on a budget of $14 million for burials and $2.2 million for administration.

But there is more to the Last Post Fund than funerals and interments. For example, the LPF maintains some interest in the dependants of the deceased and assists those suffering bereavement with advice and information about federal programs for which they might be eligible. The Fund will also continue to accept its responsibilities in commemorating the services and sacrifices of those whom it has buried. It might even take on a greater role in reminding Canadians of the debt they owe to those who came before them. In June 1998, the official objectives of the Fund were modified: the Last Post Fund was "to interest itself, to the extent possible with the means at its disposal, in the support of local Fields of Honour and other veterans' commemorative projects in Canada." This allows for a very broad interpretation and leaves the door open for future LPF involvement in a variety of activities.

In May 1999, the Fund posted its own website on the internet (www.lastpostfund.ca). This instantaneous means of world-wide communication will enable the Fund to explain and publicize its services in a manner unheard of only a decade earlier. The website permits veterans' families to submit applications directly to the nearest LPF branch by electronic mail.

As the LPF entered the twenty-first century, it could rely on a growing perpetual care fund of $1.5 million to maintain the Field of Honour and uphold the dignity of those buried there. The Field will be maintained long after the last burial has taken place there. In fact, the nation-wide care and restitution of veterans' graves, markers, and cemetery plots will be an ongoing concern of the LPF, requiring the Fund's unique expertise to manage effectively. Perhaps the quiet resting places of these men and women who served Canada or its allies to secure peace and freedom for future generations will together form the most visible and obvious legacy of the Last Post Fund. In decades to come, Canadians yet unborn will pass some of the over 100,000 well-tended Last Post Fund grave markers and gaze on the words meant especially for their eyes: "Lest We Forget".

APPENDIX A

NATIONAL PRESIDENTS OF
THE LAST POST FUND, 1909–2000

1909–1914 Reverend Canon John M. Almond
1914–1920 Commander J.T. Walsh
1920–1922 Dr. W.H. Atherton
1922–1924 A.S. Clarson
1924–1932 General Sir Arthur Currie
1932–1939 Colonel (Venerable Archdeacon) John M. Almond
1939–1942 Major John H. Molson
1942–1955 Norman Holland
1955–1957 Commodore Paul Earl
1957–1963 Lieutenant-Colonel Stuart Rolland
1963–1974 Senator Romuald Bourque
1974–1975 Major-General J.P.E. Bernatchez
1975–1978 Reverend Canon A.W. Wilcox
1978–1980 Brigadier-General J.A. de Lalanne
1980–1982 Colonel J. Redmond Roche
1982–1984 Lieutenant-Commander E. James Lattimer
1984–1988 Lieutenant-General Gilles A. Turcot
1988–1989 Major J.O. McArthur
1989–1992 Colonel Richard J. Connor
1992–1995 Lieutenant Mark Devlin
1995–1996 Captain (N) Peter G.A. Langlais
1996–1998 Colonel Harvey Bishop
1998–2000 Brigadier-General Jacques Morneault

APPENDIX B

COMMEMORATIVE CEREMONIES
FIELD OF HONOUR,
POINTE CLAIRE, QUÉBEC

GUESTS OF HONOUR SINCE 1945

1945 Colonel H.C. Osborne, Secretary-General,
Imperial War Graves Commission (Canada)

1946 Brigadier W.J. Home, District Officer Commanding,
Military District No. 4 (Montreal)

1947 Air Vice-Marshal C.M. McEwen

1948 Rear-Admiral F.L. Houghton

1949 Governor General Viscount Alexander of Tunis

1950 Brigadier-General J. Guy Gauvreau

1951 Lieutenant-General G.G. Simonds,
Chief of the General Staff

1952 Lieutenant-Governor Gaspard Fauteux

1953 Air Marshal C.R. Slemon, Chief of the Air Staff

1954 Commodore Paul Earl, Dominion Council,
Last Post Fund

1955 Governor General Vincent Massey

1956 R.O. Campney, Minister of National Defence

1957 Major-General J.P.E. Bernatchez, General Officer
Commanding, Québec Command

1958 Senator Sarto Fournier, Mayor of Montreal

1959 Lieutenant-Governor Onésime Gagnon

1960 Major-General J.V. Allard

1961 Air Commodore J.B. Harvey

1962 Lieutenant-Governor Paul Comtois

1963 Vice-Admiral H.S. Rayner, Chief of the Naval Staff

1964 Alan A. Macnaughton, Speaker of the
House of Commons

1965 Lieutenant-General R.W. Moncel, Comptroller General,
Canadian Forces

1966 Roger Teillet, Minister of Veterans Affairs

1967 Major-General J.P.E. Bernatchez, National
Vice-President, Last Post Fund

1968 Leo Cadieux, Minister of National Defence

1969 Governor General Roland Michener

1970 J.E. Dubé, Minister of Veterans Affairs

1971 Lieutenant-Governor Hugues Lapointe

1972 Arthur Laing, Minister of Veterans Affairs

1973 J.S. Hodgson, Deputy Minister of Veterans Affairs

1974 Brigadier-General J. de Lalanne, Québec Branch,
       Last Post Fund
1975 Lieutenant-General Stanley Waters, Commander,
       Mobile Command
1976 Lieutenant-General Jacques Chouinard, Commander,
       Mobile Command
1977 Douglas McDonald, Dominion President,
       Royal Canadian Legion
1978 Governor General Jules Léger
1979 Lieutenant-General J.J. Paradis, Commander,
       Mobile Command
1980 Major-General Charles Belzile, Commander,
       Mobile Command
1981 Colonel J.R. Roche, National President, Last Post Fund
1982 Brigadier-General P.V.B. Grieve, Commonwealth
       War Graves Commission
1983 General Jacques Dextraze, former Chief of the
       Defence Staff
1984 Lieutenant-Governor Gilles Lamontagne
1985 Governor General Jeanne Sauvé
1986 Major-General J.A.G. de Chastelain, Deputy Commander,
       Mobile Command
1987 Lieutenant-General Gilles Turcot, Québec Branch,
       Last Post Fund
1988 Major-General Kent Foster, Deputy Commander, Mobile
       Command
1989 Lieutenant-General J.A. Fox, Commander,
       Mobile Command
1990 Jean-Guy Hudon, M.P., Parliamentary Secretary
       for the Minister of National Defence
1991 Colonel J.R. Roche, Québec Command, Last Post Fund
1992 J.D. Nicholson, Assistant Deputy Minister,
       Veterans Affairs Canada
1993 Major-General Armand Roy, Commander,
       Land Forces Québec Area
1994 Colonel Conrad F. Harrington, former
       Chancellor of McGill University
1995 Governor General Roméo Leblanc
1996 Lieutenant-General J.M.G. Baril, Commander, Canadian
       Army
1997 Lieutenant-Governor Lise Thibault
1998 General J.M.G. Baril, Chief of the Defence Staff
1999 Clifford Lincoln, Member of Parliament, Lac-Saint-Louis

APPENDIX C

LAST POST FUND BURIALS 1909–1934

Fiscal Year	B.C.	Alta	Sask	Man	Ont	Qué	N.B.	N.S.	P.E.I.	NF	U.K.	U.S.	Tot.
1909 to 1922	—	—	—	—	—	276	—	—	—	—	—	—	276
1923	19	7	1	8	33	27	1	—	—	—	—	—	96
1924	14	9	5	16	42	25	2	—	—	—	—	—	113
1925	19	15	2	23	51	40	1	1	—	—	—	—	152
1926	26	13	5	41	57	36	5	4	—	—	—	—	187
1927	28	27	13	24	62	31	3	4	—	—	—	—	194
1928	41	24	13	42	65	46	3	6	2	—	—	1	242
1929	42	27	24	43	74	47	6	4	1	—	—	—	267
1930	53	36	18	42	99	51	—	11	—	—	—	—	311
1931	54	39	28	52	123	60	1	5	1	—	1	—	364
1932	86	48	32	55	143	55	4	7	2	—	—	—	432
1933	91	57	37	82	159	75	7	13	1	—	1	—	523
1934	84	61	43	79	184	77	7	11	—	—	—	—	546
1935	111	65	38	64	212	98	7	12	1	—	—	—	608
1936	110	59	51	99	224	85	14	10	3	—	1	1	657

Appendix C (con't)
LAST POST FUND BURIALS 1937–1955

Fiscal Year	B.C.	Alta	Sask	Man	Ont	Qué	N.B.	N.S.	P.E.I.	NF	U.K.	U.S.	Tot.
1937	144	72	46	81	257	116	12	21	3	—	—	22	774
1938	156	87	51	93	267	100	20	14	6	1	2	48	845
1939	143	91	44	101	283	99	10	26	5	—	1	55	858
1940	195	75	54	100	305	113	12	18	2	—	1	54	929
1941	245	71	52	106	314	122	19	20	5	—	—	45	999
1942	257	77	56	114	304	119	15	26	—	—	—	31	999
1943	200	91	54	117	282	114	17	18	4	—	—	42	939
1944	188	55	40	108	288	111	12	11	5	—	—	22	840
1945	179	65	28	93	208	78	6	13	2	—	—	25	697
1946	173	60	31	57	181	76	6	8	1	—	—	22	615
1947	199	61	46	38	201	78	8	11	4	—	—	10	656
1948	258	54	47	60	212	75	6	21	1	—	—	15	749
1949	227	55	44	62	209	99	15	7	—	—	—	20	738
1950	266	54	44	56	254	70	12	22	5	—	—	21	804
1951	245	67	44	55	219	68	17	12	9	12	1	17	766
1952	232	60	34	57	226	64	17	16	3	10	—	23	742
1953	205	76	36	54	248	80	18	15	6	6	2	27	773
1954	185	85	31	53	223	89	16	17	12	7	—	20	738
1955	177	80	31	53	242	104	25	20	5	4	2	26	769

Appendix C (con't)
LAST POST FUND BURIALS 1956–1975

Fiscal Year	B.C.	Alta	Sask	Man	Ont	Qué	N.B.	N.S.	P.E.I.	NF	U.K.	U.S.	Tot.
1956	196	92	37	58	253	80	19	26	8	4	2	29	804
1957	202	83	35	68	225	95	19	18	11	6	2	24	788
1958	184	70	31	71	297	101	22	21	7	4	4	13	825
1959	185	91	48	70	289	93	36	35	9	12	4	20	892
1960	202	104	42	88	285	97	26	22	22	12	1	22	923
1961	208	104	40	81	350	117	30	21	9	9	3	11	983
1962	238	88	39	74	325	112	35	24	16	7	7	13	978
1963	240	78	31	58	372	128	42	32	12	6	15	17	1031
1964	226	86	28	91	307	138	45	29	9	10	5	13	987
1965	213	81	35	77	320	138	35	33	11	3	7	7	960
1966	202	84	44	105	380	164	55	28	15	7	3	13	1100
1967	197	128	41	88	405	174	53	43	15	8	7	18	1177
1968	219	95	30	97	405	163	40	44	19	11	11	7	1141
1969	194	96	20	77	323	179	17	36	10	1	8	8	969
1970	167	102	28	84	287	185	29	30	8	2	11	16	949
1971	209	172	22	77	338	255	30	34	11	2	9	16	1175
1972	209	177	41	64	300	261	27	29	9	3	22	10	1152
1973	186	191	27	78	314	265	31	22	17	2	10	14	1157
1974	172	161	26	46	301	293	26	22	6	1	12	14	1080
1975	178	184	20	44	283	231	16	11	6	2	10	8	993

Appendix C (con't)
LAST POST FUND BURIALS 1976-1979

Fiscal Year	B.C.	Alta	Sask	Man	Ont	Qué	N.B.	N.S.	P.E.I.	NF	U.K.	U.S.	Tot.
1976	150	220	13	41	242	214	16	11	7	2	9	3	928
1977	196	310	25	61	258	305	23	16	12	4	9	8	1227
1978	240	356	20	75	237	292	19	17	6	4	6	6	1278
1979	205	350	18	43	210	274	10	13	1	2	7	7	1140

* Due to a change in data recording procedures, the statistics for the period 1980-1999 are best expressed by total burials only.

LAST POST FUND BURIALS 1980-1999

Fiscal Year	Total Burials	Fiscal Year	Total Burials
1980	1288	1991	4118
1981	1205	1992	5911
1982	1029	1993	6989
1983	1061	1994	6438
1984	1108	1995	6815
1985	1241	1996	3459
1986	1340	1997	3166
1987	1624	1998	2975
1988	1744	1999	3371
1989	2444		
1990	3415	Total since 1909	105576

NOTE ON SOURCES

This book is meant to be both an informed and an informative history of the Last Post Fund. It is not a scholarly account, nor has the author exhaustively canvassed national, provincial, municipal, or cemetery archives across Canada for information on the LPF. Nevertheless, the bulk of this narrative relies on primary sources held at the national office of the Last Post Fund in Montreal. This archival documentation provided the building blocks for this book and included correspondence files, financial data, statistical and chronological summaries, internal memoranda, biographical sketches, and annual reports. Some early LPF publications such as booklets, brochures, pamphlets, and mimeographs shed light on the founding, organization, and operation of the Fund. Most branches of the Fund also sent whatever historical material they had for the preparation of this book.

Unfortunately, important archival material related to the early decades of the Fund's operations, which had been at the Gate of Remembrance at the Field of Honour, had deteriorated or been damaged beyond use. Officers of the Fund destroyed masses of mouldy correspondence long before this book project was even conceived. More positively, the national minute books of the Fund all survive, and these proved an essential source of information, especially for the post-1960 period, for which other archival material is extremely scant. Another valuable source was the LPF's extensive collection of newspaper and magazine clippings about the Fund. Some, covering the years 1909-1922, are still arranged in the original scrapbook put together by the founder, Arthur Hair. The LPF also possesses an outstanding photographic collection, from which almost all photos used in this book are drawn.

The National Archives of Canada yielded some useful material, although much of the 'paper trail' linking the Department of Veterans Affairs with the LPF was also to be found in the LPF's archives. There is undoubtedly additional relevant material to be found in Ottawa.

Some published primary sources proved helpful, including the *Debates* of the House of Commons, *Who's Who in Canada*, and the *Canadian Parliamentary Guide*. Secondary sources included books and articles either referring to the Last Post Fund or relating to the historical context in which the organization operated for 90 years. The only secondary source that makes more than passing reference to the Fund's founding and operations is *Silent Witnesses* (1974), by John Swettenham and H.F. Wood. Walter Woods's excellent book on veterans' civil re-establishment after 1945, *Rehabilitation: A Combined Operation* (1953), devotes several pages to explaining the operations of the Fund. Desmond Morton and Glenn Wright, in *Winning the Second Battle: Canadian Veterans and the Return to Civilian Life 1915-1930* (1987), refer to the Last Post Fund several times, but only in passing. None of the standard biographies of Sir Arthur Currie, president of the Last Post Fund from 1924 to 1932, mentions his close association with the LPF. Only Daniel Dancocks, in his biography of Currie, has noted that the LPF was one of many organizations with which Currie was affiliated. Fortunately, material held at the National Archives of Canada has been more forthcoming on Currie's links to the Fund. Finally, a recent collection of essays edited by J.L. Granatstein and Peter Neary, *The Veterans Charter* (1998) contains some excellent contributions by Desmond Morton, Terry Copp, and James Struthers having relevance to the operations of the Last Post Fund.

SELECT BIBLIOGRAPHY

Bowering, Clifford. *Service: The Story of the Royal Canadian Legion, 1925-1960.* The Legion. Ottawa. 1960.

Canada. *The Veterans Charter: Acts of the Canadian Parliament to assist Canadian Veterans.* King's Printer. Ottawa. 1946.

Copp, Terry. *The Anatomy of Poverty: the Condition of the Working Class in Montreal, 1897-1929.* McClelland and Stewart. Toronto. 1974.

Crerar, Duff. *Padres in No Man's Land: Canadian Chaplains and the Great War.* McGill-Queen's University Press. Montreal. 1995.

Dancocks, Daniel G. *Sir Arthur Currie: A Biography.* Methuen. Toronto. 1985.

England, Robert. *Discharged: A Commentary on Civil Re-establishment of Veterans in Canada.* Macmillan. Toronto. 1943.

Gaffen, Fred. *Forgotten Soldiers.* Theytus Books Ltd. Penticton, B.C. 1985.

Granatstein, J.L., and Neary, Peter, eds., *The Veterans Charter.* McGill-Queen's University Press. Montreal. 1998.

Guest, Dennis. *The Emergence of Social Security in Canada.* 3rd edition. University of British Columbia Press. Vancouver. 1997.

Hale, James. *Branching Out: The Story of the Royal Canadian Legion.* The Legion. Ottawa. 1995.

Jenkins, Kathleen. *Montreal: Island City in the St. Lawrence.* Doubleday. Garden City, New York. 1966.

Linteau, Paul-André. *Histoire de Montréal depuis la Confédération.* Boréal. Montréal. 1992.

Miller, Carman. *Painting the Map Red: Canada and the South African War 1899-1902.* McGill-Queen's University Press and the Canadian War Museum. Montreal. 1993.

Morris, Philip H., ed. *The Canadian Patriotic Fund: A Record of its Activities from 1914 to 1919*. n.p. 1920.

Morton, Desmond, and Wright, Glenn. *Winning the Second Battle: Canadian Veterans and the Return to Civilian Life 1915-1930*. University of Toronto Press. Toronto. 1987.

Nicholson, G.W.L. *Canadian Expeditionary Force 1914-1919*. Queen's Printer. Ottawa. 1964.

Parr, Joy. *Labouring Children: British Apprentices to Canada, 1869-1924*. Croom Helm. London. 1980.

Pettigrew, Eileen. *The Silent Enemy: Canada and the Deadly Flu of 1919*. Western Producer. Saskatoon. 1983.

Prentice, Alison, et. al. *Canadian Women: A History*. Harcourt Brace Jovanovitch. Toronto. 1988.

Seymour, Mark R. *Conservation for Military Monuments, Cemeteries and Battlefield Sites*. Heritage Network Press. Hamilton, Ontario. 1991.

Shipley, Robert. *To Mark Our Place: A History of Canadian War Memorials*. NC Press Limited. Toronto. 1987.

Stacey, C.P. *Arms, Men and Governments: The War Policies of Canada, 1939-1945*. Queen's Printer. Ottawa. 1970.

Struthers, James. *No Fault of their Own: Unemployment and the Canadian Welfare State 1914-1941*. University of Toronto Press. Toronto. 1983.

Swettenham, John, and Wood, H.F. *Silent Witnesses*. Hakkert. Toronto. 1974.

Vance, Jonathan F. *Death So Noble: Memory, Meaning and the First World War*. University of British Columbia Press. Vancouver. 1997.

Ward, G. Kingsley and Gibson, Edwin. *Courage Remembered*. Her Majesty's Stationery Office. London. 1989.

Woods, Walter S. *Rehabilitation: A Combined Operation*. Queen's Printer. Ottawa. 1953.

Wooton, Graham. *The Official History of the British Legion*. Macdonald and Evans. London. 1956.